The ADHD Awakening

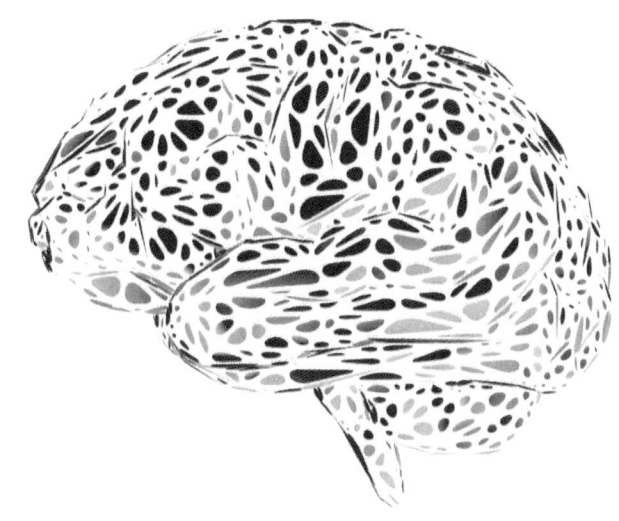

The ADHD Awakening

A Woman's Guide to Thriving After Diagnosis

SARA KELLY

HOUNDSTOOTH
PRESS

COPYRIGHT © 2026 SARA KELLY
All rights reserved.

THE ADHD AWAKENING
A Woman's Guide to Thriving After Diagnosis

FIRST EDITION

ISBN   978-1-5445-5014-5 *Hardcover*
          978-1-5445-5013-8 *Paperback*
          978-1-5445-5015-2 *Ebook*
          978-1-5445-5091-6 *Audiobook*

For my children, my greatest motivation and my deepest joy.

And for every late-diagnosed woman who has ever felt like she was too much and not enough at the same time.

You are seen. You are understood. You are not alone.

Contents

Preface 9
1. Why Women Are Overlooked 15
2. Struggling to Cope with Undiagnosed Adult ADHD 33
3. Getting Diagnosed and Mourning Lost Time 45
4. Hiding in Plain Sight with the ADHD Mask 59
5. Unlearning the "Not Good Enough" Mentality That Dominates Internal Narratives 89
6. Why Our ADHD Brains React So Intensely to Rejection ... 111
7. Perfectionism and Burnout 133
8. Emotional Flooding and Anxiety 153
9. Mastering Emotional Regulation as an ADHD Woman 177
10. Owning Your ADHD and Letting Go of Comparison 203
11. Create a Thriving Life That Works for You 225
12. The ADHD Awakening: We Are More Than Enough 257
    Acknowledgments 275

Preface

I NEVER SET OUT TO WRITE A BOOK ABOUT ADHD IN WOMEN.

At first, I was simply trying to make sense of *myself*, why certain things had always felt harder than they seemed to be for other people, why I could push myself to succeed in some areas of life while completely falling apart in others, why I felt like I was constantly *trying harder* than everyone else but still coming up short.

When I was finally diagnosed with ADHD as an adult, I felt an avalanche of emotions: relief that there was a reason for my struggles, grief for the years I spent blaming myself, and curiosity about what this meant for my past, present, and future.

As I dug deeper into the research, I started seeing my own experiences reflected back at me over and over again. And it wasn't just in medical journals or clinical descriptions; it was in conversations.

I saw it in the women I worked with. In coaching calls, support groups, and personal messages, I kept hearing the same phrases:

- Why has no one ever told me this before?
- I thought I was the only one who struggled like this.
- How did I go my whole life without realising this was ADHD?

These weren't just coincidences. They were patterns of women struggling silently—not because they weren't capable but because they had been navigating life with an invisible obstacle they didn't even know was there.

That realisation changed everything.

What started as personal research on why I ticked the way I did became something bigger: a deeper study of ADHD through both science and lived experience, followed by my work as an ADHD coach. I've witnessed the frustration, shame, and exhaustion that unmanaged ADHD can bring, and I've *felt* it personally. But I've also seen how powerful it is when women stop fighting their brains and start understanding them.

WHY THIS BOOK EXISTS

Many books about ADHD focus on clinical research, symptoms, or strategies, but few truly capture what it *feels like* to live with an ADHD brain. Even fewer reflect the unique experience of late-diagnosed ADHD in women, the way it hides behind coping mechanisms, the way it gets mislabelled as anxiety or depression, the way it's dismissed as being *just a personality trait*.

This book is here to fill that gap.

It is built on two things: research and real life. The strategies, insights, and patterns you'll read about are drawn from evidence-based studies, but also from the lived experiences of countless women who have navigated ADHD in ways that textbooks don't always capture.

To protect privacy, all names have been changed, and identifying details have been altered or generalised. No single story in this book belongs to one person. Collectively, these experiences reflect a reality that many ADHD women share.

WHY YOU'LL NOTICE SOME REPETITION

ADHD affects every area of life: our work, our relationships, our emotions, our self-esteem, even how we see time itself. But one of the biggest challenges is that many of us don't realise just how many areas it touches.

For most of us, ADHD doesn't show up as one big problem. It shows up as a hundred small frustrations that we've spent our lives working around without realising they were all connected.

That's why, as you move through this book, you may notice that some themes repeat. You might read about executive dysfunction in one chapter only to see it come up again in a different context later. The same is true for emotional regulation, time blindness, perfectionism, and the exhausting mental load that comes with managing ADHD every single day.

This isn't a mistake. It's intentional.

ADHD isn't something that fits neatly into categories. Instead, it weaves itself into everything. And many of us don't fully understand *just how much* it affects us until we see those same patterns reflected across different parts of our lives.

So if you ever find yourself thinking, *Wait, didn't we talk about this already?* Yes, we probably did. But now we're seeing it from another angle. Understanding ADHD isn't about memorising facts. It's about recognising yourself in these patterns, over and over again, until the bigger picture finally clicks into place.

WHO THIS BOOK IS FOR

My hope is that this book finds its way into the hands of:

- Women who have spent their lives feeling *different* without understanding why.
- Women who have been dismissed, misdiagnosed, or told they're simply *not trying hard enough*.
- Women who have created elaborate masks to hide their struggles—often at great personal cost.

I want these pages to be more than just words. I want them to be a mirror that helps you see yourself clearly, maybe for the first time.

But this book isn't just for those of us with ADHD. I also hope it reaches:

- Partners, friends, and family members who want to understand.
- Teachers, employers, and professionals who work with ADHD women every day.
- Anyone who has ever wondered why the brilliant, creative, driven woman in their life also seems to struggle in ways that don't quite make sense.

Understanding is the foundation of support, and support is what allows ADHD brains to thrive.

HOW THIS BOOK IS STRUCTURED

The journey through these pages begins with my own story. The first three chapters are deeply personal. They chronicle my lived experience before my ADHD diagnosis, the struggles I couldn't name, the coping mechanisms I built without understanding why I needed them, and the moment everything finally made sense.

I've shared these intimate parts of my journey not for self-indulgence, but because I know that recognition is often the first step toward understanding. Perhaps you'll see fragments of your own experience reflected in mine.

I also want to share that I'm on the autism spectrum. When someone has both ADHD and autism, it is commonly known as AuDHD, though that is not a medical term. Studies estimate that between 30 percent and 50 percent of people with autism also meet the criteria for ADHD, and many with ADHD may also fall somewhere on the autism spectrum.[1]

After these initial chapters, the book transitions to explore the collective experience of late-diagnosed women. While my story serves as an entry point, this isn't just about me. It's about the patterns, challenges, and strengths that connect us all.

---

[1] Yael Leitner, "The Co-Occurrence of Autism and Attention Deficit Hyperactivity Disorder in Children—What Do We Know?," *Frontiers in Human Neuroscience* 8 (April 2014): 268, https://doi.org/10.3389/fnhum.2014.00268.

These later chapters draw from research, professional insights, and the voices of women who have walked similar paths. Their experiences, woven together with evidence-based understanding, create a tapestry that illustrates what it truly means to navigate life with an ADHD brain that society hasn't always recognised.

The first three chapters focus on story and context because before you begin the work of change, you need to see the bigger picture. Recognising yourself in these early chapters can feel deeply validating, showing you that what you've struggled with has a name and an explanation. The self-coaching exercises begin in chapter four once that foundation has been set.

Whether you recognise yourself in every word or in just a few passages, my hope is that this structure, from personal to universal, helps illuminate both the individuality and the commonality of our experiences.

A FINAL WORD OF GRATITUDE

To every woman who has ever felt *alone* in her struggles, this book is for you.

To those who have bravely shared their experiences with me, your voices have shaped these pages, and your privacy has been honoured.

And to every person reading this, whether for yourself or someone you love, thank you. Your willingness to learn is part of what makes the world a place where neurodiversity is recognised, understood, and embraced.

Chapter One

Why Women Are Overlooked

I WAS FIVE YEARS OLD WHEN I STOOD IN FRONT OF MY KINDERgarten class and announced, "My mom is dead."

It was show-and-tell day. While other kids held up their favourite toys, I stood stiff in a plaid wool dress that scratched at my skin and clung to my tights. I kept tugging at it, trying to focus on the fabric, on the moment, on what I was about to say.

To me, this was just a truth. Something important. Something worth sharing. I thought it might even make me special—set apart in a way the others would notice. Their moms were alive. Mine wasn't. Surely that meant something.

I expected wide eyes. Maybe even awe.

Instead, I got silence. Then snickers.

Then came the whispers, the awkward glances, and, finally, laughter. The kind that doesn't feel playful. The kind that makes your throat close. My teacher didn't say much. She just stood there, stunned. I remember the pause—too long, too quiet—before she forced a smile and moved on to the next child as if it hadn't happened.

I was frozen in place, flooded with shame I didn't yet have words for.

My little hands twisted the hem of my dress under the fluorescent lights as heat crawled up my face. I could hear the giggles behind me. My ears burned. No one asked a single question. No one told me they were sorry.

Instead of feeling seen, I felt exposed.

That day, I learned something most ADHD girls learn young: When you share your truth, people don't always respond with understanding. Sometimes they recoil.

Later, some of the kids told me I was lying. "Your mom isn't dead. We've seen her!" They meant my stepmother. But I couldn't explain that to them, not in a way they'd believe. In their eyes, I had said something bizarre. Wrong. Out of bounds.

I hadn't lied. But I learned to question my own words anyway.

When I told my stepmom what had happened, hoping for comfort, she rolled her eyes. "Why would you say that?" she snapped, as if I'd embarrassed her. As if I should have known better.

But I didn't because no one had taught me the rules, especially the unspoken ones.

Girls with ADHD are often driven by connection. That day, I wasn't trying to shock anyone. I was trying to *connect*. But the truth didn't land. It made people uncomfortable, and I felt punished for it.

Many ADHD women remember moments like this when blurting out the truth led to confusion, rejection, or embarrassment. These moments often trigger shame, sensitivity, and self-blame. And the aftermath isn't fleeting. It can shape how we communicate for decades.

EARLY SIGNS OF ADHD

Looking back, I can see that sharing something so personal in that moment was likely my ADHD brain trying to make sense of big emotions and connect with others—even if my attempt wasn't received exactly the way my five-year-old self intended it to be. But as they are for so many late-diagnosed women, the signs were either missed, misunderstood, or dismissed as personality quirks.

I was impulsive—not in a reckless way but in an unfiltered, "blurt out whatever I was thinking" way. I couldn't grasp the nuances of what was "appropriate" to say and what wasn't. My emotions ran hot and fast. If I was excited, I was ecstatic. If I was upset, the world was ending. I felt everything intensely, but no one ever explained why.

When I read about ADHD in women for the first time, I couldn't get my tears to stop. Girls with ADHD are often misdiagnosed with anxiety or depression instead. We don't typically bounce off the walls like boys do, so nobody notices us struggling.[2] Our symptoms tend to be internal—emotional overwhelm, hypersensitivity, feeling like we're drowning in our own feelings. It hit so close to home it was almost painful to read.

I finally started seeing a therapist when I was in my forties, and she helped me understand that what I'd experienced my whole life had a name. The emotional intensity, the inability to filter my thoughts, and the overwhelming feelings that seemed to flood my entire body weren't character flaws. They were symptoms of ADHD that had gone unrecognised, particularly because I was a girl.

Children with ADHD experience emotional dysregulation at extreme levels. What might seem like a small inconvenience to a neurotypical child can feel devastating to an ADHD brain. Our emotions don't trickle in gently; they flood.

Studies show that children with ADHD feel emotions more intensely than neurotypical children and struggle to regulate them due to differences in brain activity, particularly in the prefrontal cortex.[3] Emotions hit hard, and when we don't have the necessary coping skills, the feelings often erupt in explosive ways.[4]

Individuals with ADHD often also struggle with something called social pragmatics, or the unspoken rules of conversation and knowing

---

[2] J. J. Sandra Kooij, *Adult ADHD: Diagnostic Assessment and Treatment*, 3rd ed. (Springer, 2013).

[3] Russell A. Barkley, ed., *Attention-Deficit Hyperactivity Disorder: A Handbook for Diagnosis & Treatment*, 4th ed. (Guilford Press, 2015).

[4] Gabor Maté, *Scattered Minds: The Origins and Healing of Attention Deficit Disorder* (Vintage Canada, 2000).

what's "appropriate" to share.⁵ We often overshare without realising it because we're driven by connection. We tell the truth. We blurt. We express feelings as they come because we want someone, anyone, to understand us.

And when rejection follows, it cuts deep.

Early signs of ADHD, especially in girls, can be varied and complex. We may experience something called rejection sensitivity dysphoria (RSD), where moments of rejection or embarrassment aren't just fleeting; they feel catastrophic.⁶ We often demonstrate impulsive behaviour as well as emotional dysregulation and hyperintensity. We struggle to fit in because these behaviours are seen as "bad" or signs of not paying attention rather than indicators of a neurological condition.

When these signs and symptoms go unnoticed or are criticised instead of treated, we can experience lifelong feelings of shame and not being good enough.

Looking back on myself as a child, I see all of them. Reflection was a painful process, but it was also the first step in dropping the shame and learning how to thrive.

SUGAR AND BRUSSELS SPROUTS: IMPULSIVE BEHAVIOUR AND EXECUTIVE FUNCTION CHALLENGES

The first time I stuck my finger in the sugar bowl, it felt like the best secret in the world.

It sat on the kitchen counter in a ceramic dish, the kind with a little lid that never quite fit perfectly. When no one was looking, I would quietly lift the top and dip my finger inside, scooping up the fine white grains and licking them off. They melted instantly on my tongue, a quick burst of sweetness, a tiny moment of pleasure in a house where joy was rare.

---

5 Barkley, ed., *Attention-Deficit Hyperactivity Disorder*.

6 William Dodson, "How ADHD Ignites RSD: Meaning & Medication Solutions," *Additude*, last modified September 5, 2025, https://www.additudemag.com/rejection-sensitive-dysphoria-and-adhd/.

I don't remember when it started, but I do remember why I kept doing it.

It wasn't just about the sugar. It was about control.

There were so many things I couldn't control: when I got punished, how long a punishment lasted, whether my dad showed up when he said he would, whether my stepmom was in a good mood or a bad one. But this? This was mine. This was a small act of rebellion, something I could do just for me.

Looking back, I see it for what it was: dopamine-seeking behaviour.

Dopamine is the neurotransmitter that helps regulate motivation, pleasure, and attention, and people with ADHD typically have lower baseline levels of it.[7] As a result, the brain is always looking for quick sources of stimulation, whether that comes from a cookie, a risky joke, or breaking a rule just to feel something. When I look back, that sugar bowl was not just about sweetness. It was a small and accessible way to self-soothe. Many women with ADHD recognise similar patterns in their own childhoods, especially if their emotional needs were overlooked or they were living in an unpredictable or emotionally unsafe environment.

Kids with ADHD often chase dopamine however they can, even in small, subconscious ways. Sugar, with its instant energy spike, is one of the easiest targets. Research shows that people with ADHD tend to crave sugar more than neurotypical individuals because their brains constantly seek stimulation and reward.[8]

Dopamine seeking in kids with ADHD can show up in all kinds of ways, many of them easy to miss unless you know what you are looking for. It's not just the child who eats too much sugar. It's also the child who cannot stop tapping their pencil or spinning in circles, the one who constantly interrupts or blurts out answers, or the one sneaking screen time or junk food when no one is watching. These behaviours

---

7   Nora D. Volkow et al., "Evaluating Dopamine Reward Pathway in ADHD: Clinical Implications," *JAMA* 302, no. 10 (2009): 1084–91, https://doi.org/10.1001/jama.2009.1308.

8   Maté, *Scattered Minds*.

might look like bad habits or defiance, but they are often unconscious attempts to stimulate the brain's reward system.

When a child seeks sugar, fidgets, sneaks screens, or pushes limits, they are often subconsciously trying to wake up or calm down their nervous system. These behaviours are crude attempts to feel steady or focused, not signs of bad character. Seeing them this way changes how we respond and how we remember our own childhoods.

I didn't know any of this at the time. I just knew that the sugar made me happy for a moment.

It wasn't the only sneaky thing I did to feel in control. I hated Brussels sprouts even more. My stepmom had a rule that I couldn't leave the table until I finished them, no matter how long it took. So I found a solution: I started spitting them behind the couch.

It was risky but worth it. I'd sit there, chewing as slowly as possible, waiting for a moment when she wasn't looking. Then, when I was sure I was in the clear, I'd quickly turn my head and let the mashed-up sprouts drop onto the floor behind the couch.

I can still smell that couch if I think about it—a scratchy brown fabric that always smelled of dust and cigarette smoke. I'm sure at some point the Brussels sprouts started to rot back there. I'm pretty sure she found them eventually, though I've blocked out what happened after. The wooden spoon, I'm guessing. It was always the wooden spoon.

I didn't realise until much later that these little acts of defiance, these tiny moments of reclaiming control, were actually my way of coping with an environment that felt overwhelming and unsafe.

Children with ADHD often engage in behaviours that seem odd, impulsive, or even deceptive to the adults around them, but there's almost always an underlying reason. Studies show that kids with ADHD are more prone to lying not because they're inherently dishonest but because they are more likely to act on impulse, forget details, or try to avoid shame-based consequences.[9]

---

[9] Barkley, ed., *Attention-Deficit Hyperactivity Disorder*.

My ADHD brain wasn't thinking about the long-term consequences of deception. I was just trying to protect myself in the moment.

ADHD brains constantly seek stimulation, and sometimes that means finding pleasure in the smallest, simplest things, like sugar crystals melting on your tongue. This was another example of dopamine seeking, but it was also impulsivity in action. The urge to act came fast, without any real pause to consider what might happen next.

That is the nature of ADHD impulsivity. It is not a lack of morals or discipline but a neurological difference in how the brain weighs short-term reward against long-term consequences. Research shows that children with ADHD often have difficulty delaying gratification and tend to choose immediate rewards over larger, delayed ones, even when they understand the trade-off.[10] They often react first and reflect later, especially when they are overwhelmed or trying to soothe themselves. Whether they blurt something out in class, take a risk they cannot explain, or reach for a quick hit of comfort, they are usually attempting to regulate an under-stimulated or emotionally overloaded nervous system. It might look like misbehaviour, but it is often survival.

I did not have the words for it at the time, but looking back, I realise the way I dealt with Brussels sprouts was an example of executive function challenges. When faced with something I hated, my ADHD brain did not think, *Just eat them and get it over with*. It thought, *How can I avoid this entirely?*

Executive dysfunction is one of the core challenges of ADHD, and it shows up in ways that are often misunderstood. It is the reason so many seemingly simple tasks feel physically impossible to start or follow through on. It affects the brain's ability to plan, organise, start, shift between, and complete tasks. That disconnect between knowing and doing is not a character flaw. It is neurological. The part of the brain responsible for managing these tasks, the prefrontal cortex, works less

---

10   Miranda R. Marco, "Delay and Reward Choice in ADHD: An Experimental Test of the Role of Delay Aversion," *Neuropsychology* 23, no. 3 (2009): 367–80, https://psycnet.apa.org/doi/10.1037/a0014914.

efficiently in people with ADHD, which makes everyday demands harder to navigate.[11]

In those moments slouching at the kitchen table staring at those Brussels sprouts, my brain was not assessing short-term discomfort versus long-term consequence. It just froze. I could not bring myself to do the *thing*, so I avoided it. Not by throwing a tantrum or refusing to eat, at least in this case. I found a work-around. I hid them. And that felt like problem-solving. Because in a way, it was. Executive dysfunction often pushes us into avoidance, not because we are lazy or defiant but because the steps required to tolerate or complete something unpleasant feel completely out of reach in that moment. It does not look like struggle from the outside. But it is.

FEELING TOO MUCH: EMOTIONAL DYSREGULATION AND SOCIAL CONFUSION

For most of my childhood, I didn't understand my own reactions. I felt things too much, too fast, and for too long. Something small could knock me sideways, and I had no idea how to come back to baseline. That is what emotional dysregulation looks like. It is not just being "sensitive" or "dramatic." Emotional regulation is the brain's ability to notice a feeling, make sense of it, and adjust our response in a way that fits the situation. In ADHD, that system often misfires.

Children with ADHD struggle to regulate both the intensity and duration of their emotions. When something feels bad, it can feel unbearable. When something feels exciting, it can take over completely. There is little pause between the feeling and the reaction. Research shows that emotional impulsiveness and poor self-regulation are tied to impairments in the brain's executive functioning, particularly in the prefrontal cortex.[12] I was often overwhelmed by social situations, confused by unspoken rules, or crushed by the smallest hint of rejection. I did not yet know how to

---

[11] Russell A. Barkley, *Executive Functions: What They Are, How They Work, and Why They Evolved* (Guilford Press, 2012).

[12] Barkley, ed., *Attention-Deficit Hyperactivity Disorder*.

de-escalate or process what I was feeling. It all landed at once and without warning. That inability to regulate and recover is one of the earliest signs of ADHD in girls, but it is also one of the most frequently missed.

At home, I struggled to understand why I felt things so powerfully. One moment, I'd be playing happily; the next, I'd be in a full meltdown over something that seemed small. I felt things so deeply but didn't have the tools to regulate them. Instead, I internalised the reactions of those around me. If my emotions were "too much" for others, then maybe something was wrong with me.

I learned early that my reactions confused people. My sister and I would chase each other through the house, screaming at the top of our lungs when we fought. The intensity of our conflicts was overwhelming, but I couldn't stop myself from reacting with full force. The volume, the energy, the desperation to be heard and understood felt uncontrollable. Looking back, I realise that my emotional regulation was nonexistent, and I had no idea how to de-escalate.

I still remember one particular fight over a Strawberry Shortcake doll when I was about six. My sister had taken it without asking (at least that's how I remember it), and something in me just snapped. I chased her through the house, shrieking so loudly that my throat hurt afterward. I couldn't form words, just pure rage sounds. My body felt hot all over, and my heart pounded so hard I thought it might break through my chest. It was like being possessed.

When my stepmom finally separated us, she looked at me with a mixture of disgust and confusion, like she couldn't understand what was wrong with me. "Why do you always have to be so dramatic?" she asked. I didn't know. I just knew that in that moment, it felt like the Most Important Thing in the World.

That's what emotional dysregulation looks like in a kid with ADHD. But it doesn't always show up as yelling. Sometimes it's crying over something small, going completely quiet, or running away to hide. Some kids hit. Some cling. Some fall apart over something they can't explain. And it has nothing to do with being dramatic. It's what happens when the feeling is too much and they don't know what to do with it.

This is one of the earliest forms of masking that ADHD girls develop: learning to suppress, downplay, or redirect emotions to avoid being labelled "dramatic" or "too sensitive." But emotional regulation isn't about trying harder; it's a neurological challenge rooted in ADHD brain function.[13] Our brains struggle to pump the brakes once emotions are triggered, making small disappointments feel like world-ending catastrophes.

STRUGGLING TO FIT IN: SOCIAL CONFUSION AND MISSED CUES

Beyond emotional dysregulation, I also struggled to pick up on social cues, making interactions confusing and often painful. My tendency to interrupt, overexplain, or miss subtle nonverbal signals made it difficult to form strong connections with peers. I wanted to belong, but it always felt like I was speaking a different social language.

I remember a birthday party incident when I was about eight. One of the popular girls in my class invited literally everyone, except me. When I asked her why, right in front of other kids on the playground (because impulse control wasn't my strong suit), she looked me dead in the eye and said, "Because you're weird and you talk too much."

I can still feel the physical sensation of those words hitting me, like someone had punched me in the stomach. My cheeks burned hot with shame, and I could hear the other kids snickering behind me. I didn't know what to say. I just stood there, mouth slightly open, unable to form words for once in my life.

That moment haunted me for years. I replayed it over and over in my head, trying to figure out what made me "weird," trying to understand what about me was so fundamentally wrong that I deserved to be excluded.

Looking back, I wasn't trying to be difficult. I just didn't understand the rules. I didn't realise how I came across or that asking that question

---

13 Barkley, ed., *Attention-Deficit Hyperactivity Disorder*.

in front of everyone would make it far worse for me. I missed what other kids picked up on so easily. The shift in tone, the body language, the silent message to drop it. That's part of ADHD too. Social cues go over your head, and by the time you realise you've missed them, the damage is done. And when I was hurt, I couldn't just brush it off.

I started counting my words after that, literally keeping track in my head: "That's ten sentences I've said. Maybe I should stop talking now."

Making friends always felt like trying to follow a complicated dance where everyone else knew the steps but me. I either came on too strong, sharing too much too fast, or I held back completely, paralyzed by the fear of saying the wrong thing. There was no middle ground.

In class, I was the kid whose hand shot up for every question (when I was paying attention). I couldn't contain my excitement when I knew the answer. My whole body would practically levitate out of the chair, arm stretched so high it hurt, as I whispered, "Ooh! Ooh! I know! I know!" But that same enthusiasm made me a target on the playground.

My elementary school teachers often described me as "bright but scattered" or "intelligent but needs to apply herself." Report cards were full of comments like "Talks excessively in class" and "Has difficulty waiting her turn." No one ever connected these dots. No one ever said, "Hey, maybe there's a neurological reason this kid can't sit still or stop interrupting."

Instead, I was labelled as the dramatic, emotional, too-much girl. The weird one. The one who couldn't quite fit in no matter how hard she tried.

I didn't realise then that what I was experiencing had a name. That there were others like me. That my brain was wired differently, not broken.

It took decades before I found that understanding, before I learned that ADHD in girls often hides behind these masks of anxiety, emotional intensity, and social confusion.

But the signs were there all along, hidden in plain sight—in that kindergarten classroom, in those sugar bowl raids, in those desperate attempts to fit in.

This is what ADHD often looks like in girls. It is emotional, confusing, and easy to miss. These girls are rarely the ones being sent to the principal's office. They are the ones being told they are too sensitive, too talkative, too dramatic, or just "a bit much." They often try hard to behave, to do well, to fit in. And when they can't, they blame themselves.

Because these traits don't match the stereotype of ADHD, they get overlooked. The intensity, the overthinking, the social slipups—none of it is random. But no one was connecting those dots back then, especially not for girls.

I wasn't bad. I wasn't broken. I was just different. But no one knew how to see it.

What I was experiencing at home didn't make it any easier.

GROWING UP IN CHAOS: ADHD IN AN UNSTABLE ENVIRONMENT

I could always tell what kind of night it was going to be by the way my stepmom set down her cup of Diet Pepsi. If it was gentle, I exhaled. If it clanked against the table, sending a ripple through the liquid, my stomach tightened.

My father, when he was around, was the fun dad. The dad who brought home unexpected gifts and let us stay up past bedtime. He was a kaleidoscope of a person: brilliant, charismatic, and deeply flawed. Looking back now, I'm almost certain he had undiagnosed ADHD too. Like me, he was a victim of child abuse, suffering at the hands of his father who was so terrible that my dad's paternal grandmother eventually paid for my grandmother to divorce him.

He was undeniably smart, a true mechanical genius who could fix almost anything. People respected his skills, even when they couldn't rely on his punctuality or follow-through. That was my dad: capable of brilliance but incapable of consistency.

Some of my fondest memories are tinged with the knowledge I now have as an adult. I remember him taking me out in an aluminum boat with a pull engine, a bucket of KFC between us as we motored across the water. Only years later did I realise we were heading to his drug dealer's house. At the time, it just felt like an adventure with my dad.

The sound of that boat motor still lives in my ears—the puttering rhythm, the way it skipped sometimes when the water got choppy. I trailed my fingers in the cold lake water as we cruised along, the wind pushing my hair back, the sun warm on my face. There was a freedom on those boat rides that I didn't feel anywhere else.

The problem was, sometimes he didn't come home at all. On those nights, my stepmom would shake me awake, her voice clipped and urgent. "Get dressed. We're going to find your father." I'd pull on my clothes in the dark as my little sister rubbed her tired eyes, and we'd pile into the car. The streets at night felt eerie, headlights bouncing off pavement, my stepmom gripping the wheel tight as she scanned parking lots and bars.

I remember the smell of those nights—the cold air coming through the car vents, the lingering scent of my stepmom's hairspray, the faint odour of beer on her breath. Sometimes we'd drive for what felt like hours, stopping at different pubs where she'd leave us in the car while she went in to look for him. I'd stare out the window at the neon signs, watching people stumble out into the parking lots, wondering if my dad would be among them.

It became normal, this cycle of searching, of never knowing what version of home I'd be returning to. But normal didn't mean easy. The inconsistency of my father's presence and my stepmom's moods wired my brain for hypervigilance. I had already learned to read people's emotions with uncanny precision, a skill developed out of necessity.

When my parents fought, it was usually at night, long after I went to bed. Their voices cut through the walls, sharp and relentless, pulling me from sleep and leaving my body rigid with dread. I'd squeeze my eyes shut, pulling the covers over my head, pressing my hands against my ears. But nothing could block it out completely. I'd lie there, stiff and small, waiting for it to end.

In those moments, I would talk to my mother in heaven. I imagined her sitting beside me, running her fingers through my hair, whispering that everything would be okay. I didn't have memories of her. She was gone before I was old enough to remember. But I held onto the fantasy that she would have protected me, that she would have made me feel safe. Instead, I had to comfort myself, whispering silent prayers to a mother I never got to know. I still talk to my mom today, usually while hiking. Sharing my deepest secrets with her gives me a sense of home, like she's with me, grounding me, offering comfort and understanding, even though she's not physically here.

When I was eight or nine, my father finally left for good. But he didn't take me with him. I stayed with my stepmom, left to navigate her unpredictable storms alone.

I hated my dad for leaving. No, that's not right. I loved him desperately, *and* I hated him for leaving. Both things were true at the same time. I wanted him to stay more than anything, but some small, wise part of me also knew that when he was there, things were even more unpredictable.

My dad was a cautionary tale, yes, but also a reminder of human complexity, of how brilliance and self-destruction can exist in the same person, how potential can go tragically unrealised when the right support isn't there. In many ways, getting my own diagnosis and treatment as an adult was a tribute to him by breaking the cycle he couldn't escape.

Growing up in that kind of chaos shaped how my ADHD showed up and how easily it was missed. In a home where the adults were reactive, unpredictable, or emotionally checked out, my symptoms didn't raise flags. I was anxious, impulsive, sensitive, and emotionally overwhelmed most of the time. But no one asked why. I just blended in. My stepmom thought I was dramatic. My teachers thought I was bright but scattered. No one connected the dots.

ADHD has a strong genetic component. Studies show that if a child is diagnosed, they likely have at least one biological parent who meets the criteria as well.[14] As I've mentioned before, I'm almost certain my dad had

---

14 Stephen V. Faraone et al., "Molecular Genetics of Attention-Deficit/Hyperactivity Disorder," *Biological Psychiatry* 57, no. 11 (2005): 1313–23, https://doi.org/10.1016/j.biopsych.2004.11.024.

it. He was brilliant, inconsistent, emotionally intense, and often lost in his own world. And an undiagnosed or untreated parent creates an unstable environment that makes it even harder to identify what is going on with the child.[15] The line between trauma and neurology gets blurry fast.

Girls are more likely to be missed. They are diagnosed later and less frequently than boys, especially when they don't have obvious hyperactivity.[16] Instead of getting support, they get labels—too sensitive, too talkative, too emotional. They over-function or fall apart quietly. Either way, they often go unnoticed.

And not every girl with ADHD grows up in a chaotic home. You don't need trauma to develop the same symptoms. Even in stable households, girls with ADHD often carry an invisible weight. They may cry easily, interrupt without meaning to, try too hard to fit in, or retreat when they feel misunderstood. But because they are not disruptive, they are rarely flagged. The struggle is still there. It is just hidden.

SUMMER SALVATION: MY GRANDPARENTS' HAVEN

While my home life was often chaotic and cold, I had one saving grace: my grandparents. Every summer, I travelled from Vancouver Island where I lived with my dad and stepmom to spend weeks with my grandparents at their home in Edmonton, and it felt like stepping into a different world entirely.

My grandparents were everything my stepmom wasn't: warm, patient, and genuinely delighted by my presence. Their home smelled like blueberry pies and homemade doughnuts, treats my grandmother made specially for my visits. The moment I arrived, my grandmother would wrap me in a hug so tight it felt like she was trying to squeeze all the love she had into me at once. My grandfather, with his weathered hands and gentle smile, would ruffle my hair and call me his "little trouble-

---

15   Susan Young et al., "The Economic Consequences of Attention-Deficit Hyperactivity Disorder in the Scottish Prison System," *BMC Psychiatry* 18 (2018): 210, https://doi.org/10.1186/s12888-018-1792-x.

16   Stephen P. Hinshaw and Katherine Ellison, *ADHD: What Everyone Needs to Know* (Oxford University Press, 2016).

maker," but the warmth in his eyes told me that in his world, trouble was something to cherish.

They lived in a modest house with a sprawling garden that my grandfather tended with meticulous care. Every morning, I joined him as he watered his tomato plants and strawberry bushes, listening intently as he taught me the names of various birds that visited the feeder. He had infinite patience for my endless questions, never once making me feel like I was too much or too loud.

My grandmother had a special tradition that made me feel loved in a way I rarely experienced at home. She served me blueberry pie for breakfast. "The ingredients in the pie make the breakfast balanced," she'd say with a wink while passing me the plate. These small rebellions against conventional rules made me feel special, like we shared a delicious secret.

She taught me to bake her famous pies and doughnuts, allowing me to measure ingredients and mix batters even though it meant flour dusting every surface of her kitchen. When I inevitably made a mess or got distracted halfway through, she didn't scold me. Instead, she laughed and said, "That's why we wear aprons, my dear," then guided me back to the task with gentle reminders.

Looking back, I can see how much of my ADHD showed up in those moments. The impulsiveness, the messiness, the big emotions, the constant need for stimulation and connection. But instead of shutting it down, my grandparents made space for it. They gave me the kind of safety that kids with ADHD need in order to thrive. I was allowed to be curious, intense, playful, scattered, and completely myself without fear of getting it wrong.

That made the difference. Not perfect parenting. Not strict routines or behaviour charts. Just being in an environment where I didn't have to armour up. Research shows that when kids with ADHD feel emotionally safe and supported, their symptoms become easier to manage, and their self-esteem improves.[17] So many of us spend our entire childhoods

---

17 Betsy Hoza, "Peer Functioning in Children with ADHD," supplement, *Ambulatory Pediatrics* 7, no. 1 (2007): 101–106, https://doi.org/10.1016/j.ambp.2006.04.011.

trying to contort ourselves into who we think we are supposed to be. I didn't have to do that there. And for a child like me, that was everything.

At their house, I never had to walk on eggshells. I never had to monitor my emotions or my words. I was allowed to be fully myself—curious, dramatic, energetic, and sometimes overwhelmed. They seemed to understand instinctively what I needed, providing structure without strictness, freedom without chaos.

In those summer months with my grandparents, I got glimpses of what it might have been like to grow up in a home where love was unconditional, where my existence wasn't a burden but a gift. They couldn't completely erase the pain of my day-to-day life, but they gave me something precious. A template for what family could be. A vision of what I deserved. When I was sixteen, I ran away from my stepmom's home, and my grandparents took me in. My grandfather told me shortly after I moved in that having me with them was like having their daughter back.

I think a lot of ADHD kids carry that same weight, even in homes that are more stable than mine was. When your emotions are too big, when you get in trouble for blurting things out, when you need constant reminders just to finish your homework, it's easy to start believing that you are the problem. That you are too much, too hard, too exhausting.

My grandparents gave me the opposite of that. They made me feel like I belonged just by existing. Like I wasn't something to manage. And once I felt that, even for a few weeks at a time, I could never unknow it.

Even now, decades later, I can close my eyes and feel the warmth of my grandmother's kitchen, hear my grandfather's deep chuckle, taste the sweet-tart flavour of blueberry pie at breakfast. They showed me that I was worthy of love exactly as I was. A lesson that helped me survive the much harder ones life had in store.

But ADHD doesn't disappear just because no one names it. The signs were always there. They just kept shape-shifting to match whatever season of life I was in.

In elementary school, I was the girl who got good marks but couldn't stay organised to save her life. Later, I was the woman who overcommitted, over-delivered, and then crashed hard. The one who seemed capable and confident on the outside but was secretly drowning in chaos, shame, and exhaustion.

I didn't have the words for any of it. All I knew was that something felt off. And for years, I believed it was me.

What I didn't know then was that the same brain wiring that made me impulsive, emotional, and misunderstood as a kid was still driving so many of the struggles I faced as an adult.

The symptoms didn't fade. They just evolved into missed appointments, emotional outbursts I couldn't explain, and a constant sense that I was failing at things other women seemed to manage effortlessly. By the time I became a wife and a mother, I found it harder to hide the cracks. I was trying so hard to hold it all together, but inside, I felt like I was coming undone.

I didn't know yet that ADHD was still with me. I didn't know it had always been with me. But everything was about to come to the surface.

Chapter Two

Struggling to Cope with Undiagnosed Adult ADHD

IN THE FALL OF 2019, I ASKED MY HUSBAND OF SEVENTEEN YEARS for a divorce. At the time, I had no idea that ADHD had played such a significant role in my relationship. I only knew that something felt deeply misaligned.

Our life together had become a constant source of stress and disappointment. He had always made a good living, yet bill collectors called because I forgot to pay the bills. My desk was a gigantic doom pile, filled with unopened mail, scattered notes, and misplaced important documents that made perfect sense to me but looked like chaos to him. These issues weren't just minor annoyances. They created real consequences that strained our relationship to a breaking point. He was often critical of my forgetfulness and disorganisation, and over time, our dynamic had begun to resemble a parent–child relationship. This is a common pattern in ADHD relationships, where one partner takes on the role of the "responsible one" while the other is seen as unreliable.[18]

Beyond the organisational struggles were deeper incompatibilities that I didn't fully understand at the time. To cope with the overwhelming stress and the loneliness of spending so much time on my own while married, I often turned to alcohol at night as a way to shut off my brain. The constant mental chaos, the endless list of things I had forgotten or needed to do, and the emotional exhaustion of feeling like I was always failing all became too much. A glass of wine helped quiet the noise, but soon, one glass turned into two, then three.

ADHD brains struggle with dopamine regulation, and individuals with ADHD are at a higher risk for substance use as a form of self-medication.[19] I didn't see it as a problem at the time; I saw it as survival. But looking back, I realise I was trying to numb the executive dysfunction, the overstimulation, and the emotional roller coaster that came with simply existing in a neurotypical world.

I've since learned that I'm also on the autism spectrum, though I didn't know it at the time. Sensory sensitivities played a large role in my frustration. My husband often hummed, sang, or repeated annoying little jingles, which sent me into near meltdown. I know now that ADHD and sensory sensitivity often go hand in hand, though my reactions may have been amplified by my autism.[20] But back then, I just knew I couldn't handle it. Small things that other people might have ignored felt unbearable. Even the sound of him chewing was enough to make my skin crawl, my pulse quicken, and my entire body tense with irritation. It felt like a relentless, inescapable noise, amplifying in my head until I had to either leave the room or fight the overwhelming urge to scream. This sensitivity, I later learned, is called misophonia, a condition that causes certain sounds to trigger intense emotional responses.

---

18 Dodson, "How ADHD Ignites RSD."

19 Timothy E. Wilens et al., "Does ADHD Predict Substance-Use Disorders? A 10-Year Follow-Up Study of Young Adults with ADHD," *Journal of the American Academy of Child & Adolescent Psychiatry* 50, no. 6 (2011): 543–53, https://doi.org/10.1016/j.jaac.2011.01.021.

20 Martin L. Kutscher, *ADHD: Living Without Brakes* (Jessica Kingsley Publishers, 2009).

I want to pause for a moment to add context. Some of what I describe might be shaped by both ADHD and autism, since they often overlap. But this story is grounded in my experience with ADHD. You do not need an autism diagnosis to relate to it. Sensory sensitivities, emotional overwhelm, executive dysfunction, and rejection sensitivity can all show up in ADHD on their own. Not every part of my story will match yours, and that's okay. ADHD looks different in all of us, especially in women. If some pieces resonate and others don't, you are still in the right place.

I also struggled with emotional dysregulation, just as I had as a child, which meant my reactions were often disproportionate to the situation. I raised my voice, got angry over things that didn't seem to bother other people, and fell into an all-or-nothing thinking pattern where I believed my perspective was the only valid one. At the time, I wasn't capable of stepping back and considering other viewpoints—it was like my brain was locked into one rigid way of seeing things. I've done a lot of work since then, but in my marriage, this led to constant friction and made productive conflict resolution nearly impossible.

Adding to the strain, my then-husband worked out of town and was home for only four to eight days a month. This meant that much of the responsibility for raising our children fell on me. Parenting requires an immense amount of executive functioning: keeping track of schedules, appointments, meals, schoolwork, and emotional support. Separately, all these were already difficult for me due to my ADHD. The mental load felt crushing at times, and I often worried that I was failing. I felt like I was constantly running behind, unable to catch up, while other moms seemed to manage it all effortlessly. The inconsistency made it hard to feel connected in our relationship or marriage.

I didn't have the words for it then (a common theme throughout this book), but I was experiencing the full weight of ADHD's impact on emotional connection. My brain was so overstimulated by the day-to-day chaos that it had little capacity left for warmth or vulnerability. I wasn't trying to withdraw emotionally. I was just surviving. And when your nervous system is in constant overdrive, even basic intimacy can feel like one more thing you're expected to perform rather than something you have the bandwidth to give.

When my husband was gone, I felt isolated and struggled with the weight of responsibilities I found overwhelming. When he was home, the tension between us was palpable. In hindsight, I can see that neither of us had the tools to make the relationship work, but at the time, I just felt like I was failing at something else that other people seemed to navigate effortlessly.

I was terrified because I didn't know if I was making a mistake or not. I knew I wasn't happy, but I also questioned if I could ever be happy. Everything always felt so hard. Everyone else seemed to have it easier than I did. What if the divorce still left me with the deep sadness and loneliness I had always felt? What if the grass wasn't greener on the other side?

At the time, I didn't have the words to explain why the disorganisation, the overwhelm, and the emotional volatility kept showing up in my marriage. I only knew that his frustration made me feel broken.

HOW THE SIGNS AND SYMPTOMS OF ADHD SHOW UP IN UNDIAGNOSED ADULTS

Back then, I had no idea ADHD was behind so much of what I was struggling with. I just thought I was bad at life. I couldn't keep up with bills, routines, or conversations. I was either doing everything all at once or stuck doing nothing. And I blamed myself for all of it.

That's how it shows up for a lot of women. Not as hyperactivity (as it often does for boys). Not as "trouble focusing" in the way people expect. But as constant pressure. Emotional ups and downs. Guilt. Exhaustion.

The signs are often invisible from the outside. Internally, it's a different story. You might:

- Run late or lose track of time completely.
- Struggle to start tasks, even small ones.
- Avoid things that feel overwhelming, then scramble at the last minute.

- Start a bunch of things and finish none of them.
- Forget appointments, birthdays, groceries, names, your train of thought mid-sentence.
- Snap at people, then feel ashamed.
- Push yourself to do everything perfectly to make up for how chaotic things feel.
- Lie awake at night reviewing everything you forgot, said wrong, or didn't finish.

This is executive dysfunction. It affects how you plan, remember, prioritise, regulate emotions, and manage time. And when it goes unrecognised, it chips away at your confidence, your relationships, and your ability to feel competent.

Most women who are diagnosed later in life have spent years being told they are too sensitive, disorganised, lazy, dramatic, or unreliable. A lot of them first get diagnosed after their child does. Others only find out after a major life shift that pushes them past what they can manage. A new baby. A divorce. A job that requires more structure than they have ever had.

None of this means we are not trying. It means our brains work differently. And the way ADHD shows up in women often gets missed.

Research backs this up. The criteria were designed around how ADHD shows up in boys, not women. Girls are more likely to internalise their symptoms, and women are more likely to be diagnosed with anxiety or depression instead.[21] A Canadian report also found that many women wait decades for a diagnosis. Often they are dismissed or misdiagnosed again and again before anyone connects the dots.[22]

If any of this sounds familiar, that's enough to keep exploring. You

---

[21] Manisha Madhoo and Patricia O. Quinn, "A Review of Attention Deficit/Hyperactivity Disorder in Women and Girls: Uncovering This Hidden Diagnosis," *The Primary Care Companion for CNS Disorders* 16, no. 3 (2014), https://doi.org/10.4088/pcc.13r01596.

[22] "Girls and Women with ADHD: Our Missed Forgotten and Most Vulnerable," Centre for ADHD Awareness Canada, 2021, https://caddac.ca/wp-content/uploads/Girls-and-Women-with-ADHD-FINAL-1.pdf.

do not have to tick every box. And you are not imagining how hard it has been.

THE ADHD-MARRIAGE TRAP: FEELING LIKE A BURDEN

I still remember the pit in my stomach when I realised I had forgotten—again. The bill sat unopened on my desk, buried beneath a mountain of receipts, sticky notes, and half-finished to-do lists. The due date had come and gone. Late fees had been added. And now I had to tell my husband.

It wasn't just about the bill. It was the pattern. The cycle of my forgetting, his reminding, my promising to be better, and then, inevitably, something slipping through the cracks. It was the feeling of watching disappointment flicker across his face, the frustration in his voice as he asked, "How hard is it to just write things down?"

I wanted to scream, "I DO WRITE THINGS DOWN! I do write things down!" But what good would it do? My brain didn't work like his. The reminders got lost. The systems he swore by felt like shackles to me. Yet every mistake, every forgotten deadline, every missed bill chipped away at my sense of competence. I wasn't just failing at adulting; I was failing him.

The household responsibilities felt endless: bills, groceries, laundry, school forms, hockey practise, doctor's appointments. The mental load of running a household while also tending to the constant needs of our kids was overwhelming. I wanted to be the mom who had it all together, who showed up to every basketball game, who never forgot a permission slip, who had an actual budget. But I wasn't.

People with ADHD often struggle with executive dysfunction, which, as just mentioned, affects our ability to organise, plan, and manage time effectively.[23] This can lead to missing deadlines, forgetting responsibilities, and feeling overwhelmed by the mental load of daily life. Many of us with ADHD compensate by overcommitting in one area, like work

---

23 Barkley, ed., *Attention-Deficit Hyperactivity Disorder*.

or academics, while unintentionally neglecting others, leading to deep-seated guilt and self-criticism.[24]

I was also in university at the time, putting every ounce of my energy into my studies. I didn't realise it then, but hyperfocus (a common ADHD phenomenon where you become so absorbed in something that you inadvertently neglect other responsibilities) had me pouring everything into school and left nothing for parenting duties. I missed too many of my daughter's basketball games, too many moments I can't get back.

Everything felt like too much all the time. I kept trying to catch up, but the more I pushed, the more things unravelled, and in many ways, my kids paid the price. My brain couldn't keep pace with the moving parts of daily life, and I had no explanation for why. It just felt like I was always dropping the ball, always letting someone down, and always falling short, no matter how hard I tried.

That guilt is something I still carry. Therapy has helped me process these feelings, and I've worked hard to rebuild those relationships. My children have forgiven me, and for that, I am endlessly grateful.

At some point, my marriage stopped feeling like an equal partnership and started feeling like he was the responsible one, and I was the one who needed managing.

Many ADHD marriages fall into this type of a parent–child dynamic, where the neurotypical partner takes on the role of the responsible one while the ADHD partner is perceived as unreliable.[25] Over time, this dynamic can lead to resentment, shame, and a deepening sense of failure for the ADHD partner, reinforcing a cycle of avoidance and low self-esteem.

For me, it was the little things. The way he reminded me to clean off my desk. The way he insisted we sit down together to create a budget, an exercise I dreaded so much that even thinking about it made me squirm.

---

24 Madhoo and Quinn, "A Review of Attention Deficit/Hyperactivity Disorder in Women and Girls."

25 Melissa Orlov, *The ADHD Effect on Marriage: Understand and Rebuild Your Relationship in Six Steps* (Specialty Press, 2010).

The way I could tell, even when he didn't say it outright, that he wished I was more organised, more structured, more responsible.

I handled the money during this time, but I constantly doubted my ability to manage it well. For a long time, I struggled with the fear of making financial mistakes, and every late bill, misplaced document, and unfinished task reinforced my belief that I wasn't capable of handling responsibility. I told myself it was easier this way, but deep down, I felt like a child in my own marriage.

I didn't overcompensate. Instead, I shut down. The constant cycle of disappointing him, of feeling like I wasn't pulling my weight, made me retreat inward. The shame was paralyzing. I started avoiding conversations about money, about responsibilities. Out of sight, out of mind. If I didn't look at the unopened mail, if I didn't acknowledge the mess, maybe it wouldn't be so overwhelming.

But avoidance only made things worse. The guilt piled up. And to escape the noise in my own head, I drank. It wasn't about the alcohol itself. It was about shutting my brain off, quieting the relentless self-criticism, giving myself a few hours when I didn't have to think about all the ways I was falling short.

NOT ALONE

I'm not alone in this. When I started talking to other late-diagnosed women, I heard the same themes over and over again.

A friend told me that her husband calls her "the tornado" because no matter how much she tries to stay on top of things, clutter and unfinished projects seem to follow her everywhere.

Another woman shared that her partner stopped trusting her with finances altogether after she forgot to pay their mortgage twice. She's now locked out of the banking apps, left to feel like a child asking for an allowance.

One mother confessed that she once forgot her daughter's birthday party invitations in the car for weeks. By the time she found them, the party date had passed. The shame was unbearable.

These stories aren't just coincidences. They're patterns of undiagnosed ADHD shaping marriages and relationships in ways we never expected.

If I could go back and tell my past self anything, it would be this: You are not broken.

I can see now how much of my struggle was related to undiagnosed ADHD. My executive dysfunction and time blindness (the inability to feel or track the passage of time) were just part of the equation. The emotional dysregulation that turned a simple reminder into a full-blown internal shame spiral made communication increasingly difficult, and the relationship between myself and my husband continued to deteriorate despite our efforts.

I spent years internalising blame, believing I was failing at things that should be easy. But ADHD makes the invisible parts of life—planning, remembering, organising—exponentially harder. And when you don't know why you're struggling, it's easy to believe that the problem is you.

An early diagnosis, or even just understanding how my brain worked, could have changed everything. It wouldn't have made me perfect, but it would have given me the tools to advocate for myself instead of drowning in shame.

I know that now. And I'm grateful for the growth, therapy, and self-awareness that have allowed me to move forward. But I still wish I could have seen myself with more compassion back then. Because the truth is, I was trying. I was always trying.

ISOLATION AND FEAR: MOVING OUT ALONE

The weight of my new independence hit me all at once on moving day. I was in the lobby of the new condo I bought surrounded by moving boxes. My fifteen-year-old stood next to me, watching as I tried to force my breathing to slow down. The high ceilings and cold tile floors stretched around me, making me feel impossibly small.

My chest tightened. My vision tunnelled. My mind jumped between a hundred unfinished tasks: utilities to set up, furniture to assemble, emails to answer. The weight of everything I had to manage on my own crashed over me all at once. And all during COVID-19.

Tears burned at the backs of my eyes, but I swallowed them down. My child was watching. I couldn't break down in front of them.

But inside, I was unravelling.

The moment the door of my new place clicked shut behind me, the silence swallowed me whole. For the first time in years, no one else's presence filled the space. No background chatter, no footsteps down the hall, no one calling my name. Just me. Alone.

I stood in the middle of my new apartment, surrounded by unopened boxes, and felt the weight of reality settle onto my shoulders. This was what I had fought for—freedom, independence, a fresh start. But in that moment, all I felt was terror.

It was 2020, and the world outside was just as isolating as the one inside these walls. The pandemic had forced everyone into solitude, but for me, it felt like a cruel twist of fate. Moving out of my marriage had been daunting enough, but doing it at a time when support systems were crumbling, when connection was reduced to pixelated Zoom calls, made it nearly unbearable. There was no safety net, no distractions, no external structure to cling to.

I sank onto the couch, staring at the blank walls, and let the emptiness close in around me. I hadn't realised how much I had depended on the noise of other people to keep my mind from turning on itself. Now, there was nothing to drown out the thoughts spiralling in my head.

In my apartment alone at night, the silence became unbearable. My mind refused to shut off, replaying old conversations, obsessing over mistakes, filling the empty space with relentless self-doubt. I had wanted this. I had craved the ability to create a life on my own terms. But I hadn't expected it to feel so heavy.

I lay awake, staring at the ceiling, wondering if I had made a mistake. What if I wasn't capable of doing this alone? What if I had traded one kind of suffocation for another?

For years, I had relied on my marriage to provide structure, even if it had been an unhealthy one. My husband had been the one to remind me of appointments, to keep the household running when my executive dysfunction got the best of me. Now, every forgotten bill, every misplaced key, every undone task was all on me.

ADHD brains struggle with self-imposed structure. We rely on external scaffolding like jobs, partners, and school schedules to keep us on track. When that structure disappears, we can easily become overwhelmed and stuck in paralysis.[26] Studies show that ADHD adults often struggle with transitions because our brains crave predictable patterns, but we lack the internal mechanisms to create and maintain them.[27]

At the same time, I was self-employed, and I could see my business slipping through my fingers. The lack of structure, the unpredictability of income, and the sheer terror of watching everything I had built unravel left me feeling completely untethered. Where was I supposed to focus my energy? How was I supposed to keep my head above water when my brain felt like it was drowning in fear and uncertainty?

I had always struggled with transitions, but this was a shift so monumental it felt like the ground had disappeared beneath me. Moving out wasn't just about finding a new place to live; it was about learning to exist entirely on my own terms for the first time in seventeen years.

I had spent years trying to fix myself, trying to do life the way everyone else seemed to. But living without a safety net finally forced me to look deeper. I wasn't just overwhelmed. I wasn't just emotional or disorganised. I had ADHD. And suddenly, everything started to make sense.

---

[26] Barkley, ed., *Attention-Deficit Hyperactivity Disorder*.

[27] Edward M. Hallowell and John J. Ratey, *ADHD 2.0: New Science and Essential Strategies for Thriving with Distraction—from Childhood Through Adulthood* (Ballantine Books, 2021).

Chapter Three

Getting Diagnosed and Mourning Lost Time

MY ADULT DAUGHTER WAS DIAGNOSED WITH ADHD IN HER EARLY twenties, and around the same time, we found out my fifteen-year-old son had it too. I remember feeling completely bewildered. Looking back, I remembered teachers had hinted at the possibility of their ADHD during parent–teacher interviews, but I'd brushed it off. My internal barometer was distorted because I was living with undiagnosed ADHD myself. And then there was my dad. Generationally we were the blind leading the blind.

I started researching. I wanted to understand my kids better, to be the kind of mom who actually knew how to support them.

I didn't expect that a casual TikTok scroll would unravel my entire self-perception in under a minute.

One night, when I was in a haze of exhaustion, I came across a video titled "Signs of ADHD You Didn't Know Were ADHD." I tapped it, half distracted, expecting to learn something useful for my kids. Instead, I found myself staring into a mirror I didn't know existed.

The creator described experiences that felt uncomfortably personal:

chronic procrastination, emotional intensity, impulsivity, the strange paradox of hyperfocus and complete inertia. My stomach twisted. *Wait... that's me.*

I scrolled to the comments. Thousands of women, all saying the same thing.

"I thought I was just lazy."

"Why does this explain my entire life?"

"How am I finding out I have ADHD from a social media app?"

The algorithm had figured me out before I had. Each new video unlocked something buried deep inside me, memories of feeling "too much," of fighting through tasks that others breezed through, of internalising failure as a personal flaw. TikTok, of all places, was exposing the truth: I wasn't lazy. I wasn't just "bad with time." I wasn't broken.

And I wasn't alone.

For years, ADHD was thought to be a childhood disorder, specifically one that affected hyperactive little boys bouncing off the walls. The quiet, daydreamy girls? The overwhelmed moms who held everything together (except for their own minds)? We slipped through the cracks.

ADHD presents differently in women than in men. It often hides in perfectionism, overachievement, or chronic overwhelm. Research confirms that women with ADHD are diagnosed, on average, five to ten years later than men, if at all.[28] Many are first diagnosed when their children are evaluated, after finally seeing their struggles reflected in their kids.

I was one of those.

THE ADHD MASK: PRETENDING TO BE FINE

One of the main reasons so many women go undiagnosed is because we learn to hide the struggle. Not because we're okay but because we're expected to be. From a young age, girls are taught to be polite, helpful, quiet, and emotionally contained. That doesn't leave much room for

---

[28] Madhoo and Quinn, "A Review of Attention Deficit/Hyperactivity Disorder in Women and Girls."

impulsivity, messiness, or overwhelm. So instead of asking for help, we learn to push through it. We become experts at performing what looks like "fine," even when we're anything but.

Depending on our cultural background, the pressure to appear capable, composed, or self-sacrificing might be even stronger. In some families, showing struggle isn't an option. So we mask harder.

Masking is a survival tactic. Women with ADHD become experts at camouflaging our struggles, mimicking neurotypical behaviour to fit in.[29] We write endless to-do lists we never follow. We set alarms, and we hit the snooze. We apologise constantly for forgetting, interrupting, losing things, being "too sensitive."

But masking comes at a cost. It drains our energy, erodes our self-esteem, and often leads to burnout. The worst part? No one sees the struggle beneath the surface. They only see a woman who *should be trying harder*.

DIAGNOSIS GRIEF: THE WHAT-IFS AND REGRETS

The night after I saw the TikTok video, I barely slept. I went down an ADHD rabbit hole, researching everything I could find. The emotional outbursts, the overwhelm, the forgetfulness, the struggle to maintain relationships, the feeling of constantly trying harder than everyone else but never keeping up—these weren't personal failures. They were symptoms.

For the first time, I saw myself clearly. And along with that clarity came a wave of relief.

For years, I had secretly feared I was developing Alzheimer's or dementia because my forgetfulness seemed to be getting worse. I would forget conversations, misplace important items, or completely blank on things I knew I should remember. Learning that ADHD, especially when compounded by emotional dysregulation, impacts memory and cognitive function was both reassuring and heartbreaking.[30]

---

29 Dodson, "How ADHD Ignites RSD."
30 Barkley, ed., *Attention-Deficit Hyperactivity Disorder*.

I wasn't broken. I had simply never been given the tools to manage my brain effectively.

The more I learned, the more I mourned. Where would I be if I had known sooner? What opportunities had I missed? What if I had never carried the belief that I just wasn't good enough?

I wasn't the only one asking these questions. One woman I spoke to, diagnosed in her forties, described it perfectly: "It's like realising you've been playing a game without knowing the rules. And now I finally have the rule book, but I can't go back and replay the game."

Her words stuck with me. I had spent my life berating myself for struggles I didn't understand. School had been a battlefield—easy at first, then impossible as demands grew. Math was a nightmare (now I know that dyscalculia, a learning disability linked to ADHD, was likely at play).[31] Reading comprehension was a struggle due to working memory deficits.[32] And when I couldn't keep up, I internalised it as failure. My stepmom, a bookkeeper by trade, got so frustrated with me when I couldn't grasp math concepts. To me, my academic struggles were proof that I wasn't bad just at numbers. I was bad at everything.

But it was never about intelligence. My brain just worked differently.

COMING TO TERMS WITH ADHD: MOVING FORWARD

Receiving an ADHD diagnosis as an adult brings a whirlwind of emotions—relief, grief, anger, even self-doubt. But the key to moving forward is learning to reframe the past with self-compassion. Instead of blaming myself, I've had to recognise that I was navigating life with an undiagnosed neurodevelopmental condition in a world that wasn't built for me.

My journey to reframing and healing has included:

---

[31] Elizabeth A. Boetsch et al., "Psychosocial Correlates of Dyslexia Across the Life Span," *Development and Psychopathology* 8, no. 3 (1996): 539–62, https://doi.org/10.1017/S0954579400007264.

[32] Erik G. Willcutt et al., "Neuropsychological Analyses of Comorbidity Between Reading Disability and Attention Deficit Hyperactivity Disorder: In Search of the Common Deficit," *Developmental Neuropsychology* 27, no. 1 (2005): 35–78, https://doi.org/10.1207/s15326942dn2701_3.

- **Educating myself:** ADHD-friendly resources such as *ADHD 2.0* by Edward M. Hallowell and John J. Ratey (2021) or *Scattered Minds* by Gabor Maté (2000) provided invaluable insight into how ADHD affects executive function, memory, and emotions. Though I do not agree that ADHD is solely the result of trauma, Maté's work helped me understand the impact of childhood experiences on ADHD symptoms. At the same time, research overwhelmingly supports that ADHD is a neurodevelopmental condition with strong genetic roots, influenced but not caused solely by environmental factors.
- **Connecting with other late-diagnosed women:** Finding community was life-changing. Support groups, online spaces, and ADHD coaches offered validation and practical strategies I never knew existed.
- **Reframing my past with self-compassion:** Instead of "I was lazy," I've learned to say, "I struggled because I didn't have the right tools." Instead of "I was flaky," I recognise, "I had undiagnosed executive dysfunction."
- **Adopting ADHD-friendly strategies:** Visual timers, body doubling, external accountability, and dopamine-based motivation techniques have made my daily life easier.

I believe in exploring all avenues of support for ADHD management. There's no single "right way" to approach ADHD. Instead, what matters is finding the combination of strategies that works for my unique brain.

For some of us, medication provides life-changing symptom relief. For others, therapy offers crucial emotional processing and coping skills. Coaching can provide practical strategies and accountability. Community support reduces isolation. And lifestyle adjustments, from nutrition to exercise to sleep hygiene, create a foundation for better functioning.

The key is approaching the ADHD journey with openness and self-compassion, recognising that support needs may evolve over time. What serves me today might need adjustment tomorrow, and that's perfectly normal for a brain that thrives on novelty and change.

COACHING AND DISCOVERING ABLEISM IN TRADITIONAL METHODS

I remember the exact moment I realised traditional coaching methods weren't ADHD-friendly. Back in 2015, before I knew I had ADHD, I hired a business coach while I was working in the real estate industry. He had a great reputation, charged a high-ticket price, and believed strongly in personal accountability. But every session, I dreaded showing up. Not because I didn't want to succeed but because I knew I would throw together the "homework" he assigned me the morning of our call. No matter how much I wanted to do better, my brain wouldn't cooperate. The tasks felt overwhelming, and following through in a rigid, linear way was impossible.

That experience showed me firsthand how traditional coaching methods failed my ADHD brain. At the time, I was the client, but the frustration and sense of failure stayed with me years later when I trained as a coach.

Desperate to find an approach that actually worked, I pursued a health and life coach certification myself in 2021, the same year I discovered I have ADHD. Instead of clarity, I found myself frustrated again. The way they taught us to coach felt just like what I had experienced in real estate. It was structured, linear, and focused on accountability in ways that didn't align with how my ADHD brain functioned. I kept thinking, *If this feels this hard for me, how is this supposed to help others?*

Then came the conversation that changed everything. I was speaking to a woman I barely knew, and she casually mentioned, "You talk about ADHD a lot. Have you ever considered focusing on the ADHD niche?"

The ADHD niche? I had never even heard of such a thing.

That offhand comment sent me down another rabbit hole of discovery. I started investigating ADHD coaching on LinkedIn, reaching out to people. Over the next few months, I interviewed seventy-five women with late-diagnosed ADHD.

A clear, undeniable pattern emerged in our struggles:

- Low self-esteem

- Rejection sensitivity dysphoria (RSD)
- Perfectionism
- Imposter syndrome
- Emotional dysregulation

This wasn't just about external issues like productivity or getting things done. This was an inside game, affecting the beliefs, self-talk, and emotional patterns shaping how we showed up in the world.

That inner voice is like our navigation system. She'll either be your biggest cheerleader, or she'll tell you you're too much, not enough, and everything in between.

I had already felt it in my bones, but speaking to these women confirmed what I knew deep down: Traditional coaching methods weren't built for ADHD brains. That business coach I hired had never once considered executive function deficits, emotional dysregulation, or the unique motivational wiring of ADHD brains, and why would he? A neurotypical business coach wouldn't understand or accommodate for executive functioning challenges.

That method was all about:

- Setting a goal and sticking to it.
- Pushing through resistance with willpower.
- Relying on self-discipline and consistency.

If this didn't work for me, how the hell would it work for the average ADHDer?

THE BREAKTHROUGH: WHAT ACTUALLY WORKS FOR ADHD BRAINS

The more I worked with ADHD women, the clearer it became: We don't need more willpower; we need different strategies.

Here's what the research says about the specific struggles experienced by people with ADHD when they encounter traditional coaching:

- **Executive Dysfunction:** "Traditional coaching methods assume access to consistent executive function, something that people with ADHD struggle with."[33]
- **Rejection Sensitivity:** "When accountability systems are built around shame or 'just trying harder,' they can trigger deep rejection sensitivity, making ADHD clients disengage."[34]
- **Emotional Dysregulation:** "People with ADHD experience emotions more intensely and have difficulty regulating them, making traditional self-discipline-based methods ineffective."[35]
- **The Cost of Masking:** "Women with ADHD often mask our struggles, leading to chronic stress, exhaustion, and feelings of fraudulence."[36]

Everything I read matched what I had already seen. My initial coaching training didn't reflect anything I was actually dealing with. It didn't speak to executive function challenges, emotional overwhelm, or the way motivation works when your brain is wired like mine. It was rigid and full of rules that made no sense for the way I think and process. If it felt that hard for me, I knew it couldn't work for the women I was trying to help.

So I let go of traditional coaching expectations. I paid attention to what was showing up in real conversations. I started learning more about how ADHD brains function, how nervous systems respond to pressure, and why traditional accountability methods fall flat. I threw out the structure that had never worked and started building something that did.

I watched my clients break free from shame, learn to implement the power of the pause, and shift how they reacted to overwhelm. They told me these modalities really worked. And why? Because they were designed with ADHD in mind.

---

[33] Barkley, ed., *Attention-Deficit Hyperactivity Disorder.*

[34] Dodson, "How ADHD Ignites RSD."

[35] Hallowell and Ratey, *ADHD 2.0.*

[36] Madhoo and Quinn, "A Review of Attention Deficit/Hyperactivity Disorder in Women and Girls."

A neurotypical coaching approach requires sticking to a rigid schedule, using willpower, and pushing through resistance.

An ADHD-friendly alternative employs flexible systems, body doubling, externalising tasks with visuals, and redefining "progress."

This wasn't about just coaching differently. This was about creating a fundamental shift in how we as ADHD women saw ourselves—not as broken, not as failures, but as people who needed the right tools to thrive. Redefining success is key to that shift. "Success for ADHDers isn't about rigid discipline, it's about creating systems that align with how our brains function best."[37]

And when ADHDers believe in ourselves, the real transformation begins. That's what the rest of this book is here to do. The answer isn't to push harder or follow a plan that doesn't fit you. It's about learning how your brain actually works, getting softer with yourself, and building tools that fit *you*. You'll see how to shift your perspective in ways that make life feel less like a fight and more like something you can finally work with.

BREAKING THE MOULD: BUILDING A LIFE THAT WORKS FOR MY ADHD BRAIN

Armed with my new understanding of how my brain functioned, I didn't just start coaching others. I also approached rebuilding my own life differently. The shift didn't happen overnight. It took months of trial and error, of failing and trying again. I had to learn to create structure in a way that worked for my ADHD brain. I did this through external reminders, body doubling, and forgiving myself for the days that didn't go as planned.

I started small. A sticky note by the door reminding me to grab my keys. A checklist with daily tasks taped to the fridge. A commitment to texting a friend once a day so I didn't disappear into isolation.

Over time, I've discovered several ADHD-friendly strategies that have

---

[37] Dodson, "How ADHD Ignites RSD."

transformed my daily functioning. Calendars and reminders have become nonnegotiable tools that alleviate the burden of forgetting appointments or deadlines. Sticky notes placed strategically in plain sight (though occasionally buried under papers) serve as visual anchors for important tasks.

Perhaps the most transformative practise has been implementing the "power of the pause," a cornerstone technique in ADHD coaching. This simple act of stopping and waiting before responding requires only one thing to remember: pause. When emotions run high or decisions feel urgent, I intentionally create space before acting. This single practise has prevented countless impulsive decisions and emotional outbursts.

Similarly, my "twenty-four-hour rule" for heated communications has saved me from regrettable emails and text messages. When I feel emotionally charged about responding to someone, I draft my thoughts but wait a full day before sending anything. I also now refuse to engage in conversations when either party is emotionally dysregulated. Instead, I directly ask for space if I'm overwhelmed or invite the other person to reconnect once they've regulated their emotions.

Like me, many ADHD adults benefit from visual reminders, accountability partners, and breaking tasks into micro steps. Research shows that when we externalise information through alarms, notes, or habit stacking, we're more likely to follow through.[38] Learning to work with our brains, rather than against them, is key to long-term success.

Eventually, the silence stopped feeling like a threat and started feeling like peace. The fear of being alone transformed into the realisation that I was, for the first time, truly in control of my own life.

One of the hardest expectations to let go of was how I handled my emotions. I spent years trying to contain them, believing that meltdowns were a sign of weakness. But the truth is, I'm allowed to feel. If I'm "too much" for someone, that's a them problem, not a me problem. I now live by two mantras: "What you think of me is not my business" and "Progress over perfection." These are more than just words; they are survival tools.

---

38 Hallowell and Ratey, *ADHD 2.0*.

For years, I felt like a square peg in a round hole. The constant friction, the pressure to fit in wore down my edges, leaving me feeling battered and broken. But I finally realised the problem wasn't me. It was the mould I was trying to force myself into.

Now my goal isn't to have people like me. It's to love myself and create inner peace.

Unlearning people-pleasing was a process. I used to believe that saying yes to everything made me more likable. Now I know that boundaries don't push people away. They build bridges. Saying no is not rejection. It's self-respect. And no is a complete sentence. The moment I embraced that, everything changed.

I also used to think independence meant handling everything on my own. Now I understand that ADHD-friendly independence means setting up the right kinds of support, whether that's creating accountability systems, outsourcing tasks, or just having people in my corner who understand how my brain works.

My ADHD brain wasn't built for isolation, but that doesn't mean I can't learn how to create a life that works for me. I don't have to do it perfectly. I just have to keep going.

Because on the other side of fear is freedom. And I deserve to claim it, as do you.

AN UNEXPECTED HAPPY ENDING

In 2022, my ex-husband and I unexpectedly found our way back to each other. We are still divorced but have rebuilt our relationship in a way that works for us. Now we're just partners in crime, committed to each other in a monogamous relationship, free from the expectations that once weighed us down.

Our relationship today is fundamentally different. Understanding ADHD has transformed how we interact. He now sees my patterns through a neurodivergent lens and responds with accommodation instead of judgment. This isn't about giving me a pass or lowering expectations. It just gives context for behaviours that don't fit the neurotypical mould. (Autism plays a part too, but ADHD is where the biggest shifts have happened for both of us.)

On my side, I no longer shut down or get defensive when he offers reminders or suggestions. We've learned to check in and clarify what the other person actually means instead of jumping to conclusions. My ADHD sometimes shows up as interrupting without meaning to or completely missing something he said because my brain drifted. That used to cause tension. Now we both understand it's not carelessness or disrespect. It's just how my brain works. The same goes for my autistic tendency to speak directly. It can come off as blunt, but he no longer reads it as rudeness or criticism. He gets that it's just how I communicate.

This mutual understanding has allowed us to build something new, a relationship free from the expectations that once weighed us down, focused instead on genuine connection and acceptance. Sometimes the path to finding each other requires first losing what wasn't working, then finding ourselves before we can truly see each other clearly.

SHIFTING THE FOCUS: FROM MY STORY TO OUR STORY

Getting my ADHD diagnosis was life-changing, but it was only the first step. Understanding my brain helped me make sense of so many past struggles, but what truly transformed my life was realising that I wasn't alone. The patterns I saw in myself—masking, self-doubt, perfectionism, and overwhelm—were the same struggles echoed by countless other ADHD women.

That was when I knew this journey wasn't about just me.

Although I may still share some of my own experiences throughout this book, my focus is shifting. This isn't just my story. It's our story. It's about the shared experiences of ADHD women who have spent years feeling misunderstood. It's about the research that validates what we've intuitively known all along. And most importantly, it's about the practical, ADHD-friendly strategies that help us move forward, not by forcing ourselves to fit into neurotypical expectations but by embracing how our brains actually work.

This is where our collective journey truly begins. The discoveries I've made about managing ADHD, building relationships that honour our neurodiversity, and creating systems that work with our brains instead of against them aren't just personal wins. They're insights that might help you too.

Because ultimately, the most powerful realisation in my ADHD journey wasn't just understanding my own brain. It was discovering I was part of a community of incredible, resilient, creative women who had been navigating similar challenges all along. Women who, like me, had spent years thinking they were broken, only to discover they were simply wired differently.

Together, we're rewriting the narrative around ADHD. We're creating new pathways to thrive in a world that wasn't built for us. And we're proving that with the right understanding, strategies, and support, our ADHD brains aren't just manageable; they're extraordinary.

In the chapters that follow, I'll dive deeper into the specific challenges we face as ADHD women and, more importantly, the strategies that actually work for our uniquely wired brains. Because while getting diagnosed may be the beginning of understanding, learning to embrace and work with our ADHD is the true journey that continues to unfold with each passing day.

It's a journey we don't have to take alone.

Chapter Four

Hiding in Plain Sight with the ADHD Mask

"IF I HAVE TO FAKE ONE MORE POLITE SMILE, I MIGHT ACTUALLY scream."

A coaching client named Claire shared this with me during our Zoom interview as she was gripping her pen so tightly it left deep marks on the paper and pressed into the callous that had clearly formed from years of this habit.

She would force herself to nod at the right moments, her smile tight, her head aching from the effort of holding it all together. The voices around her blurred—she should be paying attention, but all she could think was, *I can't keep this up much longer.* From the outside she looked like she belonged here, like she had it all under control.

Inside, she was unravelling.

"Did I send that email? What was the deadline for that project? I hope I didn't sound rude just now." The thoughts stacked on top of each other, her brain running damage control in real time. She was watching, adjusting, second-guessing. Rehearsing her responses before she even knew if she'd need them.

She told me when she made it back to her office from a meeting, she dropped into her chair, the tension finally leaving her shoulders. A ninety-minute meeting left her feeling like she just ran a marathon.

She knew this wasn't normal.

Claire didn't struggle with her job because she wasn't capable. She struggled because every task took twice the effort. Following discussions, managing priorities, and suppressing her natural impulsivity demanded relentless, exhausting self-monitoring. Yet no one saw it.

ADHD masking is the invisible labour of appearing neurotypical. The constant, silent calculations—when to nod, when to hold back a comment, when to pretend you're fine when your brain is anything but.

The cost is chronic exhaustion, burnout, and a slow erosion of self-trust.

ADHD masking refers to the conscious or unconscious strategies we employ to hide our symptoms and conform to societal expectations. This phenomenon is particularly prevalent among women with ADHD, who often feel compelled to suppress behaviours like impulsivity, inattentiveness, or hyperactivity to align with traditional gender norms. Although no studies have directly linked ADHD masking to chronic cortisol elevation, research on emotional suppression and stress physiology suggests that long-term masking may place a significant strain on the body's stress-response systems.[39]

To really understand the impact of masking, we need to look at when it starts, how it shows up over time, and why so many of us don't even realise we're doing it. It's not something that appears overnight. It builds slowly, often beginning in childhood and shaping how we move through the world.

---

[39] Marisa Mylett, "'I Wish I Could Just Be Myself': Social Camouflaging, Internalized Stigma, and Internalizing Mental Health Problems in Adult ADHD" (MA thesis, Simon Fraser University, 2022), https://summit.sfu.ca/item/35794.

THE DEVELOPMENT OF MASKING ACROSS LIFE STAGES
ADOLESCENCE: THE ONSET OF CAMOUFLAGE

"I remember the exact moment I realised I needed to be different," Alison said, her voice carrying the weight of decades spent pretending. "I was thirteen, sitting in math class, and I asked what my classmates thought was a 'stupid' question. The laughter still rings in my ears. After that, I stopped raising my hand."

From then on, Alison became a quiet observer, a social anthropologist studying the neurotypical world. Instead of taking notes on algebra, she tracked the mannerisms of the popular girls: how they spoke, how they moved, how they seemed effortlessly in control.

"I memorised their patterns like a survival manual," she admitted. "If I wanted to fit in, I had to be like them."

For many of us with ADHD, this realisation happens at some point in adolescence. We begin to understand that our natural behaviours aren't "acceptable." Some, like Alison, imitate social confidence. Others study the quiet, academically successful girls, hoping that discipline will make them blend in. Different masks, same pain.

By our teenage years, the pressure to be composed, focused, and socially aware becomes relentless. Many of us feel it before we can even name it: the way teachers expect us to sit still and pay attention, the way friends seem to navigate social dynamics effortlessly while we're still replaying something we said an hour ago.

So we adapt. Some of us become obsessive notetakers, colour-coding everything to make up for our forgetfulness. Others start memorising social scripts, watching how the "put-together" girls behave and mimicking them. We learn to laugh at the right times, nod even when we've lost track of the conversation, and work twice as hard just to appear as organised as everyone else.

But behind it all, we're exhausted.

Samantha shared her route. "I created colour-coded systems for everything. My notebooks were pristine. I'd spend hours making study guides that looked perfect." She let out a small laugh, but there was an edge to it. "Everyone thought I was incredibly organised and focused, but the truth was, I was compensating. What took others an hour took me three because I couldn't focus. I was exhausted all the time, but no one knew because on the outside, I looked like I had it all together."

I once saw one of Samantha's notebooks. It was a work of art, perfectly formatted, highlighted in complementary colours, every section neatly underlined. But when I asked her about that class, she admitted she remembered almost nothing. All her mental energy had gone into making her notes look perfect, not absorbing the material.

ADULTHOOD: THE PAIN OF CONCEALMENT

Masking doesn't stop after high school. As responsibilities multiply, so does the pressure to appear competent. Many ADHD women build entire careers on the illusion of having it all together, while privately, they're drowning.

Donna, an attorney who responded to my LinkedIn outreach, carried herself with the kind of confidence I've always envied. Sharp. Commanding. Effortlessly in control. At least that's the image she projected.

But during our interview, the professional mask slipped.

"In court, I'm known for being sharp, quick on my feet, and meticulously prepared," she told me. "What my colleagues don't see is that I stay up until two in the morning triple-checking everything because I'm terrified of making a mistake." She paused, absentmindedly twirling her glass. "They don't see me crying in my car from exhaustion or the panic attacks I have before big meetings."

Her words hit me like a punch to the gut, not just because of their weight but because of how deeply familiar they feel.

Then she said something that stayed with me long after our conversation ended: "I've built this reputation as someone who's always on top of things, but maintaining that image is killing me slowly."

In a follow-up conversation, she told me she started therapy. It was helping, she said, but decades of masking don't unravel overnight.

Societal norms frequently dictate that women should be organised, attentive, and emotionally stable. These expectations pressure women with ADHD to hide their symptoms more diligently than men, leading to underdiagnosis and misdiagnosis. Research indicates that women with ADHD receive diagnoses an average of ten years later than men with similar symptom severity, largely due to effective masking.[40]

THE HIDDEN COSTS OF MASKING

While masking might offer temporary relief from judgment, it comes at a cost that can build quietly over the years until it becomes impossible to ignore: anxiety, depression, a fractured sense of self.

I've struggled with anxiety for as long as I can remember, but it wasn't until my ADHD diagnosis that I started connecting the dots. I wasn't just anxious. I was exhausted from constantly monitoring myself, filtering my words, adjusting my reactions. And I'm far from alone.

Earlier in the book, I shared what it was like to hold things together during my divorce while everything inside me was unravelling. I also talked about the shame I felt after not being invited to that birthday party, and how hard I tried to act like it didn't matter. That wasn't just emotional stress. That was masking. And it takes a toll.

Jenna's story really stuck with me. For years, she was misdiagnosed with anxiety and depression. Then a perceptive therapist finally caught what everyone else had missed.

"My therapist eventually realised that my anxiety wasn't the real issue. It was the result of decades of masking," she told me. "I was always on high alert, making sure I didn't talk too much, didn't interrupt, didn't space out. That kind of self-policing wears you down. Eventually, I just broke."

Her story isn't rare. It's one I've heard over and over. It's the same one I've lived myself. Women misdiagnosed for years before realising ADHD was the missing piece. It says a lot about how the medical system has overlooked ADHD in women. Quinn notes that "females with ADHD may develop better coping strategies than males to mask their symptoms,"

---

40 Madhoo and Quinn, "A Review of Attention Deficit/Hyperactivity Disorder in Women and Girls."

which lowers the likelihood of recognition and diagnosis.[41] That delay can mean years of being treated for the wrong thing and believing the problem is just us.

But masking doesn't just take a toll on our mental health. It chips away at our sense of identity. When you spend a lifetime shaping yourself into what other people expect, you start losing sight of who you actually are.

I felt that disconnect growing throughout my adult life. There was a gap between the version of me that people saw and the one buried under layers of pretending.

Maya, a writer I spoke with, put it into words in a way that really hit home.

"After decades of playing a part, I genuinely didn't know who I was anymore. I had a different persona for work, for friends, for family. Each one was carefully crafted to hide my ADHD traits. When my therapist asked me what I truly enjoyed or what my actual personality was like, I couldn't answer. That terrified me."

Her words hit me hard. She described something I had felt but never named: that deep, quiet grief of losing yourself under years of performing normal. And how could you not, when the world keeps telling you you're getting it wrong? Too much in some moments, not enough in others.

For many of us with ADHD, this isn't just social awareness. It's survival. Masking is the exhausting act of suppressing our natural behaviours to fit in. It's mimicking neurotypical social patterns, over-preparing to avoid failure, and carrying a mental checklist of "acceptable" behaviours. And while it can help us navigate the world, it comes at a steep cost: burnout, anxiety, and the painful disconnect from our authentic selves.

The idea of "fake it till you make it" is a misleading trap that many ADHD women fall into. It's reinforced by toxic positivity culture. And I include myself in that!

---

41 (Patricia O. Quinn and Manisha Madhoo, "A Review of Attention-Deficit/Hyperactivity Disorder in Women and Girls: Uncovering This Hidden Diagnosis," *Primary Care Companion for CNS Disorders* 16, no. 3 (2014), https://doi.org/10.4088/PCC.13r01596.

The stories women have shared with me about the lengths they've gone to appear "normal" are sometimes heartbreaking. One recounted going to work with the stomach flu because she was so afraid of being seen as lazy or making excuses. "I infected three coworkers and eventually had to leave anyway when I couldn't stop throwing up," she wrote. "That's what masking does. It makes us do irrational things just to appear 'worthy.'"

Another described preparing for a job interview by memorising "normal" responses to questions about organisation methods, knowing her actual chaotic-but-functional system would be judged harshly.

Sandy, a school counselor who participated in my research, described masking as "constantly translating myself into a different language. I monitor everything, my gestures, my tone, how long I've been talking, whether I'm making enough eye contact but not too much. By the end of the day, I'm not just tired; I'm empty."

Research has shown that ADHD masking is more common in women, largely due to social expectations. Unlike boys, who are often diagnosed based on external hyperactive symptoms, girls with ADHD tend to internalise their struggles and develop compensatory behaviours. Over time, this effort to appear "normal" can lead to chronic stress, anxiety, and even identity confusion.

Neurological studies show that masking activates regions of the brain associated with performance monitoring and cognitive control while suppressing regions related to spontaneous self-expression. This creates a neurological state similar to constantly performing onstage, requiring heightened vigilance and self-monitoring. MRI studies demonstrate that sustained masking effort correlates with reduced activity in regions responsible for authentic emotional processing and increased activity in those associated with social conformity.[42]

Many women in the MRI study expressed relief at understanding the neurological basis of why masking feels so exhausting. "It actually helped me

---

42 Lucy Ann Livingston et al., "Compensatory Strategies Below the Behavioral Surface in Autism: A Qualitative Study," *The Lancet Psychiatry* 6, no. 9 (2019): 766–77, https://doi.org/10.1016/s2215-0366(19)30224-x.

feel less broken somehow," one participant wrote. "It's not that I'm 'too sensitive' or 'can't handle normal life.' My brain is literally working overtime."[43]

This sentiment came up repeatedly in different forms. The validation that comes from understanding our experiences through a neurological lens rather than a moral or character-based one can be profoundly healing for many women with ADHD.

RECOGNISING ADHD MASKING AND BEGINNING TO UNMASK

For many, getting diagnosed with ADHD is only the beginning. The harder part comes after, when you realise how much of your personality has been shaped by masking. You start to wonder, *Who am I without the filtering, the pretending, the constant effort to seem "fine"?* That's where unmasking begins. It's not a single moment. It's a slow, often uncomfortable process of reclaiming what's real.

Unmasking isn't about abandoning every coping mechanism. It's about deciding which ones empower us and which ones hold us back. It's a process of self-discovery and self-acceptance, and for many of us, it's terrifying.

One woman I interviewed told me about her efforts to unmask more often.

"It's terrifying," she admitted. "Last week, I actually told my boss I was having an 'ADHD day' and needed to work from home, where I could pace and talk to myself without bothering anyone. I nearly hyperventilated before sending that email. Ten years ago, I would have rather died than admit that."

Vanessa, a professor who responded to my survey, shared a similar experience. She began her unmasking journey gradually, testing the waters in spaces where she felt safe.

"I started with close friends, people I knew would accept me," she said. "I gave myself permission to fidget during our coffee dates instead of sitting perfectly still. I stopped rehearsing what I wanted to say before speaking."

---

[43] Livingston et al., "Compensatory Strategies Below the Behavioral Surface in Autism."

She hesitated here, as if debating whether to continue.

"And I actually told them about my ADHD and how hard I'd been working to hide it," she finally said. "Their acceptance was like oxygen to me."

Her words stayed with me. I made a mental note to text her a follow-up, which, in true ADHD fashion, meant I forgot entirely—that is until three weeks later when I had an *oh crap* moment and scrambled to text her back like no time had passed.

She replied within minutes. Warm, understanding, zero judgment. She even laughed about it, telling me she does the same thing. That one moment reminded me how powerful it can be to unmask with the right people. Knowing the real story behind your quirks and gaps shifts the whole dynamic. You stop bracing for judgment. You start letting yourself be seen.

THE GRADUATED UNMASKING PLAN

For many ADHD adults, unmasking isn't as simple as "just being yourself." Years or even decades of suppressing natural behaviours for social acceptance make the process complicated. The Graduated Unmasking Plan offers a structured way to ease into authenticity while balancing real-world social dynamics.

This approach involves the following steps:

1. **Perform a safety assessment:** Identify environments from safest to most challenging.[44]
2. **Select natural behaviours:** Choose one to three ADHD-related behaviours you usually suppress but would like to express.[45]

---

[44] Ludmila N. Praslova, "The Strain of Masking: Reclaiming Our Neurodivergent Selves," *Psychology Today*, last modified July 20, 2025, https://www.psychologytoday.com/us/blog/positively-different/202411/the-strain-of-masking-reclaiming-our-neurodivergent-selves; and Ioanna Stavraki, "What Is ADHD Masking? Signs You Are Masking & How to Deal with It," Simply Psychology, last modified January 26, 2024, https://www.simplypsychology.org/adhd-masking.html.

[45] "ADHD Masking in Adults: Signs, Risks and How to Unmask," Kantoko, May 18, 2025, https://www.kantoko.com.au/articles/adhd-masking-in-adults; and Cat Salladin, "What Does It Mean to Unmask Neurodivergence?," NeuroSpark, accessed September 17, 2025, https://www.neurosparkhealth.com/blog/what-does-it-mean-to-unmask-neurodivergence.

3. **Start in the safest spaces:** Practise authentic expression only in environments with the highest safety rating.[46]
4. **Prepare a script:** Create brief, confident responses for potential questions about behavioural changes.[47]
5. **Activate your support system:** Engage one to two trusted people as "authenticity allies" who understand and support your unmasking goals.[48]
6. **Gradually expand:** As your comfort grows, expand authentic expression into additional environments.[49]

This structured method acknowledges the emotional and social risks of immediate, full unmasking. Research shows that many ADHD and autistic individuals fear stigma when revealing their natural behaviours, which can lead to heightened anxiety and social exclusion.[50] However, when individuals gradually introduce their authentic selves into safe environments, they build confidence and resilience.[51]

One participant described her experience with unmasking stimming behaviours. "I love to rock back and forth when I'm thinking, but I've always suppressed it in public. I started allowing myself to do it at home, then with my closest friend, then in small team meetings." She added with a laugh, "I'm not ready for the boardroom yet, but I'm getting there."

I found myself nodding in agreement, remembering all the small motions I've suppressed, the way I rub my index finger along my bottom

---

46 Praslova, "The Strain of Masking"; and Ed Taylor, "Unmasking in Relationships: Safety, Shame, and Being Seen," Tiimo, May 28, 2025, https://www.tiimoapp.com/resource-hub/unmasking-adhd-in-relationships.

47 Salladin, "What Does It Mean to Unmask Neurodivergence?"; and Stavraki, "What Is ADHD Masking?"

48 Taylor, "Unmasking in Relationships"; and Janina Maschke, "Unmasking with ADHD," *Psychology Today*, January 31, 2025, https://www.psychologytoday.com/us/blog/empowered-with-adhd/202501/unmasking-with-adhd.

49 "ADHD Masking in Adults: Signs, Risks and How to Unmask," Kantoko; and Maschke, "Unmasking with ADHD."

50 Lotte Van Putten et al., "Is Camouflaging Unique for Autism? A Comparison of Camouflaging Between Adults with Autism and ADHD," *Autism Research* 17, no. 3 (2024): 460–73, https://doi.org/10.1002/aur.3099.

51 Steven K. Kapp et al., "'People Should Be Allowed to Do What They Like': Autistic Adults' Views and Experiences of Stimming," *Autism* 23, no. 7 (2019): 1782–92, https://doi.org/10.1177/1362361319829628.

lip when thinking, the bouncing leg, the need to touch interesting textures. Small freedoms that neurotypical people take for granted.

Build Self-Awareness

The first step in our unmasking journey is noticing when we're masking. Many of us have been doing it for so long that it's become automatic. Masking, also known as camouflaging, involves consciously or subconsciously hiding ADHD symptoms to conform to societal expectations or avoid stigma. This behaviour can become so habitual that individuals may not realise they're doing it.[52]

"I sometimes don't even realise I'm doing it until I get home and feel the physical relief of letting the mask drop," a woman I interviewed shared.

To start identifying these patterns, ask yourself:

- Am I filtering my words to avoid judgment?
- Am I mimicking someone else instead of being myself?
- Do I feel exhausted after socialising?
- Do I force myself to be hyper-organised or perfect to compensate for ADHD struggles?

Masking requires significant mental energy and can lead to stress, anxiety, and burnout. The constant effort to monitor and adjust behaviours consumes mental resources, leading to exhaustion over time.[53]

Keeping a journal of these observations can be incredibly insightful, at least in theory. One woman in my study laughed as she admitted, "I start strong for three days and then forget about it for six months!" A relatable struggle for many of us with ADHD. We're pros at starting journals, only for them to end up in the ever-growing journal graveyard.

---

[52] Flynn Williams, "What to Know About ADHD Masking," Medical News Today, June 19, 2023, https://www.medicalnewstoday.com/articles/adhd-masking.

[53] Williams, "What to Know About ADHD Masking."

That's another thing I've learned through this research: Our challenges aren't character flaws. They're shared experiences, manifestations of how our brains work. And there's something deeply comforting in that realisation.

Challenge the "Rules" We've Created

Many of us operate under silent rules we've developed over the years:

- I have to be on time, or people will see me as unreliable.
- I can't ask for help, or people will think I'm lazy.
- I need to double-check everything to avoid making mistakes.

These unspoken rules often stem from a desire to conform to neurotypical standards and avoid the shame and stigma associated with ADHD.[54]

As one participant put it, "I realised I had this invisible rule book governing my entire life, but I didn't write the rules."

Darcy, who works in design, shared a breakthrough moment: "I had this rule that I could never mention ADHD at work because people would think less of me. When I finally disclosed to my manager, not only was she supportive, but she helped me restructure my workflow in ways that played to my strengths. All those years of hiding for nothing!"

Her experience wasn't universal. Several women reported negative reactions to disclosure, but these experiences highlight an important question we all need to ask ourselves: Are these rules helping us, or are they rooted in fear?

A quick reality check can help:

- Where did this rule come from?

---

[54] Kathleen G. Nadeau, "Why ADHD Is More Challenging for Women," CHADD, Attention Magazine, June 2023, https://chadd.org/attention-article/why-adhd-is-more-challenging-for-women/.

- Who actually told me this was true?
- Is there any flexibility in how I approach it?

Disclaimer: While many workplaces are becoming more understanding of ADHD, experiences with disclosure can vary. If you're unsure whether disclosure will be well received, consider factors like company culture, leadership attitudes, and legal protections. If HR isn't a safe option, seeking advice from trusted colleagues, external mentors, or legal resources can help you make an informed decision.

Reframe ADHD as a Strength

For many women in my study, this was the hardest shift to make. After years of trying to "fix" themselves to fit neurotypical expectations, the idea of embracing ADHD traits felt counterintuitive.

But instead of masking our natural tendencies, what if we leaned into them?

- If we interrupt in conversations, we can acknowledge our excitement rather than shaming ourselves.
- If we fidget, we can use it as a tool for focus rather than suppressing it.
- If we struggle with structure, we can lean into flexible planning methods rather than forcing rigid systems.

Unmasking and embracing ADHD traits can lead to a more authentic and fulfilling life. This is about shifting the narrative from viewing these traits as deficits to recognising them as unique strengths.[55]

---

[55] Soheil Mahdi et al., "An International Qualitative Study of Ability and Disability in ADHD Using the WHO-ICF Framework," *European Child and Adolescent Psychiatry* 26 (2017): 1219–31, https://doi.org/10.1007/s00787-017-0983-1.

WHY ADHD WOMEN WHO "SEEM FINE" ARE OFTEN STRUGGLING THE MOST

Some of the most accomplished women I interviewed also described the most intense internal struggles.

From the outside, many of us look like we have it all together. We're successful in our careers. We're resourceful. We've always found ways to make things work. Maybe we've been praised for our ability to multitask, for our creativity, for our drive. People see our wins—the new job, the impressive networking skills, the ability to pivot when needed—and assume that means we're thriving.

But what they don't see is the exhaustion of keeping up appearances. They don't see the missed deadlines, the unread emails piling up, the late-night panic of trying to finish what should have been a simple task. They don't see the silent self-doubt, the anxiety that comes from knowing we're always one forgotten step away from disaster.

One interview that particularly struck me was with Olivia, an event planner with ADHD who presents a flawlessly organised facade to clients.

"My events run like clockwork. No one would ever guess that behind the scenes, I'm in complete chaos. I set a hundred reminders. I stay up all night triple-checking details. And I've developed elaborate systems to compensate for my executive dysfunction. People tell me how 'naturally organised' I am, and I just smile and nod while feeling like a complete fraud."

As soon as she said it, I nodded, a wave of recognition washing over me. I knew that struggle firsthand. For ADHD women who seem outwardly capable, the battle often plays out in silence. The better we become at masking our challenges, the less likely others are to believe we need support—and that in itself can be profoundly isolating.[56]

I recognised these capable women because I was one of them. For about a year, I took a shot in real estate, and I was *good* at it. I wasn't just selling homes; I was selling an image. A version of myself that looked confident, capable, and completely in control.

---

[56] Dodson, "How ADHD Ignites RSD."

I threw myself into the business, going all in on the high-energy, high-stakes world of door-knocking. While other agents hesitated, I pounded the pavement, introducing myself to strangers, turning cold leads into warm conversations, and closing deals. I knew how to read people, build trust, and create momentum. In just one year, I landed twenty-five sales, all from sheer persistence, social finesse, and a willingness to do what most people avoided.

From the outside, I looked like I had it all figured out. But inside, I was constantly teetering on the edge of burnout.

Then reality caught up with me.

One day, I made a mistake on a contract. A big mistake. The kind that could have gotten me sued. I had errors and omissions insurance, but that didn't stop the gut-wrenching panic that set in. The legal paperwork of real estate was a nightmare. A labyrinth of fine print, deadlines, and technical jargon. Every contract felt like a ticking time bomb, waiting for me to miss some crucial detail.

I spiralled. Had I ruined everything? Would I get sued? Had I just destroyed my career?

I obsessed over the error, replayed every scenario in my head, and didn't sleep for three days straight. The weight of responsibility, of keeping up the appearance of competence while secretly drowning, was crushing.

In the end, everything worked out. But I knew I was done.

The stress of keeping up with contracts, deadlines, and legal fine print made real estate unsustainable for me. The very things that made me excel—the energy, the people skills, the chase—were the same things that drained me.

I could sell houses all day long, but the back-end responsibilities—the organisation, the fine details, the follow-through—were my breaking point.

And I know I'm not alone in this. Again and again, I've seen the same story play out for ADHD women. We mask our struggles so well that no one sees them. We thrive in areas that are interactive, high energy, and dynamic. But when it comes to the back-end work, tedious details, executive function demands, and hidden labour, that's where we break.[57]

And often, it's not a lack of skill. It's the sheer weight of keeping up the mask that eventually pushes us to walk away.

Success doesn't mean ease for us ADHD women. Many of us assume that if we are achieving outward success, our struggles must not be "real" ADHD. But ADHD isn't about what we can do. It's about how we do it and what it costs us. Research shows that ADHD individuals who maintain outward success often have elevated stress hormones and higher rates of stress-related health conditions despite their achievements, showing the physiological toll of compensating for ADHD challenges.[58]

This insight resonated strongly with the women I interviewed and mirrors my own experience in real estate. Several had been told they "couldn't possibly have ADHD" because they were successful in their careers or academics. One woman, a surgeon, was told by a colleague that her ADHD diagnosis must be a mistake because she "couldn't have made it through medical school with ADHD."

Hearing that kind of invalidation stings almost as much as the daily struggles themselves.

Remember, this is an inside game. Looking like we have it together on the outside means nothing when we're fighting an internal battle as ADHD women.

Living this way comes at a price. Through my interviews, several clear patterns emerged.

BURNOUT

Burnout is more than stress. It's the point where your brain and body start to give out from carrying too much for too long. It shows up as bone-deep exhaustion, emotional flatness, and a growing sense that

---

57 Barkley, ed., *Attention-Deficit Hyperactivity Disorder*.

58 Kenneth Blum et al., "Attention-Deficit-Hyperactivity Disorder and Reward Deficiency Syndrome," *Neuropsychiatric Disease and Treatment* 4, no. 5 (2008): 893–917, https://doi.org/10.2147/NDT.S2627.

nothing you do matters. For ADHD women, it's common because we're constantly working against systems that don't support how our brains work.

Monica, a marketing director, shared her breaking point.

"I was the person who always delivered, no matter what. But I was running on pure adrenaline for years. One day, my body just shut down. I couldn't get out of bed for weeks. The doctor said it was severe adrenal fatigue from chronic stress."

Constantly pushing through ADHD challenges without support leads to deep exhaustion. The effort it takes to seem fine drains us mentally and physically.[59] Nearly 80 percent of the women I interviewed reported experiencing at least one major burnout episode that required time off work or significant life changes.

IMPOSTER SYNDROME

Imposter syndrome shows up when your achievements feel like accidents and you live with a quiet fear that someone's about to find you out. For ADHD women, it often comes from years of masking our struggles while appearing competent on the outside.

"I'm convinced that someday everyone will realise I'm a fraud," admitted Rachel, a professor with ADHD. "I've published papers and won teaching awards, but all I can think about is how close I came to missing deadlines or how many all-nighters I pulled to compensate for my executive dysfunction. If my colleagues knew how much I struggle behind the scenes, would they still respect me?"

Because our struggles are invisible to others, we start questioning whether our success is real. This theme of imposter syndrome appeared in virtually every interview I conducted.

---

[59] Maté, *Scattered Minds*.

ANXIETY AND EMOTIONAL EXHAUSTION

Living with ADHD means carrying an invisible weight. The fear of missing something important. The shame of needing reminders for things others seem to manage easily. The guilt of disappointing people, even when you're doing your best. Over time, this creates a baseline of chronic stress that wears you down.

Stephanie, an accountant with ADHD, put it like this: "It's like background radiation. Even when everything seems fine, there's this constant buzz of anxiety. I'm always bracing for something to go wrong, for someone to realise I'm not actually as capable as they think."

Research confirms this pattern. One study found that ADHD in women is strongly linked with chronic stress, anxiety, and internalised shame due to years of coping with unmet expectations and being misunderstood.[60]

HYPER-INDEPENDENCE

One of the most common patterns I saw in the women I interviewed was the pressure to handle everything alone. Not out of pride but out of survival. When you're constantly dismissed or misunderstood, you stop expecting support. You start believing that needing help is weakness, and independence becomes your default.

If no one sees our struggle, they won't offer help. But when we do ask for support, we may be dismissed because we "seem fine." Over time, this leads to the belief that we have to do everything alone.

Karen, a single mother with ADHD, shared, "I've become so independent out of necessity that I don't know how to ask for help anymore. People see me managing a career and raising kids alone, and they assume I'm superwoman. The truth is, I'm drowning, but I've forgotten how to reach for a lifeline."

Her words stayed with me. How many of us have become so skilled at coping that we've lost the ability to connect authentically and ask for what we need?

---

60 Madhoo and Quinn, "A Review of Attention Deficit/Hyperactivity Disorder in Women and Girls."

BREAKING THE CYCLE: A DIFFERENT APPROACH

So what actually works for us? Instead of forcing ourselves into neurotypical strategies, the key is finding ADHD-friendly systems—ones that work with our brains, not against them.

BUILDING EXTERNAL SUPPORT SYSTEMS

Once we stop trying to do everything alone, the next step is figuring out what kind of support actually works. For ADHD women, that often means building systems outside ourselves to help manage what's happening inside. Whether it's reminders, accountability, or practical help, these structures can make the difference between spinning our wheels and making real progress.

Jessica, an entrepreneur with ADHD, came up with an unconventional solution.

"I formed what I call my 'executive function board of directors,' a small group of friends and colleagues who each help with different aspects of my business. My detail-oriented friend reviews contracts before I sign them. My time-management-savvy colleague helps me set realistic deadlines. We all play to our strengths."

Having accountability partners who understand ADHD is crucial for sustainable success. Several women described similar scaffolding systems, external structures that support their internal challenges.

REFRAMING SUCCESS

After years of chasing neurotypical standards, many of us hit a point where we start asking a different question: What if success isn't what we were taught to believe? For the women I spoke to, redefining success wasn't about lowering the bar. It was about making it real, sustainable, and rooted in self-respect.

"I used to think success meant doing everything perfectly and independently," said Natalie, a therapist with ADHD. "Now I define success as knowing when to ask for help, when to let things go, and how to prioritise my well-being alongside my achievements."

Letting go of perfectionism and defining success on their own terms was perhaps the most transformative shift for many women in my study.

CREATING DOPAMINE-FRIENDLY WORKFLOWS

One of the biggest game changers for the women I interviewed was learning to work *with* their brain instead of against it. When we understand how dopamine affects focus and motivation, we can stop forcing ourselves into systems that don't fit. The key is creating workflows that support how our brains actually function.

Andrea, a writer with ADHD, saw a dramatic change in her productivity when she stopped forcing herself into a rigid structure and started working with her brain.

"I broke up with traditional nine-to-five schedules. Now I work in intense ninety-minute blocks followed by real breaks. I gamify boring tasks by setting timers and giving myself small rewards. I schedule my most creative work during my peak energy times. My output has actually increased since I stopped fighting my brain's natural patterns."

The women who reported the highest satisfaction with their work had all found ways to restructure their days to align with their natural energy patterns. Finding ways to make the "boring" parts of work more engaging isn't just helpful; it's necessary.

PRACTISING SELF-COMPASSION

For many high-functioning ADHD women, the turning point wasn't about doing more. It was about softening the way they spoke to themselves. The women in my research kept coming back to one thing: self-compassion. Not as a nice idea but as a necessary shift in how they managed their day-to-day struggles.

"The game changer for me wasn't a productivity hack; it was learning to talk to myself with kindness," said Michelle, a nurse with ADHD. "I stopped berating myself for ADHD moments and started recognising how hard I'm working to manage them. The less energy I spend on self-criticism, the more I have for actually addressing challenges."

Many of the women I interviewed described shifting from self-criticism to self-compassion as the hardest but most important change. Recognising that struggling doesn't mean failing is crucial for our well-being.

For so many of us with ADHD, holding it together on the outside doesn't reflect what's happening inside. I know that feeling well.

OWNING OUR ADHD AND LIVING AUTHENTICALLY

For many women I spoke with, learning about ADHD wasn't just an explanation. It was a turning point. Years of self-blame started to loosen their grip, making room for something new: self-acceptance.

Diane, a consultant diagnosed in her forties, described it in a way that stuck with me.

"Learning about ADHD was like discovering a secret manual to a game I had been playing on hard mode my entire life," she said. "Before my diagnosis, I was convinced I was just broken. My forgetfulness, my impulsivity, my struggles with organisation all felt like personal failings, not a brain-based difference."

Her words resonated deeply. Many of us spent years believing we just weren't trying hard enough. That we were somehow less than. No matter how much effort we put in, we still missed appointments, lost track of tasks, and felt like we were constantly one step behind.

Earlier, I talked about my struggles with working memory and dyscalculia. But for most of my life, I didn't know those challenges had names. I just thought I was falling short, no matter how hard I tried.

That belief grinds you down. It sinks into your bones, whispering that you're not enough. It follows you into every classroom, every workplace, every conversation where you second-guess yourself before anyone else can. It doesn't just wear you down; it erodes you, slowly, until you start to believe that struggle is just who you are.

So many of us internalised the idea that we were simply "bad" at certain things. But the truth is, we weren't given the right support. Our brains weren't broken. We just needed the right tools.

This is why early diagnosis is so critical, not just because it provides tools for managing ADHD but because it offers the validation needed to break free from the lifelong sense of brokenness that so many of us have carried.

But ADHD isn't a measure of intelligence. It's a challenge of executive function. Understanding that our disorganisation isn't a personal failing and that our dopamine-seeking behaviours, like turning to stimulation for regulation, are simply our brains' way of searching for balance can be incredibly liberating.[61]

The shift from self-blame to self-acceptance has neurological benefits. Brain-imaging studies show that self-criticism activates threat centres in the brain, while self-compassion activates care systems. For our ADHD brains already dealing with executive function challenges, self-blame further impairs cognitive performance, creating a negative spiral. In contrast, self-acceptance improves cognitive flexibility and problem-solving capacity.[62]

I found this research particularly meaningful. When I shared it with participants, many responded emotionally. The scientific validation that harsh self-talk isn't just psychologically harmful but neurologically counterproductive helped them begin to shift their inner narratives.

Alexandra, an artist who responded eloquently to my outreach, spent decades trying to contain her emotional intensity.

"I was always told I was 'too emotional,' 'too sensitive,' 'too reactive.' I exhausted myself trying to flatten my emotional landscape to make others comfortable. The day I realised that my emotional depth was actually connected to my creativity was the day I started to heal."

For many women in my study, one of the hardest expectations to let

---

[61] Dodson, "How ADHD Ignites RSD."

[62] Kristin D. Neff and Roos Vonk, "Self-Compassion Versus Global Self-Esteem: Two Different Ways of Relating to Oneself," *Journal of Personality* 77, no. 1 (2009): 23–50, https://doi.org/10.1111/j.1467-6494.2008.00537.x.

go of was how they handled emotions. They had spent years trying to contain them, believing that emotional intensity was a sign of weakness or immaturity. But the truth is, we're allowed to feel deeply. If we're "too much" for someone, that's not our problem to solve.

Sarah, a teacher, found freedom in boundaries.

"I used to say yes to everything out of fear of rejection. I'd overcommit, burn out, then hate myself for not being able to follow through. Learning that no is a complete sentence changed everything for me. Setting boundaries doesn't push people away. It builds healthier relationships."

For years, many participants felt like they were playing a game where the rules were never designed for them. The constant friction, the pressure to fit in wore down their edges, leaving them feeling battered and broken. But eventually, they realised the problem isn't us; it's the mould we've been trying to force ourselves into.

REBUILDING OUR LIVES TO ACCOMMODATE OUR ADHD

After diagnosis, many of us immersed ourselves in learning everything we could about ADHD. Those of us with AuDHD (both autism and ADHD) often became our own special interest. We needed to understand ADHD, not just for the sake of knowledge, but as a path to self-compassion.

The more we learn, the more we soften toward ourselves. It isn't about lowering expectations. It's about reshaping them to align with how our brains actually function.

After her diagnosis, Tamara completely redesigned her workspace to support her focus. She works as a paralegal and shared truly thoughtful insights in our conversations.

"I realised traditional organisation systems weren't working for me, so I created what my family jokingly calls my 'ADHD command centre.' Everything is visible: clear bins, open shelving, colour-coding everywhere. What looks chaotic to others is actually perfectly functional for my brain because I can see everything at once."

She even included photos of her workspace with her interview responses. What might seem disorganised to a neurotypical person made perfect sense when she explained her system. Nothing was hidden away. Everything was colour-coded and visually accessible.

For many of us, the most surprising part of making ADHD-friendly changes was that, for the first time, we didn't feel guilt. We felt liberated. Instead of forcing ourselves to fit into rigid neurotypical structures, we started designing lives that actually worked for our brains.

Lauren, a small-business owner whose responses were refreshingly blunt, transformed her approach to time management.

"I threw out traditional scheduling approaches and created a system based on energy levels rather than clock time. I work in 'sprints' when my focus is strong, and I build in recovery periods. I've stopped fighting my brain's natural rhythms. As a result, I'm actually more productive and much happier."

One of the biggest game changers for many participants was changing their self-talk. Where we once tore ourselves down for having ADHD challenges, we learned to break tasks into manageable steps to avoid overwhelm. We stopped demanding perfection and shifted our focus to progress. While we do our best to implement helpful strategies, we also remind ourselves that self-compassion is just as important as the strategies themselves.

Emma, a psychologist diagnosed with ADHD in her forties, put it best: "The greatest gift of my late diagnosis wasn't the medication or the strategies, though those helped. It was the permission to be exactly who I am, to work with my brain instead of against it. I'm not broken; I'm different. And different can be wonderful."

I'm Not Broken and Neither Are You

Unmasking our ADHD is a revelation, but it also comes with grief. Many of us have built our identities around who we thought we needed to be, not who we actually are. Shedding that mask means confronting years of perfectionism, self-doubt, and deeply ingrained beliefs about worth.

One participant emailed me after our interview, "I keep thinking about our conversation and realising how much of my life has been spent trying to be someone I'm not. There's freedom in letting go of that, but there's also sadness for all the energy I wasted, all the joy I missed by hiding myself."

Her words capture something essential about this journey. As exhausting as masking is, letting go doesn't come easily. Even after we understand why we do it, the fear of being "too much" lingers. The pressure to meet unrealistic expectations, to be productive, to have it all together, to constantly prove ourselves doesn't just disappear overnight.

But we don't need to fix ourselves. We deserve to show up as we are. No apologies necessary.

SELF-COACHING EXERCISES: MASKING

These exercises are here to support your unmasking process, not to grade or evaluate you. You're not doing them wrong if you don't have clear answers right away. Use them as tools for self-awareness, not self-criticism. Let them guide you toward small, intentional changes that feel safe and doable. This isn't about overhauling who you are. It's about getting closer to who you've always been underneath the mask.

THE MASKING INVENTORY ASSESSMENT

Masking is something many of us do without even realising it. It's an automatic survival strategy. But the first step toward authentic living is recognising when and how we're masking.

A structured inventory can help with this process by tracking:

- **Masking Behaviours:** Specific ways you alter your natural self in different settings (work, social, family).
- **Triggers:** Situations or people that make you feel the need to mask more.
- **Energy Cost:** How draining each masking behaviour feels, rated on a scale from 1 to 10.
- **Necessity Evaluation:** Which masks are truly needed to function and which are just habits rooted in fear.
- **Authenticity Opportunities:** Identifying safe situations in which you can experiment with reducing masking.

Noticing these patterns can be a real wake-up call. Masking becomes so second nature that we often don't even realise we're doing it. It's just how we've learned to move through the world. But research shows, and I've seen firsthand in my own life and through the women I've spoken with, that constantly adjusting ourselves to meet expectations is *exhausting*. Many women with ADHD describe spending their entire day trying to "get it right," only to collapse in private, completely drained.⁶³

Studies also suggest that women are more likely to internalise ADHD struggles, leading to anxiety, depression, and burnout.⁶⁴ The pressure to appear in control can make it harder to recognise our own needs. It can be even harder to ask for support.

Building awareness around masking isn't about dropping all social filters overnight. It's about figuring out where we can reclaim space for our real selves.

THE AUTHENTIC SUCCESS FRAMEWORK

You can use this framework to align your achievements with your overall well-being. It acknowledges that success without sustainability isn't truly success and provides practical steps to maintain achievement without sacrificing health.

I initially adopted this framework after experiencing burnout two years ago and refined it based on feedback from research participants and my training at the ADD Coach Academy.

1. **Success Audit:** Evaluate your current accomplishments by considering both external recognition and internal satisfaction.
2. **Cost Accounting:** Identify the hidden costs—physical, emotional, and relational—associated with your current success patterns. Research indicates that women with ADHD often adopt compensatory behaviours to meet societal expectations, leading to increased stress and potential burnout.⁶⁵
3. **Values Clarification:** Determine what truly matters to you versus

---

63 Clive A. Kelly, Caroline Kelly, and Ruth Taylor, "Review of the Psychosocial Consequences of Attention Deficit Hyperactivity Disorder (ADHD) in Females," *European Journal of Medical and Health Sciences* 6, no. 1 (2024): 10–20, https://doi.org/10.24018/ejmed.2024.6.1.2033.

64 George Sachs, "ADHD in Women: Removing the Mask," Sachs Center, accessed September 17, 2025, https://sachscenter.com/unmasking-adhd-in-women/.

65 Madhoo and Quinn, "A Review of Attention Deficit/Hyperactivity Disorder in Women and Girls."

goals pursued due to societal conditioning or as compensation for perceived shortcomings. Clarifying personal values can lead to more authentic and fulfilling success.[66]
4. **Support Needs Assessment:** Identify specific supports you need—not just desire—for sustainable success. A comprehensive assessment of needs can inform strategic planning to reduce mental health service disparities.[67]
5. **Success Metric Redesign:** Create new personal definitions of success for yourself that incorporate well-being alongside achievement. Aligning health strategies with personal values ensures that success metrics promote overall health and satisfaction.[68]

THE TRUE NORTH IDENTITY RECLAMATION

This systematic approach can aid you in recovering your authentic identity while acknowledging the complex reality that some strategic masking may still be necessary in certain contexts.

1. **Pre-Mask Exploration:** Identify traits, interests, and tendencies from childhood before significant masking began. Reflecting on early behaviours can help reconnect with our true identity.[69]
2. **Permission Statements:** Create personalised declarations of self-acceptance for ADHD traits (e.g., "I give myself permission to think nonlinearly"). Embracing neurodiversity fosters self-acceptance and reduces the need for masking.[70]
3. **Strength Translation:** Reframe perceived ADHD "weaknesses" as

---

66   Kathleen G. Nadeau and Patricia O. Quinn, *Understanding Women with AD/HD* (Advantage Books, 2002).

67   California Institute for Mental Health, *Stakeholder Recommendations for Mental Health and Substance Use Disorder Services Presented to the California Department of Health Care Services and Its County Partners* (June 2013), https://www.dhcs.ca.gov/Documents/StakeholderRecommen_forMHSUD.pdf.

68   State of Wisconsin Department of Health Services, *Maternal and Child Health Services Title V Block Grant* (2024), https://www.dhs.wisconsin.gov/mch/blockgrant/mch-blockgrant-2024.pdf.

69   Williams, "What to Know About ADHD Masking."

70   ADDA Editorial Team, "ADHD Masking: Does Hiding Your Symptoms Help or Harm?" ADDA, August 1, 2024, https://add.org/adhd-masking/.

potential strengths in appropriate contexts. Recognising and leveraging these strengths can enhance self-esteem and authenticity.[71]

4. **Relationship Inventory:** Evaluate which relationships support authenticity and which require masking. Understanding the dynamics of these relationships is crucial for mental well-being.[72]

5. **Expression Experiments:** Design small, safe opportunities to express previously masked aspects of self. This approach encourages genuine self-expression and reduces the emotional toll of masking.[73]

6. **Legacy Reflection:** Consider what would be lost if our unique neurological perspective remained hidden. Embracing our true identity allows for meaningful contributions and personal fulfillment.[74]

---

[71] "7 ADHD Strengths and Benefits," Touch-Type Read & Spell, accessed September 17, 2025, https://www.readandspell.com/us/adhd-strengths.

[72] Nadeau, "Why ADHD Is More Challenging for Women."

[73] Sharon Saline, "Moms with ADHD: Nurturing Your Power of Authenticity," *Dr. Sharon Saline* (blog), accessed September 17, 2025, https://www.drsharonsaline.com/blog/2021/05/moms-with-adhd-nurturing-your-power-of-authenticity.

[74] Alexandra Gerlach, "The Lost Girls: Unmasking ADHD in Adult Women," Pharmacy Times, October 29, 2024, https://www.pharmacytimes.com/view/the-lost-girls-unmasking-adhd-in-adult-women.

Chapter Five

Unlearning the "Not Good Enough" Mentality That Dominates Internal Narratives

"why can't you just clean your room? you're such a slob."

"If you just tried, you wouldn't get such bad grades."

"You're so smart, but you're just lazy."

Rebecca could still hear these words from her childhood as if they were spoken yesterday. Now forty-two, years after her late ADHD diagnosis, her voice caught as she recalled the confusion and shame.

"My parents thought I was being defiant," she said, her voice growing quieter. "They'd see my messy room and—god, the disappointment on their faces. My dad would say, 'Do you just not care about your things?' But I did care! I'd start cleaning and then find an old journal, get completely lost reading it, and two hours later…" She spread her hands, a gesture that said it all.

Rebecca is not alone in this oversight. For many of us, childhood was filled with messages that reinforced the belief that we were fundamentally flawed. Teachers, parents, and peers often misunderstood our struggles, mistaking neurological differences for personality defects.

Megan remembered being called "the daydreamer" by her third-grade teacher. "She would snap her fingers in front of my face," Megan said. "I wasn't daydreaming. I just processed information differently. But try explaining that when you're eight! All I knew was that adults were constantly frustrated with me."

ADHD girls often struggle with executive function from an early age. But because our symptoms tend to align less with hyperactivity and more with inattentiveness, we are frequently overlooked or misinterpreted.[75] Instead of receiving support, many of us are labelled as careless, irresponsible, or simply "not trying hard enough."

Struggles with organisation, object permanence, and task paralysis are common experiences for us as ADHD women, especially in childhood. Remember walking into your room, seeing the mess, and feeling completely paralysed? Not knowing where to start? Many of us were labelled as lazy or messy when, in reality, our brains simply processed tasks differently.

Jasmine laughed, but with a sharpness. "I'd attempt to clean my room and get completely sidetracked. I'd find an old toy and suddenly, poof, I was on the floor playing instead of cleaning. Or I'd organise my books by colour, then by size, then alphabetically, and somehow my room would end up messier than when I started. My parents would check on me and assume I'd been playing instead of cleaning."

A common theme in our childhood experiences was the disconnect between effort and results. Many of us recalled spending hours attempting to organise our space, only to feel frustrated when our progress was invisible to others. This cycle of trying, failing, and being shamed reinforced the belief that we were inherently incapable.

Executive dysfunction in ADHD affects multiple cognitive processes essential for organisation. Our struggles stem from specific neurological differences:

---

[75] Madhoo and Quinn, "A Review of Attention Deficit/Hyperactivity Disorder in Women and Girls."

- **Task Initiation:** The inability to start a task, even when willing to do it.
- **Working Memory:** Holding multiple steps of a process in mind.
- **Emotional Regulation:** Managing frustration when struggling with a task.
- **Dopamine Deficiency:** A lack of intrinsic motivation for non-stimulating tasks.

Studies show that the prefrontal cortex in ADHD brains develops differently, impacting impulse control, planning, and sustained attention.[76] Additionally, our ADHD brains have lower dopamine levels, making it harder to feel motivated by routine or uninteresting tasks.[77]

This is why traditional discipline—such as grounding, yelling, or providing rewards—often failed with us. It assumed we were making a choice to be unmotivated rather than struggling with an invisible neurological barrier.

When you've been told you're too much, too scattered, too emotional, or not living up to your potential, those messages start to settle in. At first, it's other people's voices. Teachers, parents, friends. But eventually, you don't need anyone else to say it. You've already taken it on yourself.

That's how the "not good enough" story takes hold. Quietly. Over time. You stop trusting your instincts. You second-guess every decision. You start wondering if maybe you really are just lazy, messy, or unreliable. And because your ADHD isn't always visible to others, people don't see how hard you're trying. They only see what you missed or forgot.

So you learn to see it that way too.

---

76 Barkley, ed., *Attention-Deficit Hyperactivity Disorder*.

77 N. D. Volkow et al., "Motivation Deficit in ADHD Is Associated with Dysfunction of the Dopamine Reward Pathway," *Molecular Psychiatry* 16 (2011): 1147–54, https://doi.org/10.1038/mp.2010.97.

REWRITING THE NARRATIVE: PRACTICAL SELF-TALK STRATEGIES

Lisa fidgeted with her coffee cup as she spoke. "The voice in my head was brutal," she said. "Always telling me, 'You're just getting by on luck. If people knew how much you struggled with basic tasks, they'd realise you were a fraud.'" She looked up. "And the worst part? I believed it. Completely. For decades."

After her diagnosis at thirty-eight, Lisa began the difficult work of rewriting this internal narrative. "The first step was realising these beliefs weren't true. Instead, they were stories I'd been told and had internalised. The second step…" She hesitated. "That was harder. Actively replacing them with more accurate, self-compassionate talk."

For many of us, recognising that these beliefs were never true is just the beginning. We must actively replace them with self-compassionate and ADHD-friendly self-talk.

Here are some reframing examples:

- **From "I'm lazy" to "My ADHD brain needs support."** Instead of saying, "I should be able to do this like everyone else," try "My brain works differently. I need systems that are designed for the way I function."
- **From "I'm a messy slob" to "I struggle with organisation, and that's okay."** Instead of saying, "I'll never be able to keep things clean," try "I need clear, external reminders and smaller steps that make tidying manageable."
- **From "I'm unmotivated" to "I need dopamine to get started."** Instead of saying, "Why can't I just do it?" try "I need to create urgency, novelty, or excitement to help my brain engage."

Diana described what she called a "reality check" note on her phone, filled with affirmations that countered her negative self-talk. "When I feel that shame spiral starting," she said, "I read these statements: 'My brain needs different strategies, not more willpower. My worth isn't measured by my productivity. I bring unique strengths because of how I think.'" She added, "It sounds cheesy, but it works."

The kind of negative self-talk many women described isn't just psychologically harmful; it has neurological consequences. Studies show that self-criticism activates the brain's threat response and decreases activity in regions responsible for learning and growth.[78] Conversely, self-compassion activates the caregiving system, reducing stress hormones and improving executive function—something particularly crucial for our ADHD brains.

WHY ADHD WOMEN ARE CONDITIONED TO APOLOGISE AND SEEK EXTERNAL VALIDATION

Aisha tallied how many times she said sorry in a single workday. The total: forty-seven.

"I made little marks on a sticky note," she said, her eyes widening. "Sorry for asking questions. Sorry for needing time to think. Sorry for leaving at five to get my kid!" She shook her head, laughing without humour. "The worst part? I had no idea I was doing it. Completely automatic, like breathing."

Have you caught yourself apologising for things that don't even require an apology? Saying sorry for taking up space, for asking a question, for having an opinion? Many of us don't just apologise when we're wrong. We apologise for existing.

For us, this excessive apologising (and I am not just speaking as a Canadian here) and deep need for external validation isn't just a personality quirk; it's a learned survival mechanism. Years of making social missteps, being misunderstood, and struggling to meet expectations has conditioned us to believe that our natural way of being, our impulsivity, our big emotions, our forgetfulness are all inherently wrong. So we overcompensate. We apologise preemptively to soften any perceived inconvenience. We seek approval constantly to reassure ourselves that we're "doing it right."

---

78 Olivia Longe et al., "Having a Word with Yourself: Neural Correlates of Self-Criticism and Self-Reassurance," *NeuroImage* 49, no. 2 (2010): 1849–56, https://doi.org/10.1016/j.neuroimage.2009.09.019.

THE "TOO MUCH, YET NOT ENOUGH" PARADOX

Tanya remembered the conflicting messages she received throughout childhood. "In the same day—and I'm not exaggerating—my teacher would tell me I was talking too much in class, and then later say I wasn't focusing enough on my work." She ran a hand through her hair, frustration evident even in the retelling. "Too energetic, but not applying myself enough. I couldn't win! It was like, 'What do you want from me? Because I can't figure it out.'"

Many of us grew up tangled in these contradictions. "You're too loud." "You talk too much." "Why are you so emotional?" But at the same time, we were also told, "You're not trying hard enough." "You need to be more responsible." "Just focus more." It was an impossible tightrope to walk: We were constantly being told we were too much and not enough at the same time.

I knew that struggle well. I, too, was guilty of talking too much in class. By third or fourth grade, I had earned the honour of sitting at the very front of the classroom, my desk pressed up against the teacher's, illuminated like a permanent spotlight on my inability to just behave. Another layer of humiliation. Another reminder that I was different.

This paradox created a chronic sense of self-doubt. Where exactly were we supposed to fit? To navigate this impossible standard, we started masking, toning ourselves down, filtering our words, apologising, and constantly looking to others for approval.

The conflicting messages ADHD women and girls receive are neurologically confusing. Our brains are wired for consistency and predictability, and these contradictory expectations create a state of cognitive dissonance. Research shows this uncertainty activates the amygdala, increasing anxiety and heightening our need for social reassurance.[79]

When nothing you do seems quite right, you start to pre-apologise for simply existing. You learn to say sorry not because you've done something wrong but because you're bracing for the next correction.

---

[79] Matthew D. Lieberman, "Social Cognitive Neuroscience: A Review of Core Processes," *Annual Review of Psychology* 58, (January 2007): 259–89, https://doi.org/10.1146/annurev.psych.58.110405.085654.

Camila cringed remembering a family dinner from when she was eight. "I blurted out, 'Aunt Jenny's food tastes awful!'" She sounded embarrassed even now. "The table went silent. My mom got that look. You know the one. And later came the excruciating conversation about 'thinking before speaking,' which basically translated to 'Why can't you just be normal?'"

Camila dropped her hands, her expression serious. "After that, I became this hypervigilant kid. I'd literally rehearse conversations before family gatherings. I'd apologise before offering an opinion. I lived in constant fear of saying the wrong thing."

Our ADHD brains struggle with impulse control, working memory, and reading subtle social cues. This means we often interrupt, overshare, or misinterpret situations. Imagine being that child who blurts out honest but awkward comments, only to be met with stares and awkward silence. Instead of receiving gentle correction, many of us were made to feel ashamed. Over time, we started apologising automatically, instinctively, to prevent rejection before it could happen.

THE LINK BETWEEN ADHD AND PEOPLE-PLEASING TENDENCIES

Women with ADHD often learn to seek external validation for every decision. Maria first noticed her habit of seeking external validation when she caught herself texting three different friends about what to wear to a casual work gathering.

"It wasn't even a fancy party," she said, shaking her head. "Just drinks with coworkers. But there I was, sending photos to three people, asking 'This one or that one?' And then it hit me. I wasn't actually looking for their opinion. I was looking for permission to trust my own judgment."

Recognising the pattern reminded her that her value wasn't determined by how well she could conform.

"Now when I feel that urge to poll everyone I know, I ask myself, 'What would I decide if I just trusted myself?'"

Our need for external validation has neurological roots. Our ADHD brains have altered reward pathways, making us more dependent on immediate external feedback. Studies show that people with ADHD have reduced activity in brain regions responsible for intrinsic motivation and self-evaluation, making external validation particularly compelling.[80]

Next time we feel the pull to seek reassurance before making a decision, we can pause and ask:

- Am I asking for genuine input, or am I looking for permission to trust myself?
- What's the worst that could happen if I didn't get external reassurance?

Building self-trust is a slow process, but noticing when we're outsourcing our self-worth is the first step.

WHY ADHD BRAINS SEEK EXTERNAL VALIDATION

Madison's friends teased her about being "allergic to saying no." She volunteered for extra projects at work despite feeling overwhelmed. She agreed to social commitments even when exhausted. She put others' needs before her own, even when it cost her dearly.

"The thought of disappointing someone makes me physically ill," she said, her voice dropping. "I'm not exaggerating. My heart races. I feel sick to my stomach. It's easier to just say yes than to deal with that feeling, even if saying yes means I'm up until three trying to get everything done."

At its core, people-pleasing in ADHD women isn't just a personality trait; it's a survival mechanism. Several ADHD traits make people-pleasing more likely:

- **Rejection Sensitivity Dysphoria (RSD):** We often feel rejection more intensely than neurotypical individuals. A minor criticism,

---

80 Volkow et al., "Motivation Deficit in ADHD."

an unanswered text, or even a neutral facial expression can feel devastating. To avoid this pain, we go out of our way to please others.[81]
- **Emotional Dysregulation:** Our ADHD brains struggle to regulate emotions, making disapproval or conflict feel unbearable. Instead of facing difficult conversations, many of us default to smoothing things over, even at our own expense.[82]
- **Masking and Perfectionism:** Many of us have spent years suppressing our true selves to fit in. This can lead to over-apologising, overexplaining, and seeking approval from others to confirm our worth.[83]
- **Dopamine-Seeking Behaviour:** Validation and praise provide much-needed dopamine boosts. When our ADHD brains are low on dopamine, we can rely on external approval as a shortcut to feeling good, reinforcing people-pleasing habits.[84]

Like many other women with ADHD, Delia spent years saying yes to everything until her ADHD coach helped her reframe people-pleasing. "My coach didn't try to 'fix' me," she explained, leaning forward. "Instead, she helped me see that my desire to please others came from genuine empathy, a quality that makes me good at my healthcare job. The goal wasn't to stop caring about others but to balance it with caring for myself."

People-pleasing behaviours in ADHD women often stem from the same neural circuitry that drives our empathy and social awareness. Studies show that many ADHD individuals have heightened emotional responsiveness to others' needs.[85] The goal isn't to eliminate this sensitivity but to channel it in healthier ways.

---

[81] Dodson, "How ADHD Ignites RSD."

[82] Barkley, ed., *Attention-Deficit Hyperactivity Disorder*.

[83] Madhoo and Quinn, "A Review of Attention Deficit/Hyperactivity Disorder in Women and Girls."

[84] Hallowell and Ratey, *ADHD 2.0*.

[85] Mahdi et al., "An International Qualitative Study of Ability and Disability in ADHD Using the WHO-ICF Framework"; Jane Ann Sedgwick et al., "The Positive Aspects of Attention Deficit Hyperactivity Disorder: A Qualitative Investigation of Successful Adults with ADHD," *ADHD Attention Deficit and Hyperactivity Disorders* 11 (2019): 241–53, https://doi.org/10.1007/s12402-018-0277-6; and Philip Shaw et al., "Emotion Dysregulation in Attention Deficit Hyperactivity Disorder," *The American Journal of Psychiatry* 171, no. 3 (2014): 276–93, https://doi.org/10.1176/appi.ajp.2013.13070966.

Instead of trying to "fix" people-pleasing, we can learn to reframe it through self-awareness and strength-based strategies, including empowering self-talk and the twenty-four-hour rule.

EMPOWERING SELF-TALK

When you change your internal dialogue, you're not just being nicer to yourself. You're actually rewiring your brain.

Negative self-talk activates the brain's threat system, particularly the amygdala and parts of the default mode network.[86] This triggers a stress response—your cortisol increases, your heart rate may rise, and your brain shifts into survival mode. In this state, executive functions like working memory, planning, and emotional regulation (all already difficult with ADHD) become even harder to access.[87]

Empowering or self-compassionate self-talk activates a different system entirely. It engages the caregiving system, involving areas like the medial prefrontal cortex, which helps regulate emotional responses and increases levels of oxytocin, the hormone associated with safety and connection.[88] This reduces stress and promotes a more balanced internal state—crucial for emotional regulation and executive function in ADHD.

In other words, harsh inner talk puts your brain in shutdown mode. Compassionate inner talk helps it function.

Take these for example:

- Replace "If I say no, they'll be mad at me" with "Saying no doesn't make me a bad person. It means I'm prioritising my needs too."

---

86 Longe et al., "Having a Word with Yourself."

87 Amy F. T. Arnsten, "Stress Signalling Pathways That Impair Prefrontal Cortex Structure and Function," *Nature Reviews Neuroscience* 10 (2009): 410–22, https://doi.org/10.1038/nrn2648.

88 Olga M. Klimecki et al., "Differential Pattern of Functional Brain Plasticity After Compassion and Empathy Training," *Social Cognitive and Affective Neuroscience* 9, no. 6 (2014): 873–79, https://doi.org/10.1093/scan/nst060; and H. Rockliff et al., "A Pilot Exploration of Heart Rate Variability and Salivary Cortisol Responses to Compassion-Focused Imagery," *Clinical Neuropsychiatry: Journal of Treatment Evaluation* 5, no. 3 (2008): 132–39, https://psycnet.apa.org/record/2008-15384-002.

- Replace "I should help, or they won't like me" with "My worth is not tied to how much I do for others."

THE TWENTY-FOUR-HOUR RULE: THE POWER OF THE PAUSE

Another strategy is to take a pause. Once we start shifting our internal dialogue, it becomes easier to change our external responses too. When asked for a favour, practise saying, "Let me think about it and get back to you tomorrow." This removes the immediate pressure to say yes and gives time to assess our own capacity.

Jordan found this technique transformative. "The twenty-four-hour rule changed everything for me," she said, then laughed. "Well, not all the time. I still cave sometimes. Last month with my sister's fundraiser, I knew I was overcommitted but said yes anyway. Old habits." She shrugged. "But it helps maybe 70 percent of the time, which is huge for me. It breaks that automatic yes response and gives me time to check in with myself."

REWRITING THE STORY IN YOUR MIND: CHALLENGING NEGATIVE CORE BELIEFS AND SHIFTING TO AN EMPOWERING MINDSET

For many of us with ADHD, negative self-talk isn't just a fleeting thought; it's a constant internal dialogue. Negative core beliefs, deeply ingrained over years of masking struggles, make self-worth feel conditional. The fear of failure, rejection sensitivity dysphoria (RSD), and imposter syndrome intertwine, reinforcing a destructive pattern: *I'm not enough. I'll never be enough.*

But what if that voice is wrong?

Natalie described the relentless critic in her mind. "Even after winning a case, as an attorney, I'd think, *You just got lucky,* or *Anyone could have done that.*" She took a sip of water. "One day my partner asked me to name a single accomplishment I was proud of, and I couldn't do it. Not one thing. Everything to me was either luck or not good enough."

We spend years absorbing messages that shape our self-perception in damaging ways. These messages come from childhood, workplaces, relationships, and society at large.

"You're too much."

"You're too sensitive."

"You need to try harder."

"Why can't you just be normal?"

By the time we reach adulthood, these statements become core beliefs, unconscious narratives that dictate our self-worth. We are particularly prone to internalised failure, a cycle where past mistakes reinforce the belief that we are inherently flawed.[89]

These negative core beliefs have a neurological dimension. ADHD brains have stronger connections between the amygdala (emotional centre) and areas involved in self-perception. This means our brains are more likely to incorporate negative experiences into our identities. Additionally, working memory challenges in ADHD make it harder for us to maintain perspective on past successes when facing current struggles.[90]

REFRAMING THE NARRATIVE

Negative core beliefs feel like truths to us, but they are stories that can be rewritten.

Zoe explained how she worked with her therapist to challenge her core belief that she was "fundamentally irresponsible."

"My therapist asked me to write down all the evidence," she said, still sounding surprised. "Sure, I sometimes missed bill payments or forgot appointments. But I was also trusted with life-or-death situations at work. I'm a nurse. I raised two children. I had friendships that had lasted decades."

She shook her head. "It wasn't about ignoring my challenges. It was

---

[89] Madhoo and Quinn, "A Review of Attention Deficit/Hyperactivity Disorder in Women and Girls."

[90] Thomas E. Brown, *A New Understanding of ADHD in Children and Adults* (Routledge, 2013).

about seeing the whole picture, not just the parts that confirmed what I already believed about myself."

1. **Challenge the Thought:** When self-critical thoughts arise, such as *You're not good enough*, challenge them by asking, "Where is the evidence? Would I speak to a friend this way?" This is a core strategy in cognitive restructuring, which helps individuals replace irrational thoughts with more balanced ones.[91]
2. **Name the Pattern:** Recognising when imposter syndrome or rejection sensitivity dysphoria (RSD) is hijacking thoughts is a form of metacognitive awareness. Labelling these patterns (e.g., *This is my ADHD brain, not reality*) creates psychological distance and reduces emotional reactivity.[92]
3. **Use Dopamine-Driven Self-Validation:** Instead of relying on external praise, individuals with ADHD can boost intrinsic motivation by creating micro rewards and celebrating small wins. For example, "I finished that email despite my executive dysfunction—go me!" This aligns with research on self-reinforcement strategies in ADHD treatment.[93]
4. **Reframe Failures as Data:** Viewing mistakes as learning opportunities rather than personal failures fosters resilience. Instead of saying, "I failed," reframing it as "I learned what doesn't work for me" is consistent with CBT's approach to emotional regulation and adaptive thinking.[94]
5. **Embrace Strength-Based Thinking:** ADHD brains thrive in creative, high-interest environments. Rather than focusing on deficits, individuals benefit from leaning into strengths such as problem-solving, empathy, and divergent thinking. This strengths-based approach is

---

[91] Judith S. Beck, *Cognitive Behavior Therapy: Basics and Beyond*, 3rd ed. (Guilford Press, 2021).

[92] Robert L. Leahy, *The Worry Cure: Seven Steps to Stop Worry from Stopping You* (Harmony Books, 2005).

[93] Barkley, ed., *Attention-Deficit Hyperactivity Disorder*.

[94] Christine A. Padesky and Kathleen A. Mooney, "Strengths-Based Cognitive–Behavioural Therapy: A Four-Step Model to Build Resilience," *Clinical Psychology & Psychotherapy* 19, no. 4 (2012): 283–90, https://doi.org/10.1002/cpp.1795.

supported by ADHD research advocating for positive psychology interventions.[95]

The shift from self-criticism to self-compassion is the single most powerful mindset change we ADHD women can make. Studies show that self-compassion reduces anxiety and increases resilience in neurodivergent individuals.[96]

Instead of "I'm so lazy and forgetful," try "My brain needs external structure. What support can I set up?"

Instead of "I'll never be as good as them," try "I bring unique strengths to the table."

Lauren explained how self-compassion transformed her work performance. "The weird thing?" she said. "When I stopped berating myself for every mistake and started treating myself with kindness, my productivity actually improved. Self-criticism was consuming mental energy I needed for my job."

She paused. "It's like I had been running a program in the background of my brain. This constant criticism was using up all my RAM. When I shut that program down, suddenly I had capacity for the work itself."

This kind of self-compassion has measurable benefits for ADHD brains. Research shows it increases levels of oxytocin and reduces cortisol, creating a neurochemical environment that improves executive function. Self-compassionate individuals show greater cognitive flexibility and resilience after setbacks—crucial skills for managing ADHD challenges.[97]

---

95 Sedgwick et al., "The Positive Aspects of Attention Deficit Hyperactivity Disorder."

96 Kristin Neff, *Self-Compassion: The Proven Power of Being Kind to Yourself* (William Morrow, 2011).

97 Kristin Neff and Emma M. Seppälä, "Compassion, Well-Being, and the Hypo-Egoic Self," chap. 13 in *The Oxford Handbook of Hypo-Egoic Phenomena*, Kirk Warren Brown and Mark R. Leary, eds., (Oxford University Press, 2016).

PRACTICAL SELF-TALK STRATEGIES FOR REWIRING SELF-PERCEPTION

When was the last time you caught yourself saying, "I'm such a mess," "I'll never get this right," or "Why can't I just be normal?" If you're like most ADHD women, the answer is probably today.

Can you feel that little voice in your head that judges every misstep? Negative self-talk is a constant companion for many of us. It can be so automatic that we barely notice it happening. But what if the way we talk to ourselves isn't just a reflection of how we feel but a powerful force actively shaping our brains, our emotions, and our behaviours?

Shifting self-talk isn't about embracing toxic positivity or pretending everything is fine. It's about building a more accurate and supportive internal dialogue. Here's how to start.

NOTICE AND NAME THE THOUGHT

The first step is awareness. Start paying attention to the things you say to yourself. When a negative thought comes up, label it: "That's self-criticism." This simple act creates distance between you and the thought, allowing you to challenge it instead of accepting it as fact.[98]

Vanessa described how she started wearing a rubber band on her wrist and gently snapping it whenever she caught herself in negative self-talk. "It wasn't about punishment," she explained. "It was a physical reminder to pause and notice what I was saying to myself. That awareness was the first step to changing it."

REFRAME WITH COMPASSION

Instead of fighting the thought, try shifting it slightly toward self-compassion.

Instead of "I never finish anything. I'm such a failure," try "I struggle with task completion, but that doesn't define my worth."

---

[98] Judith S. Beck, *Cognitive Behavior Therapy: Basics and Beyond*, 2nd ed. (Guilford Press, 2011).

Instead of "I'm so lazy," try "My brain needs different strategies to get started."

Instead of "Why can't I just be normal?" try "My brain works differently, and that's okay."

INTERRUPT THE SPIRAL

If you catch yourself spiralling into negativity, disrupt the pattern by engaging your senses. Move your body. Take deep breaths. Speak an affirmation out loud. Even something as simple as placing a hand over your heart and saying "I'm doing my best" can shift your emotional state.[99]

Denise described what she called a "spiral interruption kit," a set of small sensory items she kept at her desk. "I have a lavender hand cream, a smooth stone I can hold, and a little card with phrases that help ground me. When I feel that negative spiral starting, I engage my senses first, then my rational mind. It works better than trying to think my way out of those feelings."

USE DOPAMINE-BOOSTING SELF-TALK

Since ADHD brains thrive on dopamine, you can tie your self-talk to motivation and progress.

- I don't have to do this. I *get* to do this.
- Future me will thank me for taking this step.
- I only need to start. Momentum will take over.

CREATE A SELF-TALK CHEAT SHEET

Write down supportive phrases that resonate with you, and keep them visible. When your brain defaults to self-criticism, you'll have a go-to list of responses ready.

---

[99] Daniel J. Siegel, *Mindsight: The New Science of Personal Transformation* (Bantam Books, 2010).

Hannah told me about her "neural shortcut sheet" that she kept in her wallet, on her phone, and at her desk. "I've learned that my brain follows the path of least resistance," she explained. "So I make compassionate self-talk the easiest option by having it immediately available."

As we practise these strategies, we gradually rewire our neural pathways, making self-compassion more automatic and self-criticism less frequent. The goal isn't perfection. *It's progress.* Each time we choose a kinder inner voice, we feel a small shift within ourselves. We breathe a little easier. We stand a little taller. And with each compassionate thought, we take one step closer to unlearning the "not good enough" mentality that has held us back for too long.

Remember, we aren't broken. We aren't failing. We're women with ADHD brains, learning to embrace our unique wiring while navigating a world that wasn't built for us. And that journey, even with all its challenges and victories, makes us exactly who we're meant to be.

SELF-COACHING EXERCISES: INTERNAL NARRATIVE

The following exercises will help you unlearn the stories you've been told and the ones you've absorbed about what your struggles mean. Rewriting your internal narrative has nothing to do with sugarcoating. It's about giving yourself a clearer, more accurate reflection of how your ADHD brain actually works. When you replace shame with understanding, you make room for real change to happen.

THE NEUROLOGICAL REFRAMING EXERCISE

This exercise can help you replace shame-based beliefs with a neurologically accurate understanding. Create a three-column worksheet:

1. **Childhood Label:** Record specific criticisms received (e.g., "lazy," "messy," "careless"). Negative labelling in childhood is linked to lower self-esteem and internalised shame.[100]
2. **Neurological Reality:** Identify the ADHD-related challenge behind the behaviour (e.g., "executive dysfunction affecting task initiation"). ADHD-related struggles stem from brain function, not personal flaws.[101]
3. **Compassionate Reframe:** Create a new interpretation that acknowledges both the challenge and your efforts (e.g., "I was working with an ADHD brain that made sequential tasks difficult"). Reframing reduces self-judgment and fosters self-acceptance.[102]

THE SELF-TALK REPLACEMENT PROTOCOL

This protocol can help you transform reactive self-criticism into prepared, compassionate responses that acknowledge ADHD challenges while maintaining self-respect.

---

[100] Amori Yee Mikami, "The Importance of Friendship for Youth with Attention-Deficit/Hyperactivity Disorder," *Clinical Child and Family Psychology Review* 13 (2010): 181–98, https://doi.org/10.1007/s10567-010-0067-y.

[101] Barkley, *Taking Charge of Adult ADHD*.

[102] M. Godfrey-Harris and S. C. K. Shaw, "The Experiences of Medical Students with ADHD: A Phenomenological Study," *PLoS ONE* 18, no. 8 (2023): e0290513, https://doi.org/10.1371/journal.pone.0290513.

- **Identify the Trigger:** Note the situation that typically activates the negative self-talk.[103]
- **Record the Automatic Thought:** Write down the exact words of your inner critic.[104]
- **Identify the ADHD Connection:** Link the thought to an ADHD challenge.[105]
- **Create Three Alternative Responses:** Develop three truthful but compassionate replacements.[106]
- **Practise Daily:** Proactively review and rehearse new responses before triggers occur.[107]

THE APOLOGY-TO-ACKNOWLEDGMENT CONVERSION

A simple shift in your conversation strategy can transform habitual over-apologising into confident communication. Create personalised response alternatives for common situations in which unnecessary apologies occur.

Instead of saying, "I'm sorry for talking too much," try "Thanks for listening. I got really excited about that!" Instead of "Sorry I forgot to reply," try "Thanks for your patience. I appreciate it!"

This subtle shift maintains social grace without reinforcing the idea that we've done something wrong just by existing. Practising these alternatives creates new neural pathways that eventually become automatic. Next time we feel "sorry" bubbling up for something that doesn't warrant an apology, we can pause, take a breath, and choose a response that honours both ourselves and others.

---

[103] Aaron T. Beck, *Cognitive Therapy and the Emotional Disorders* (International Universities Press, 1976).

[104] David D. Burns, *Feeling Good: The New Mood Therapy* (William Morrow, 1980).

[105] Barkley, ed., *Attention-Deficit Hyperactivity Disorder*.

[106] Neff, *Self-Compassion*.

[107] Dennis D. Tirch, *The Compassionate Guide to Overcoming Anxiety: Using Compassion-Focused Therapy to Calm Worry, Panic, and Fear* (New Harbinger Publications, 2012).

THE BOUNDARY-SETTING FRAMEWORK

This framework is designed to help people-pleasing ADHD women maintain their natural empathy while protecting their well-being. It provides structured steps to prevent overcommitment and emotional depletion:

1. **Identify our Boundary Baseline:** Determine what you genuinely have the capacity to give without self-sacrifice.[108]
2. **Create Decision Filters:** Develop three to four questions to ask before committing, such as "Do I have the energy for this?" or "What would I have to give up?"[109]
3. **Prepare Refusal Scripts:** Draft kind yet firm language to decline requests that push you past your limits.[110]
4. **Practise the Twenty-Four-Hour Rule:** For nonurgent requests, always wait twenty-four hours before saying yes to prevent impulsive commitments.[111]
5. **Schedule Recovery Time:** For the commitments you do make, ensure you build in buffer time for restoration.[112]

This framework acknowledges the strengths behind people-pleasing tendencies while introducing practical structures to prevent emotional exhaustion and burnout.

---

[108] Reinhart Missy Wilson, *The ADHDer's Guide to Saying No Without Guilt: An ADHD-Friendly Way to Say No, Reduce Overwhelm, Manage Impulsivity, and Prioritize Your Well-being* (Independently published, 2025).

[109] Suzanne H. Mitchell and Deborah Sevigny-Resetco, "Effort-Related Decision-Making in ADHD," *Journal of Psychiatric and Brain Science* 5 (2020): e200027, https://doi.org/10.20900/jpbs.20200027.

[110] Rian E. Van Heerden, "Assertiveness and Perception of Style of Assertiveness among Future South African Employees" (MA thesis, University of the Free State, 2017), https://scholar.ufs.ac.za/server/api/core/bitstreams/0709535a-7bac-4457-a4d1-ae3ed484b32b/content.

[111] Dawei Wang et al., "The Effectiveness of Revocable Precommitment Strategies in Reducing Decision-Making Impulsivity," *Social Cognitive and Affective Neuroscience* 19, no. 1 (2024): nsae093, https://doi.org/10.1093/scan/nsae093.

[112] "ADHD and People Pleasing: What's the Correlation?," The ADHD Centre.

THE CORE BELIEF EXCAVATION TECHNIQUE

This structured method is rooted in cognitive behavioural therapy (CBT) principles that help individuals identify and challenge deeply held negative beliefs. The process involves the following steps:

1. **Identify Thought Patterns:** Track recurring negative thoughts by maintaining a journal over a specified period, such as one week.[113]
2. **Find the Core Belief:** Examine each negative thought by asking, "What does this thought say about me?" Repeating this question helps uncover underlying core beliefs.[114]
3. **Trace the Origin:** Reflect on past experiences to identify when and where these core beliefs first developed, understanding their historical context.[115]
4. **Gather Contradicting Evidence:** Compile specific experiences that challenge the validity of the negative belief, promoting a balanced perspective.[116]
5. **Create a Replacement Belief:** Develop an alternative, more balanced belief that acknowledges both challenges and strengths, facilitating healthier thinking patterns.[117]

This structured examination prevents vague positive thinking and instead builds evidence-based alternative beliefs grounded in reality.

---

[113] Beck, *Cognitive Behavior Therapy*.

[114] David D. Burns, *Feeling Great: The Revolutionary New Treatment for Depression and Anxiety* (PESI Publishing, 2020).

[115] Padesky and Mooney, "Strengths-Based Cognitive–Behavioural Therapy."

[116] Leahy, *The Worry Cure*.

[117] Keith S. Dobson and David J. A. Dozois, eds. *Handbook of Cognitive-Behavioral Therapies*, 4th ed. (Guilford Press, 2019).

THE SELF-TALK TRANSFORMATION SYSTEM

This systematic approach acknowledges that changing self-talk patterns requires structure and repetition, especially for ADHD brains that benefit from external reinforcement.

1. **Complete a Baseline Assessment:** Recording negative self-talk patterns in specific situations enhances self-awareness and allows individuals to identify recurring cognitive distortions.[118]
2. **Develop Replacements:** Creating three to five accurate, compassionate alternatives for common negative thoughts aligns with cognitive restructuring, a key CBT intervention.[119]
3. **Incorporate Environmental Reminders:** Using visual cues in places where negative self-talk typically occurs helps reinforce positive cognitive shifts by associating new thoughts with familiar triggers.[120]
4. **Schedule Practise Sessions:** Scheduling daily five-minute periods to actively rehearse new self-talk patterns strengthens cognitive flexibility and supports behavioural change.[121]
5. **Find an Accountability Partner:** Sharing regular progress reports with a trusted friend or coach facilitates consistency and reinforces new thought patterns through social reinforcement.[122]

---

[118] Burns, *Feeling Great.*

[119] Beck, *Cognitive Behavior Therapy.*

[120] Christine A. Padesky and Kathleen A. Mooney, "Presenting the Cognitive Model to Clients," *International Cognitive Therapy Newsletter* 6, no. 1 (1990): 13–14, https://www.padesky.com/wp-content/uploads/2022/10/v6no_1_2_present_model-web2022.pdf.

[121] Beck, *Cognitive Behavior Therapy.*

[122] Donald Meichenbaum, *Cognitive-Behavior Modification: An Integrative Approach* (Springer, 1977).

Chapter Six

Why Our ADHD Brains React So Intensely to Rejection

I FIRST MET KAREN ON A ZOOM CALL IN 2022. SHE TOLD ME HOW she had sat at her desk, staring blankly at her computer screen, trying desperately to hold back tears. Her boss had just wrapped up their weekly check-in, nothing major, just a quick review of her latest project. Overall, the feedback had been positive. But the moment she heard the words "room for improvement," everything else faded. Her chest tightened. Her mind spiralled. One thought took over: *I'm not good enough*.

"It was like being hit by a truck," Karen explained to me later. "My chest tightened. My face got hot, and suddenly I couldn't think about anything else except what a failure I was. It wasn't just disappointment. It was this overwhelming sense of shame that consumed me completely."

What Karen experienced wasn't an ordinary reaction to feedback. It was rejection sensitivity dysphoria (RSD), an intense emotional response to perceived or actual rejection, criticism, or failure common in those of us with ADHD. Unlike general sensitivity that everyone might experience, RSD is a neurological phenomenon that triggers overwhelming feelings of shame, embarrassment, and emotional pain, often leading to anger, withdrawal, or avoidance.

Karen's experience matches what research has shown: Up to 99 percent of people with ADHD report experiencing some level of RSD, with many describing it as one of the most debilitating aspects.[123] While rejection is difficult for everyone, our ADHD brains react with disproportionate intensity, making even minor criticisms feel catastrophic. Of the seventy-five women I interviewed, all but two of them told me that they experienced RSD.

Rejection sensitivity dysphoria is not officially listed in the latest diagnostic manual (DSM-5) but is increasingly recognised by ADHD specialists as a core emotional component of ADHD. The term was popularised by Dr. William Dodson to describe the extreme emotional sensitivity and pain triggered by the perception of being rejected or criticised or falling short of expectations and goals.[124]

THE NEUROLOGICAL BASIS OF RSD IN OUR ADHD BRAINS

Elena's friends often described her as the most sensitive person they knew. A thoughtless comment could ruin her day. A perceived slight could send her spiralling for weeks. A disagreement with a loved one didn't just sting; it felt catastrophic.

"I've always been told I take things too personally," she admitted. "But it's not like I choose to feel this way. When someone criticises me, it physically hurts. My chest tightens, my stomach drops. It's like my body can't tell the difference between emotional rejection and physical pain."

For most of her life, she believed this was just a personality flaw, and she needed to "toughen up" or "grow out of it." What neither she nor the people around her understood was that her intense reactions

---

123 Dodson, "How ADHD Ignites RSD."

124 Dodson, "How ADHD Ignites RSD."

weren't a choice. They were a direct result of how her ADHD brain processed rejection.

Elena's therapist eventually helped her make sense of what was happening. In one session, the therapist pulled out a diagram and mapped out how ADHD affects rejection sensitivity. For the first time, Elena saw her experiences not as a personal failing, but as a neurological response—something she could begin to understand, manage, and, most importantly, stop blaming herself for.

ADHD affects dopamine regulation, emotional processing, and impulse control. These factors make rejection feel far more painful for us than for people with neurotypical brains. It's more than in our heads; our nervous systems perceive rejection as a real, immediate threat. That's why even minor criticism can feel devastating and why our emotional responses sometimes seem extreme even to ourselves.[125]

Dopamine, the neurotransmitter responsible for motivation, pleasure, and emotional regulation, is produced at lower levels in our ADHD brains. This deficiency means we struggle with regulating emotions, especially negative emotions like shame and rejection.[126] Our ADHD brains don't just register rejection as unpleasant. They interpret it as a direct threat to self-worth.

Research also suggests that dopamine dysregulation in ADHD brains makes us more prone to reward-seeking behaviours—meaning we crave external validation but struggle to internalise success.[127] This makes rejection particularly powerful for us.

For Elena, understanding the neurological basis of her reactions was life-changing. "For the first time, I realised my brain was wired differently, not broken, just different," she said. "It explained why rejection felt so physically painful, why criticism could derail me for days, and why I struggled to 'just get over it' like other people seemed to."

---

[125] Shaw et al., "Emotion Dysregulation in Attention Deficit Hyperactivity Disorder"; Annabel Rowney-Smith et al., "The Lived Experience of Rejection Sensitivity in ADHD—a Qualitative Exploration," medRxiv, November 18, 2024, https://doi.org/10.1101/2024.11.16.24317418.

[126] Barkley, ed., *Attention-Deficit Hyperactivity Disorder*.

[127] Volkow et al., "Evaluating Dopamine Reward Pathway in ADHD."

Her therapist also explained how her hyperactive amygdala—the brain's "alarm system"—contributed to her intense reactions. In our ADHD brains, this region tends to be overactive, meaning that even small rejections can set off a fight-or-flight response. While neurotypical brains might register criticism as "constructive," our ADHD brains often overreact, interpreting it as a serious personal attack.[128]

Adding to this challenge is the weakened prefrontal cortex function in ADHD. This brain region, responsible for rational thinking and emotional regulation, is underactive in our ADHD brains.[129] This makes it harder to override emotional reactions with logic. For example, while a neurotypical person might think, *That comment wasn't personal*, someone with an ADHD brain struggles to calm the amygdala's reaction, leading to intense emotional flooding.

"The hardest part to explain to others is how my body reacts," Elena said. "My heart races. I feel sick to my stomach, and sometimes I even get lightheaded. It's a full-body experience, not just an emotional one."

This physical response is linked to nervous system dysregulation in ADHD. Many of us with ADHD often operate in a state of heightened stress reactivity, which can result in:

- Overstimulation of the nervous system, making rejection feel physically painful.
- Difficulty shifting attention away from emotional pain, leading to prolonged distress.
- Increased likelihood of developing anxiety, depression, or avoidance behaviours due to repeated RSD episodes.[130]

One strategy I teach in my coaching practise is using what I call inviting the "logical detective" to balance the emotional part of the brain when we get stuck in rumination. When we experience something

---

[128] Dodson, "How ADHD Ignites RSD."

[129] Barkley, ed., *Attention-Deficit Hyperactivity Disorder*.

[130] Madhoo and Quinn, "A Review of Attention Deficit/Hyperactivity Disorder in Women and Girls."

upsetting like criticism, rejection, or a misinterpretation, our emotional brain (specifically, the amygdala) kicks into high gear. This part of the brain is responsible for processing threats, and for those of us with ADHD, it tends to hit the alarm button fast. Even small moments of perceived rejection can feel overwhelming, triggering spirals of shame, self-doubt, or catastrophising.

This is where the logical detective comes in.

Instead of letting the emotional brain run the entire show, we can bring in the part of the brain responsible for reasoning, the prefrontal cortex. The logical detective asks questions like: *Is there actual evidence that I did something wrong? Could there be another explanation for this situation? Would I be this hard on a friend if they were in my shoes?*

For example, when experiencing RSD, instead of thinking, *I'm overreacting. Why am I like this?* we can shift to:

- My amygdala is reacting to perceived rejection. It's trying to protect me, but it doesn't always get it right.
- My logical detective can step in and help me look at the bigger picture.
- I am feeling rejected right now. Could this be my ADHD amplifying my feelings?

This small shift doesn't invalidate emotions. It makes space for them without letting them take over. It helps us respond instead of react. And over time, practising this kind of self-talk makes it easier for us to break free from shame and build self-trust.

I like to explain it this way:

Picture your prefrontal cortex as the office manager of your brain—the one in charge of planning, organisation, and keeping everything running smoothly. Now imagine your amygdala as the fire alarm, always on high alert for potential danger. When your brain senses a threat (like social rejection), it doesn't pause to assess whether it's an awkward email or a charging bear. It just sounds the alarm.

When that alarm is blaring, the office manager can't focus on logical decision-making. That's why calming strategies like deep breathing, movement, or self-reassuring statements can help reset the alarm system and allow the prefrontal cortex to regain control.

By learning to "translate" these brain processes into simple, supportive language, we can reduce emotional overwhelm and regain our sense of agency.

WHY WOMEN WITH ADHD EXPERIENCE RSD MORE INTENSELY

Social conditioning plays a significant role in how RSD manifests. Women are typically expected to maintain social harmony and be relationally focused, creating additional pressure that can intensify rejection sensitivity. Research shows women with ADHD often internalise rejection more deeply and ruminate on it longer than our male counterparts.[131]

From an early age, many girls are encouraged to keep the peace by choosing their words carefully, prioritising others' feelings, and avoiding conflict. For ADHD women, this pressure combines with rejection sensitivity, making even minor criticism feel deeply personal. Instead of seeing it as feedback on a single action, we absorb it as a judgment of our entire character.

Sophie, a marketing director with ADHD, described how this played out in her leadership role.

"If I give feedback to my team and someone seems upset, I'll obsess about it for days. I'll rewrite emails ten times to make sure they don't sound too harsh. Meanwhile, my male colleague with ADHD just says what he thinks and moves on. We both experience rejection sensitivity, but the way we've been taught to handle social interactions is completely different."

Another factor in our more intense experience of RSD is masking and perfectionism. Many of us spend years developing elaborate compensatory strategies to hide our ADHD symptoms. We work harder than

---

[131] Madhoo and Quinn, "A Review of Attention Deficit/Hyperactivity Disorder in Women and Girls."

others to appear organised, attentive, and "normal." Receiving criticism despite these exhausting efforts can feel particularly devastating.

Maria, a teacher with ADHD, described the crushing weight of trying to keep up. "I pour so much energy into keeping my classroom organised and making sure every lesson is planned down to the last detail. But when my principal pointed out that I missed a deadline, it was like none of that mattered. I wasn't just disappointed. I was ashamed. I'd been working so hard to keep my struggles hidden, and in that moment, it felt like I had been exposed for my shortcomings. I'd failed."

For many of us women with ADHD, the fear of being "found out" makes any criticism feel like it could unravel the image we've worked so hard to maintain. When our compensatory efforts fail, despite how much energy we've poured into them, we can experience intense feelings of fraudulence and shame.

On top of that, many of us experience rejection sensitivity even more deeply because of our tendency to hyperfocus on relationships. The same intense focus that helps us dive into projects and be highly productive can also lead to overanalyzing social interactions and getting stuck in loops of self-doubt and worry.

When connection feels like survival, the brain gives social cues the same urgency it gives danger. That's why we may become intensely preoccupied with the dynamics in our relationships. Even subtle shifts in tone or body language can trigger the brain's threat response. We don't just notice them. We spiral. What might be a passing comment to someone else can completely derail our day.

Leanne, a graphic designer with ADHD, recognised this pattern in her friendships.

"I can spend hours analyzing a one-word text from a friend. If someone I care about seems distant, I can't focus on anything else. It's like my brain gets stuck in a loop of 'What did I do wrong?' I've lost entire days to this kind of thinking."

One thing that can help is consciously separating gender expectations from emotional responses. When you find yourself experiencing a strong RSD reaction, think through the two separately, like this:

- The situation that triggered RSD. ("My idea wasn't acknowledged.")
- The gender-based expectations that amplified your reaction. ("As a woman, I feel I need universal approval to be valued.")

This separation helps us recognise when social conditioning is intensifying our RSD experience and respond with more self-compassion.[132]

UNDERSTANDING "PERCEIVED" REJECTION

When I interviewed Alicia, she shared a vivid example of how quickly her thoughts could spiral when waiting for a response from a friend. She described staring at her phone, checking for the fifth time in an hour to see if her friend had replied to her text. It had been six hours since she'd suggested they get together over the weekend, and the silence was becoming unbearable.

She hates me, Alicia thought, her mind racing through every possible scenario. *I must have said something wrong the last time we talked. Maybe she's out with other friends and doesn't want me around. She's probably trying to figure out how to tell me she doesn't want to be friends anymore.*

By the time her friend replied the next morning, apologising for the delay and enthusiastically agreeing to meet up, Alicia had already spent nearly twenty-four hours anxiously spiralling, convinced she'd lost a friendship she deeply valued.

This scenario highlights one of the most challenging aspects of RSD for women with ADHD: distinguishing between real rejection and perceived rejection. For many of us, rejection doesn't just sting, it knocks the wind out of us. RSD can turn even minor social slights into overwhelming emotional experiences, making it hard to tell the difference between actual rejection and what our brains perceive as rejection.

The hypervigilance for rejection in our ADHD brains is linked to an evolutionary threat-detection system that's turned up too high. The anterior cingulate cortex, which helps process social pain, shows higher

---

[132] Nadeau and Quinn, *Understanding Women with AD/HD*.

activation in people with rejection sensitivity, meaning we literally feel social exclusion more intensely than others.[133]

Becca, a marketing professional with ADHD, put it this way: "My brain is like a rejection radar. It picks up on things that probably mean nothing, like delayed responses, neutral expressions, or offhand comments, and turns them into proof that I've messed up somehow. If my boss says, 'We need to talk later,' I don't just assume it's about a project. I'm already spiralling, convinced I'm about to be fired."

This heightened sensitivity leads to a common ADHD experience: seeing rejection where it may not exist. A friend taking longer than usual to text back, a neutral tone in an email, or a coworker not inviting you to lunch can spiral into deep feelings of being unwanted or unworthy.

Many of us with ADHD have spent years feeling like outsiders, which makes our brains hypervigilant for signs of rejection. This means we often overanalyse interactions, looking for proof that people dislike us, even when no such evidence exists.

Tara, a nurse with ADHD, recognised several common patterns of perceived rejection in her life: "I assume my husband is angry with me when he's quiet, even though he's usually just tired. I read too much into short text messages from friends. I convince myself that my coworkers don't like me because they didn't specifically invite me to lunch, even though they said, 'We're heading out if anyone wants to join.'"

These patterns of perceived rejection contrast with signs of real rejection, which tend to be more consistent and explicit:

- Repeated exclusion from social events or work discussions.
- Direct negative feedback about behaviour or work.
- Clear patterns of avoidance from someone.
- Explicit statements that your presence is unwelcome.

---

[133] Naomi I. Eisenberger and Matthew D. Lieberman, "Why Rejection Hurts: A Common Neural Alarm System for Physical and Social Pain," *Trends in Cognitive Sciences* 8, no. 7 (2004): 294–300, https://doi.org/10.1016/j.tics.2004.05.010.

The challenge for ADHD women is that perceived rejection feels just as painful as real rejection. The emotional response is the same, even when the situation doesn't warrant it.[134]

BUILDING AN "EMOTIONAL BUFFER" SO REJECTION STINGS LESS OVER TIME

Dana shared with me that one day she walked into her weekly therapy session looking visibly lighter than she had in months. "Something amazing happened," she told her therapist. "My proposal got rejected at work, and I didn't fall apart. I was disappointed, sure, but I didn't spiral into shame or question my entire worth as a person. I actually... handled it."

For Dana, who had struggled with debilitating RSD for years, this moment marked a breakthrough. It didn't happen overnight. It was the result of months spent intentionally building what her therapist called an "emotional buffer" against rejection.

Simply learning about RSD and understanding its impact on her experiences as an ADHD woman gave her newfound resilience.

Rejection hurts! There's no denying it. But for us ADHD women, RSD makes it feel unbearable. Whether it's a critical comment, a perceived social slight, or a professional setback, our ADHD brains process rejection as a threat, triggering the same fight-or-flight response as physical danger.[135]

Over time, repeated experiences of rejection, real or perceived, can leave emotional wounds that never fully heal, keeping us hypervigilant for future pain. The solution isn't to avoid rejection altogether (which isn't possible) but rather to develop an "emotional buffer": a collection of tools and strategies that lessen rejection's sting, ensuring it doesn't derail our confidence, relationships, or self-worth.

The neuroplasticity of the brain means that repetitive thoughts create

---

134 Saline, *The Emotional Experience of ADHD*.

135 Dodson, "How ADHD Ignites RSD."

stronger neural pathways. For many of us ADHD women, years of painful rejection experiences have created robust neural highways to negative self-beliefs. Building an emotional buffer involves creating new neural pathways through consistent alternative responses to rejection.[136]

Cassandra, a writer with ADHD, described her journey to build emotional resilience. "I used to believe that if someone criticised my writing, it meant I was a terrible writer and person. Rejection meant I was fundamentally flawed. Changing that narrative has been the most important part of managing my RSD."

Like Cassandra, many of us ADHD women carry deep-seated beliefs about rejection:

- If someone criticises me, it means I'm not good enough.
- If I get left out, it must be because people don't like me.
- If I fail, it means I never should have tried.

These thoughts reinforce negative core beliefs and make rejection feel personal. But rejection is often situational and not a reflection of worth. Shifting this narrative is the first step in creating emotional distance.

Michelle, a software developer with ADHD, shared how she practised reframing rejection: "When I didn't get called for a second interview, instead of thinking, *I'm not smart enough*, I practised thinking, *They were looking for a different skill set*. Instead of *No one wants me on their team*, I'd consciously shift to *This particular team wasn't the right fit*."

This reframing exercise represents a crucial step in building an emotional buffer against rejection: Because our ADHD brains are wired for external validation, rejection hits harder when we depend on others to feel good about ourselves. Building an internal validation system helps create a safety net when external approval is lacking.[137]

Jade, a teacher with ADHD, found that documenting her accomplishments helped strengthen her internal validation. "I keep a 'wins

---

[136] Siegel, *Mindsight*.

[137] Saline, *The Emotional Experience of ADHD*.

journal' where I write down things I'm proud of each day, even small things like grading all the papers or remembering to call my mom. When rejection hits and I start to feel worthless, I can look back at concrete evidence that I am competent and valuable."

Other strategies that help strengthen internal validation include:

- Reciting daily self-affirmations that specifically counter common RSD thoughts.
- Practicing self-compassion by responding to yourself as you would to a friend.
- Creating a "validation bank" of positive feedback to revisit during difficult times.

Resilience isn't about avoiding rejection. It's about minimising the suffering that comes with catastrophising a situation and then recovering faster. The stronger the emotional buffer, the quicker we ADHD women can bounce back from setbacks.

Olivia, a social worker with ADHD, created a specific "Rejection Recovery Plan" that helped her manage RSD. "When rejection hits, I have a written plan I follow automatically. First, I name what I'm feeling. For example, I might say to myself, 'This is RSD.' Then I use a physical grounding technique like running cold water over my wrists or doing jumping jacks. Next, I reach out to my ADHD support group. Having a specific plan means I don't have to think clearly in the moment when emotions are overwhelming."

For ADHD women like Dana, Cassandra, Michelle, Jade, and Olivia, building an emotional buffer against rejection doesn't happen overnight. It requires consistent practise, self-awareness, and often professional support. Over time, these strategies can transform how we experience rejection—it shifts from a devastating blow to a manageable disappointment.

Rejection will always be a part of life with ADHD, but it doesn't have to control our emotions or self-worth. By building an emotional buffer, we ADHD women give ourselves the power to respond to rejection with resilience rather than spiralling into self-doubt.

LIVING WITH RSD: FINDING FREEDOM THROUGH UNDERSTANDING

"The moment that changed everything for me wasn't when the RSD stopped. It was when I finally understood what was happening and stopped blaming myself for it," explained Rebecca, a forty-two-year-old architect diagnosed with ADHD in her late thirties.

After decades of intense emotional reactions that seemed out of proportion, relationships damaged by her sensitivity to perceived slights, and professional opportunities missed because fear of rejection paralyzed her, Rebecca finally had a name for her experience: rejection sensitivity dysphoria.

"Learning about RSD was like finding the missing piece of a puzzle I'd been struggling with my whole life," she said. "Suddenly all these painful experiences made sense. It wasn't that I was too emotional or too sensitive. It was that my brain was literally wired to experience rejection more intensely."

Recognising that RSD is a neurological experience, not a character flaw, is transformative for many of us women with ADHD. It doesn't eliminate the pain of rejection, but it does provide a framework for understanding and managing it more effectively. Naming and normalising experiences is a powerful intervention for our ADHD brains. Research in neuroscience shows that simply labelling emotional states activates the prefrontal cortex and reduces amygdala activity, helping regulate emotional responses.[138]

Trisha, a thirty-five-year-old teacher, described how this realisation shifted the way she saw herself. "For years, I thought I was just too sensitive, that if I could just toughen up like everyone kept telling me, I'd be fine. But learning that my brain actually processes rejection differently changed everything. Now, instead of beating myself up, I try to be gentler with myself when those feelings hit."

---

[138] Matthew D. Lieberman et al., "Putting Feelings into Words," *Psychological Science* 18, no. 5 (2007): 421–28, https://doi.org/10.1111/j.1467-9280.2007.01916.x.

For so many of us, the journey to managing RSD effectively includes several key insights.

Natalie, a business analyst, found power in prediction. "Once I understood my RSD patterns, I could anticipate situations that might trigger those feelings, like performance reviews or meeting new people. Being prepared doesn't prevent the feelings entirely, but it does mean they don't blindside me anymore."

Courtney, a graphic designer, discovered that disclosure is helpful in close relationships. "I've explained RSD to my partner and closest friends. Now when I'm having an episode, I can just say 'I'm having RSD about this conversation,' and they understand I need reassurance or space. It's been a game changer for my relationships."

Victoria, a nurse practitioner, learned to distinguish between feeling and acting. "The biggest realisation for me was that I can feel these intense emotions without having to act on them. I can observe, 'I'm having a rejection sensitivity response right now,' without sending the defensive text or withdrawing from a relationship. The feeling still hurts, but I don't make decisions from that place anymore."

While RSD is a real and challenging part of ADHD, it doesn't have to control our lives. With the right understanding and strategies, we can learn to manage it in a way that makes space for both growth and self-compassion.

Rebecca put it best: "RSD is still part of my life, but it doesn't run the show anymore. I can feel those big emotions without letting them swallow me whole. I can catch myself when my brain jumps to worst-case scenarios. And most importantly, I've stopped seeing my sensitivity as a weakness. It's what makes me empathetic, creative, and deeply passionate. Honestly, I wouldn't trade my brain for anything."

Learning to live well with RSD isn't about toughening up or shutting down our emotions. It's about building awareness, finding the right tools, and giving ourselves permission to exist as we are, without shame. For the women who shared their stories here, understanding RSD was the first and most powerful step toward that kind of freedom.

EMBRACING OUR SENSITIVE SELVES

"The most beautiful people we have known are those who have known defeat, known suffering, known struggle, known loss, and have found their way out of the depths. These persons have an appreciation, a sensitivity, and an understanding of life that fills them with compassion, gentleness, and a deep loving concern. Beautiful people do not just happen."

—ELISABETH KÜBLER-ROSS

As I reflect on the countless conversations I've had with women like Karen, Elena, Alicia, Cassandra, and Rebecca, I'm struck by a powerful realisation: Our sensitivity isn't simply a burden; it's also a gift.

The same neurological differences that make us feel rejection so deeply also allow us to experience connection, creativity, and compassion with remarkable intensity. Our ADHD brains don't just perceive the negative more strongly; they perceive everything more vividly. We experience the world in high definition.

I remember sitting with Mia, a writer with ADHD who had just published her first novel after years of rejection letters. "The rejections nearly broke me," she told me as she gazed toward the window. "But the depth with which I feel things is what makes my writing connect with readers. I wouldn't trade my sensitive heart, even though it's been bruised so many times."

This is perhaps the most beautiful paradox of our ADHD experience: The very quality that can cause us so much pain is also the source of our greatest strengths. Our sensitivity makes us empathetic leaders, intuitive friends, passionate advocates, and creative thinkers. We notice nuances others miss. We feel deeply for others' struggles. We care, sometimes too much, but in a world that often feels increasingly disconnected, isn't that a gift worth having?

Living with RSD doesn't mean eliminating our sensitivity. It means learning to harness it without being overwhelmed by it. It means building that emotional buffer not to numb ourselves but to create space for choice in how we respond. It means recognising that our intense emotional experiences are valid while also understanding that our perception isn't always reality.

The women I've worked with who manage RSD most effectively haven't become less sensitive. They've become more self-aware. They've learned to recognise their RSD responses, pause before reacting, question catastrophic thoughts, and soothe their nervous systems when overwhelmed. They've built communities of understanding, surrounded themselves with people who value their sensitivity, and learned to set boundaries with those who don't get it.

Most importantly, they've come to see their sensitivity not as something broken to be fixed but as an integral part of who they are. It's a quality to be managed, channelled, and even celebrated.

As we wrap up this chapter, I want to leave you with something to think about: What if your sensitivity isn't a flaw but simply part of how your brain is wired?

What if the goal isn't to shut down your emotions but to build the resilience to navigate them?

What if instead of feeling ashamed of how deeply you experience things, you approached those feelings with curiosity and compassion?

Because here's what I know for certain: You aren't alone in this experience. Across North America and around the world, millions of us are navigating these same waters, feeling deeply, sometimes hurting deeply, but also loving deeply, creating passionately, and living fully. Our sensitive hearts may make rejection harder to bear, but they also make connection more profound, joy more vibrant, and life richer with meaning.

And that, I believe, is worth every moment of effort it takes to manage our RSD.

FINDING BEAUTY IN OUR SENSITIVITY

As I sit at my desk tonight, rain pattering against the window, I'm reflecting on the countless conversations I've had with women across the world about our experiences with ADHD and rejection sensitivity.

There's something profoundly moving about the way we've all found each other—women who have spent much of our lives feeling different, misunderstood, "too much" or "not enough" and have recognised ourselves in each other's stories.

I think about my own journey with RSD. How a single critical comment could once derail me for days, months, hell, even years. How I'd rehearse conversations endlessly, analyzing every word and facial expression for signs of disapproval. How I believed, deep down, that if people really knew me—the disorganised, emotional, intense me—they would inevitably reject me.

What changed wasn't that I stopped feeling things deeply. It wasn't that I developed a "thicker skin" (whatever that means). It was that I finally understood what was happening in my brain during these moments of intense emotional pain.

And with that understanding came something precious: self-compassion.

Living with ADHD has taught me that embracing our sensitivity isn't just about managing it. It's about accepting ourselves fully. In a world that often sees emotional detachment as strength, choosing to honour our sensitivity while learning to work with it is its own kind of power.

The women who shared their stories in these pages have shown me that real change doesn't come from trying to erase our sensitivity. It comes from understanding it.

Every time we meet ourselves with self-compassion instead of criticism, every time we pause to ground ourselves instead of spiralling, every time we recognise an RSD response without letting it define us, we take back a little more of our power.

This journey isn't linear. There will be days when rejection cuts deep despite all our tools, when the tsunami of emotion feels too overwhelming to bear, when old patterns reassert themselves. But even on those days, we now have something precious that many of us lacked before: understanding. We know what's happening in our brains. We know we're not alone. And we know this storm, like all storms, will pass.

I remember sitting in a coffee shop in Vancouver with Maya, a brilliant interior designer with ADHD who had just navigated a difficult client meeting without spiralling into self-doubt. "I still felt everything," she told me, stirring her latte thoughtfully. "The criticism still stung. But it was like I was watching the feelings from a slight distance instead of drowning in them. I could see *Oh, this is RSD happening* and just… breathe through it."

That's the paradox I've witnessed again and again with the women I've interviewed and worked with: We don't become less sensitive as we heal. We become more aware, more compassionate with ourselves, more skilled at navigating the intensity of our emotions. We learn to create a buffer not to numb ourselves but to give ourselves space to choose our responses.

As you step away from this chapter, I hope you carry more than just strategies. I hope you see yourself a little differently. Your sensitivity, the way you feel things so deeply, isn't a flaw. It's what makes you attuned to the people you love, what fuels your creativity, what helps you notice what others might miss.

Resilience doesn't mean shutting that part of yourself down. It means learning how to give yourself enough space to pause, to choose your response instead of being swept up in the moment. And in that space, you can finally breathe. In that awareness, you start to feel steadier. And when you're surrounded by people who truly get it, you no longer feel like you have to explain yourself. You just belong.

We are unlearning the idea that sensitivity is something to fix. Instead, we are learning to see it for what it is: part of who we are, not something to fight against. We're letting go of self-doubt, making peace with our past, and reclaiming the parts of ourselves we once tried to shrink.

And maybe the most freeing realisation of all is that the thing we spent years trying to change was never the problem in the first place.

SELF-COACHING EXERCISES: REJECTION SENSITIVITY DYSPHORIA

RSD is way more than just feeling hurt. It's about how fast and how deep that hurt lands. For many ADHD women, even a small moment of perceived rejection can flood the system. Your chest tightens. Your brain starts spinning. You're suddenly stuck in a loop of self-doubt or shame.

These exercises are here to help you recognise that moment when it happens, interrupt the spiral, and respond in a way that's grounded and self-respecting. This won't erase RSD, but it will help you build the awareness and skills to handle it with more clarity. Start small. Be honest with yourself. And know that even naming what's happening is progress.

RECOGNITION FRAMEWORK

Having a framework helps you recognise RSD episodes as they happen. One way to do this is to create a personalised checklist of physical, emotional, and cognitive symptoms that signal you're in a rejection spiral. Common signs might include physical sensations like chest tightness or a flushed face, emotional states like shame or panic, and thought patterns like *Everyone thinks I'm incompetent*.[139]

Start by reflecting on past moments when you've felt overwhelmed by rejection. What did it feel like in your body? What thoughts came up? How did your emotions shift? Write these down in a notebook or keep a digital note on your phone that's easy to pull up when you feel that familiar wave coming on.

The goal isn't to stop the reaction but to recognise it early. Having this checklist in front of you creates just enough distance to help you pause, name what's happening, and decide how to respond rather than getting swept away by it. Use it as a grounding tool. Revisit it often so it becomes second nature.

Having this framework ready before an episode occurs helps create

---

[139] Saline, *The Emotional Experience of ADHD*.

the cognitive distance needed to respond effectively when emotions are overwhelming.

REALITY-TESTING PROTOCOL

This exercise provides a structured approach to evaluating whether rejection is real or perceived. When feeling rejected, become that detective and follow these steps:

1. **Collect Evidence:** Write down specific, observable behaviours that suggest rejection (not interpretations or feelings).
2. **Generate Alternatives:** List at least three alternative explanations for the behaviour that don't involve rejection.
3. **Assess Probability:** Rate how likely each explanation is based only on past patterns and facts.
4. **Plan an Action:** Create a small, specific action to test your perception (e.g., a direct but casual check-in with the person).

This protocol interrupts the automatic assumption of rejection and creates space for a more accurate interpretation of social situations.

REJECTION REFRAMING MATRIX

Here's an exercise that helps you systematically transform your instinctive negative interpretations of rejection into more balanced perspectives.

Create a four-column worksheet and fill in each of the columns based on what you're experiencing:

- **Situation:** Describe the rejection event objectively.
- **Automatic Thought:** Record the immediate self-critical interpretation.
- **Evidence Against:** List facts that contradict this negative interpretation.

- **Balanced Perspective:** Create a new interpretation that acknowledges both disappointment and personal worth.

For example:

- **Situation:** "I was not invited to a colleague's wedding."
- **Automatic Thought:** "No one likes me enough to include me in important events."
- **Evidence Against:** "I was invited to her birthday last month. The venue may have limited capacity. Only very close friends seem to be invited."
- **Balanced Perspective:** "Not being invited doesn't reflect my value as a person or colleague. Social circles naturally have different levels of closeness."

REJECTION RECOVERY PLAN

Create a roadmap for responding to rejection that you can implement even when you're emotionally dysregulated. This step-by-step plan should be:

- Created during a calm state, not an RSD episode.
- Written down and easily accessible, such as stored in phone notes or as a physical card.
- Practised regularly through role-play or visualisation.
- Shared with trusted supporters who can help initiate the plan when needed.

A basic template includes:

- **Recognition Phrase:** "I am experiencing RSD right now."
- **Physical Reset:** A specific sensory intervention (cold water, movement, etc.)

- **Communication Script:** Prepared language to ask for space or support.
- **Comfort Activity:** A reliable, accessible source of dopamine and comfort.
- **Reflection Prompt:** A question to ask after emotions have settled.[140]

RSD AWARENESS AND RESPONSE TRAINING (ART)

This practise can help you develop personalised protocols for your most common RSD scenarios.

Identify the three to five situations that most frequently trigger RSD for you (e.g., work feedback, relationship conversations, social media interactions). For each scenario, create a detailed response plan that includes:

- **Recognition Cues:** The earliest physical and emotional signs that RSD is activating.
- **Immediate Interventions:** Quick techniques to prevent escalation (breathing, movement).
- **Communication Templates:** Pre-written language to ask for what you need.
- **Strategic Withdrawal Plans:** How to take space appropriately if needed.
- **Reengagement Guidelines:** How to return to the situation once regulated.

---

[140] Saline, *The Emotional Experience of ADHD*.

Chapter Seven
———

Perfectionism and Burnout

I'LL NEVER FORGET MARTHA'S STORY. WHEN I FIRST MET HER, DARK circles under her eyes told me everything before she even spoke. "I was up until three again," she admitted with a tired laugh. "Working on a presentation that was probably fine six hours earlier."

As she described her night, hunched over her laptop with empty coffee cups multiplying on her desk, constantly whispering, "Just a little more," I recognised a pattern I've seen countless times. I've lived it myself.

"It was good enough," she told me, rubbing her eyes. "Hell, it was probably better than what my boss expected. But I just…couldn't stop. The thought of submitting something with even a tiny flaw made my stomach knot up."

Martha wasn't dealing with a one-time crunch for a deadline. This was her life, what she called her "normal." A pendulum swing between obsessive work and complete collapse. Pouring everything into a task until she had nothing left, then hating herself when she inevitably crashed.

This perfectionism–burnout cycle is exhausting for us ADHD

women. I heard it described the same way countless times from both the women I interviewed and in my group coaching practise. It's a relentless back-and-forth: hyperfocus one day, total shutdown the next.

We're either all in, pouring every ounce of energy into something until we're depleted, or we're so overwhelmed we can't even start.

Far from being a personality quirk or character flaw, it's how our ADHD brains handle motivation, urgency, and reward.[141]

"It's like I'm two completely different people," Martha told me, gesturing with her hands the way she always did when she was trying to make me understand something important. "When the adrenaline kicks in, I'm on fire—I mean, I feel unstoppable. But then…" She slumped in her chair. "As soon as I finish, I crash so damn hard I can barely function. It takes me days to recover, and just when I start feeling human again, boom. The cycle starts over."

I nodded because I get it. I really do.

ADHD brains are constantly hunting for dopamine, and hyperfocus delivers a hit like nothing else, but the cost is steep. Without some kind of balance, the crash that follows brings an awful combination of exhaustion, guilt, and a persistent, nagging belief that maybe we just need to try harder next time.[142]

You might notice that perfectionism and hyperfocus often show up together. They are not the same, but they feed into each other. Perfectionism is the driver, the belief that your value comes from flawless output. It pushes you to keep going long after the work is good enough. Hyperfocus is the state that makes this possible. Once locked in, you lose track of time, energy, and other priorities. Perfectionism can become a form of hyperfocus, with the goal of perfect work keeping you in the zone for hours. The cost is the same: burnout, guilt, and the cycle starting over.

ADHD brains have lower baseline dopamine levels, which negatively

---

[141] Barkley, ed., *Attention-Deficit Hyperactivity Disorder*.

[142] Dodson, "How ADHD Ignites RSD."

affect our motivation and reward processing.[143] It's why boring tasks feel like climbing Mount Everest until suddenly there's a deadline, and poof! The pressure creates a dopamine rush that makes focus possible. But this roller coaster of last-minute hyperfocus followed by total collapse absolutely wrecks our physical and mental health over time.

WHY WE OFTEN TIE OUR SELF-WORTH TO PRODUCTIVITY

One of the biggest struggles we face as ADHD women is the belief that our value is directly linked to how much we accomplish. Society praises productivity, organisation, and efficiency, traits that our ADHD makes incredibly difficult to maintain consistently. This leads many of us to internalise the idea that if we can't keep up, we are somehow failing.

Iliana, a high-achieving professional with ADHD, described how she couldn't relax unless everything on her to-do list was done. "Rest felt like failure. If I wasn't checking things off, I felt useless," she admitted during our group coaching session. This mindset often leads us to work past our limits, ignoring signs of fatigue until we completely shut down.[144]

When asked about her childhood, Iliana recalled teacher comments that followed her into adulthood: "Very bright but needs to apply herself." "Could achieve more if she paid attention." "Inconsistent effort." These weren't just assessments of academic performance; they became definitions of character. The message was clear: Her struggles weren't because of how her brain was wired but because of who she was.

As she grew older, Iliana internalised these messages, developing compensatory strategies and working twice as hard as everyone else, staying up later, checking and rechecking her work. She became an overachiever as a defence mechanism. "If I could just be productive enough, organised enough, accomplished enough, maybe I could outrun the feeling that there was something fundamentally wrong with me," she explained.

---

143 Nora D. Volkow et al., "Evaluating Dopamine Reward Pathway in ADHD: Clinical Implications," *JAMA* 302, no. 10 (September 9, 2009): 1084–91, https://doi.org/10.1001/jama.2009.1308.

144 Madhoo and Quinn, "A Review of Attention Deficit/Hyperactivity Disorder in Women and Girls."

A woman in her late thirties shared something similar during our coaching session: "I used to think my worth was tied to how much I got done. If I wasn't productive, I felt like I had no right to exist. I'd push myself to exhaustion just to feel acceptable."

Dr. William Dodson explained that our ADHD brains operate on an "interest-based nervous system," meaning we struggle with motivation unless a task is engaging, urgent, or novel. Traditional productivity models don't work for our ADHD minds, yet many of us push ourselves to fit into neurotypical expectations, feeling immense shame when we fall short.[145]

Social conditioning plays a significant role too. Women are often expected to keep everything running smoothly, manage households, remember birthdays, and coordinate social calendars, all while pursuing careers. For those of us with ADHD who struggle with exactly these types of executive function tasks, the pressure is crushing. We feel like we're failing at the very things that define "good women."

THE DOPAMINE TRAP OF OVERWORKING: WHEN BURNOUT FEELS REWARDING

"Just one more task. Just one more hour."

Countless numbers of us whisper this mantra over keyboards late at night. The strangest part? There's something intoxicating about pushing to the edge. The adrenaline rush of deadline pressure, the dopamine hit of crossing items off a list, the brief moment of triumph when pulling off what seemed impossible. In that moment, working until exhaustion doesn't feel like self-destruction. It feels like success.

Emma, a graphic designer with ADHD, described this phenomenon perfectly in our coaching group. "I would procrastinate for weeks, then hyperfocus for twelve-hour stretches, running purely on adrenaline. And when I pulled it off, it felt amazing. Like I had outsmarted my own brain."

---

145 Dodson, "How ADHD Ignites RSD."

But the crash always came. For Emma, like many of us, these periods of intense productivity were inevitably followed by days of brain fog, exhaustion, and inability to function. Yet a small, twisted part of her was proud of this. She wore her exhaustion like a badge of honour. "Look how hard I work," it seemed to say. "Look what I'm willing to sacrifice."

Sophie, a nurse and mother of two, shared her similar experience. "I'd get this burst of excitement when I had a full schedule. It made me feel important, like I was keeping up with everyone else. But when the exhaustion hit, it was brutal. I'd crash, cancel plans, and miss deadlines. Then I'd feel guilty and start the cycle all over again."

This is the dopamine trap of overworking. Burnout can feel perversely rewarding to our ADHD brains. The urgency of deadlines, the surge of last-minute productivity, and the relief of completion all provide temporary dopamine boosts that mask the underlying damage of chronic stress and exhaustion.

We are particularly susceptible to becoming "adrenaline junkies" due to how our brains process rewards. The dopamine rush from last-minute success can become addictive, creating a neurological preference for this high-stress work pattern, despite its detrimental effects on our health and well-being.[146]

Tracey thrived on the intensity of new projects at work. When a new assignment landed on her desk, she would throw herself into it completely. She would stay late, skip meals, and wake up exhausted, yet she convinced herself she was performing at her peak.

But at home, the cost was high.

Dishes piled up. Texts from friends went unanswered. Her ability to switch gears deteriorated. Her husband, once understanding, grew frustrated with her sudden disengagement. When she finally crashed, she was unable to focus on anything, struggling with overwhelming guilt and exhaustion. It took her weeks to recover, only to fall back into the cycle when the next big work project arrived.

Hyperfocus is the term for a neurobiological state driven by dopamine

---

[146] Volkow et al., "Evaluating Dopamine Reward Pathway in ADHD."

regulation. Dr. William Dodson explained that our ADHD brains operate on an interest-based nervous system, meaning that unless a task is novel, exciting, urgent, or rewarding, we have difficulty engaging with it. Once our brains are engaged, however, disengaging becomes just as difficult.[147]

For many women with ADHD, hyperfocus shows up in ways we don't always recognise right away. It might be spending hours deep in a project and forgetting to eat. It might be rewriting the same paragraph all night trying to make it perfect. It might even be getting stuck in a loop of research or overthinking that feels productive but leaves us drained. When we hyperfocus, it's like the rest of the world goes quiet. We lock in and lose track of time, and it often doesn't hit us until our body crashes or something pulls us out of it.

Additionally, research shows that people with ADHD experience weaker interoception—the ability to perceive internal body signals.[148] This is why we may not realise we are hungry, thirsty, or sleep-deprived until it becomes extreme.

Hyperfocus is often described as a superpower (a term I personally dislike), one of the few "benefits" of ADHD. And in some ways, it is remarkable. The ability to dive so deeply into a task that everything else disappears can lead to incredible creativity and productivity. But like many superpowers in comic books, hyperfocus comes with a dark side (specifically here, not being able to control it).

Kimberly, another woman with ADHD, shared how perfectionism compounded the hyperfocus problem. "Whenever I started a creative project, I would become consumed by every detail, redesigning, over-researching, tweaking endlessly. I could spend twelve hours straight working on a project while ignoring everything else, convincing myself that I was just being thorough. But the cost was steep. I consistently missed deadlines, not because I was procrastinating but because I could not stop refining."

---

[147] Dodson, "How ADHD Ignites RSD."

[148] Alisha M. Bruton et al., "Diminished Interoceptive Accuracy in Attention-Deficit/Hyperactivity Disorder: A Systematic Review," *Psychophysiology* 62, no. 2 (February 2025): e14750, https://doi.org/10.1111/psyp.14750.

This is the double-edged sword of hyperfocus. It brings incredible productivity in one narrow area, but often at the cost of balance in all others. And over time, this imbalance leads to burnout.

LEARNING TO PRIORITISE REST WITHOUT GUILT

"I wouldn't rest until I literally got sick. Like, actual flu sick. That was the only time I felt justified in doing absolutely nothing."

Melanie, a marketing executive with ADHD, shared this during one of our group coaching sessions, and I watched heads nodding around the circle. I knew that pattern too well—pushing and pushing until your body basically gives you the middle finger and forces you to stop.

For many of us, rest often feels like this forbidden luxury we haven't earned. Like we need to check off some impossible list of achievements before we're "allowed" to take a break.

But here's the thing I've learned after years of running myself into the ground: Burnout isn't some badge of honour. It's not proof that you're working hard enough. It's just destructive.

Amy, one of my long-term clients, described it perfectly over coffee one day: "I'd finally sit down after hours of running around, and literally within seconds, my brain would start screaming at me: 'What the hell are you doing? Get up! You haven't finished XYZ!'" She laughed, but there was real pain behind it. "Rest didn't feel like an option. It felt like I was failing at life."

That's the thing about rest for us. It's more than relaxation. It's about permission. And damn, we are stingy with giving ourselves that permission.

Why is rest so challenging for our ADHD brains? Part of it is dopamine deficiency. Our brains crave constant stimulation. Part is time blindness. We struggle to gauge when we need breaks. But a significant factor is the shame and guilt many of us have internalised. After years of being told we're not trying hard enough, we push ourselves to the breaking point just to feel adequate.

Janelle, a mom with ADHD, shared how she overcame her rest

resistance. "I had to literally schedule 'do nothing' time in my calendar and treat it like an important meeting. At first, I felt ridiculous sitting on my porch just staring at the trees. But after a few weeks, I started to crave that time. Now it's nonnegotiable."

Research shows that our ADHD brains need more recovery time, not less.[149] Proper rest improves executive function, emotional regulation, and overall cognitive performance.[150] By viewing rest as essential maintenance rather than an optional luxury, we can begin to release the guilt associated with "doing nothing."

REDEFINING SUCCESS IN A SUSTAINABLE WAY

Emma shared with me that she was always the "promising one." In university, she aced exams, stayed up all night perfecting assignments, and impressed professors with her creativity. But as soon as she entered the workforce, everything fell apart. The rigid schedules, the expectation of steady output, and the daily monotony left her drained. She started staying late to compensate, convinced that if she just worked harder, she could keep up.

She couldn't.

Missed deadlines and forgotten meetings piled up. Her boss started commenting on her "lack of focus," and soon, her self-worth crumbled. She quit, convinced she was failing at adulthood. Years later, after an ADHD diagnosis, she realised the problem wasn't her intelligence or work ethic.

It was the expectation that she could sustain a neurotypical work style. She had spent years chasing a version of success that was never designed for her.

---

149 Tomokatsu Kono, "Embodied Bases of Attention-Deficit/Hyperactivity Disorder," *Linkage* 2 (2024): 7–14, https://doi.org/10.32165/linkage.2.2.

150 Aayushi Sen and Xin You Tai, "Sleep Duration and Executive Function in Adults," *Current Neurology and Neuroscience Reports* 23, no. 11 (November 2023): 801–13, https://doi.org/10.1007/s11910-023-01309-8.; and Jennifer Murphy et al., "Interoception and Psychopathology: A Developmental Neuroscience Perspective," *Developmental Cognitive Neuroscience* 23 (2017): 45–56, https://doi.org/10.1016/j.dcn.2016.12.006.

For many of us with ADHD, the conventional definition of success is grounded in consistency, productivity, and efficiency, but it often feels impossible to sustain. Society often measures achievement by how well one sticks to routines, meets deadlines, and maintains order. Traditional productivity models rely heavily on consistency and willpower, which can be difficult for our ADHD brains due to fluctuating dopamine levels. Sustainable success comes from embracing flexibility, interest-based motivation, and self-compassion.[151]

But our ADHD brains thrive in bursts of energy, hyperfocus, and nonlinear thinking. These rigid expectations don't just feel unattainable; they set us up for chronic self-doubt and burnout.

Many of us who were diagnosed later in life have internalised the belief that we are "behind" in life because we struggle to meet neurotypical standards. We compare ourselves to friends, colleagues, or influencers who seem effortlessly put together, fuelling a sense of inadequacy. This pressure often leads to cycles of overworking to compensate, followed by exhaustion and shame when motivation inevitably wanes.

What if success wasn't about fitting into someone else's framework? What if it was about creating a definition that works for each of our unique brains?

Mia, an artist with ADHD, shared how she transformed her relationship with unfinished projects. "I used to abandon paintings when I lost interest. Instead of forcing myself to finish every piece, I started celebrating the process. Even if I don't complete it, I've still created something. That's success."

Samantha, a freelance writer, discovered that instead of forcing herself to work nine to five, she was most productive in short bursts. She started working in ninety-minute focus sprints with long breaks. Her output increased, and she felt less drained.

At thirty-eight, Rachel switched careers after years of struggling in corporate jobs. She now works as an ADHD coach, using her lived experience to help others. "I'm not behind," she shared. "I'm exactly where

---

[151] Barkley, ed., *Attention-Deficit Hyperactivity Disorder.*

I need to be. All those 'failures' and detours gave me the experience I need to help others now."

Rachel, Mia, and Samantha show us that stepping away from rigid expectations can open the door to more sustainable success. Each of them stopped chasing traditional measures of achievement and started building work patterns that honoured their energy, creativity, and attention. By defining success on their own terms, they found a way to be productive without sacrificing their well-being.

BREAKING THE PERFECTIONISM–BURNOUT CYCLE: MOVING FORWARD

The perfectionism–burnout cycle doesn't break itself. Changing patterns in place since childhood requires intention, self-awareness, and a willingness to be uncomfortable. But it also requires compassion, something many of us have never offered ourselves.

Rather than trying to eliminate perfectionism entirely (a perfectionistic goal in itself!), try working with it differently. Recognising its roots in ADHD, including the fear of making mistakes, sensitivity to criticism, and deep desire to prove our worth, helps us reframe these tendencies not as character flaws but as adaptations to a lifetime of feeling different without knowing why.

Strategies that help us break the cycle aren't revolutionary, but they are effective:

- Set timers when working on projects to prevent hyperfocus from consuming entire days.
- Schedule recovery time after intense work periods—actual blocks in the calendar dedicated to rest.
- Practise the "good enough" principle, deliberately submitting work that isn't perfect to challenge perfectionistic tendencies.
- Build support systems with other ADHD women who understand the struggle and provide accountability.

- Celebrate progress rather than perfection, keeping a done list instead of just a to-do list.[152]

Most importantly, treating ourselves with kindness is essential. When the critical voice starts its familiar narrative about not being enough, pausing to ask "Would I say this to someone I love?" can create perspective. The answer is almost always no. And here's a news flash that might be hard to swallow: We deserve the same gentleness we offer others.

Breaking free from the perfectionism–burnout cycle isn't about becoming less driven or ambitious. It's about channelling that drive in sustainable ways. It's about creating success metrics that honour our neurodivergent brains rather than fighting against them. It's about recognising that our worth isn't tied to productivity.

Let me repeat this: Your worth is *not* tied to your productivity.

The journey isn't linear. I still have days when the old patterns resurface. Pushing too hard, forgetting to rest, holding to impossible standards. But with increasing awareness, I can course correct before hitting complete exhaustion.

Sometimes when I think about our collective journey with perfectionism and burnout, I feel this weird mix of sadness and hope that's hard to put into words. Sadness for all those years so many of us spent thinking we were just fundamentally broken. For all the exhaustion we've dealt with trying to jam ourselves into a world that wasn't built for brains like ours.

But there's hope too. Because once you see the patterns, you can start to change them. Not perfectly (ha!), but enough to make life better.

I look at my own journey and the journeys of women like Martha. Many of us have moved from working until three in the morning and wearing our exhaustion like some twisted badge of honour to recognising when we're slipping into those old, destructive patterns. We've slowly

---

[152] Kathleen E. Hupfeld et al., "Living 'in the Zone': Hyperfocus in Adult ADHD," *ADHD Attention Deficit and Hyperactivity Disorders* 11 (2019): 191–208, https://doi.org/10.1007/s12402-018-0272-y.

learned to hear that whisper of "just one more hour" for what it really is: not motivation but a warning sign.

We're starting to see rest not as a reward we have to earn through suffering but as something our ADHD brains genuinely need to function.

None of this happened overnight for me. There were plenty of false starts. Plenty of nights I found myself right back in perfectionism's grip, polishing something that was already good enough. I'm doing it right now as I make another pass on this chapter!

But each time I catch myself, each time I manage to close the laptop and say, "This is good enough," it gets a tiny bit easier.

What I've figured out (the hard way, naturally, because I'm still navigating my own ADHD) is that for us ADHD folks, finding balance isn't about achieving some perfect zen state of equilibrium. It's about creating a rhythm that actually works with our neurodivergence instead of constantly fighting against it. It's about accepting that our energy and motivation will always have these dramatic ebbs and flows and planning around them instead of pretending they don't exist.

And maybe most importantly, it's about redefining what success even means. It's not some destination we reach by burning ourselves to the ground but a journey where we honour both our strengths (which are pretty incredible) and our very real limitations.

I'll never forget what Lisa, one of my clients, said in our final session together. She leaned back in her chair, looking more relaxed than I'd ever seen her, and said, "You know, perfectionism was my shield for so long. I thought if I could just be perfect, no one would notice how much I was struggling. But now I see that my imperfections aren't flaws. They're just part of how my brain works. And there's a kind of freedom in that."

In that freedom lies our path forward. It's messy and imperfect, with plenty of detours, but it's authentically our own.

SELF-COACHING EXERCISES: PERFECTIONISM AND BURNOUT

If there's one thing I see over and over again with ADHD women, it's that we're either pushing ourselves to the edge or completely wiped out. There's rarely a middle ground. Perfectionism keeps us sprinting, and then burnout knocks us flat.

These exercises are about disrupting that cycle. Not by forcing more discipline or motivation but by working with how your brain actually functions. Think of them as practical tools to help you slow down, reset, and redefine what success even means.

DOPAMINE BREAKS

Taking small dopamine boosts throughout the day can help you maintain more consistent energy and prevent the whole crash-and-burn thing that leaves you useless for days.[153]

I've learned the hard way that fighting against a neurological reality is pointless. We need to work with it instead of beating ourselves up.

For my clients prone to these all-or-nothing cycles (and for myself, if I'm honest), I recommend building in regular "dopamine breaks" throughout work sessions: five- to ten-minute pauses for movement, music, checking your phone, or whatever gives you a little hit of pleasure.

ALTERNATIVE METRICS

For those of us who tie self-worth to productivity, creating alternative metrics for "good days" can break this harmful pattern.

If your self-worth is tied to how much you get done, you're not alone. But this mindset quietly fuels burnout and makes it hard to rest without guilt. One way to start breaking this pattern is by tracking different metrics that reflect how you're actually doing, not just what you've produced.

Try this exercise at the end of each day:

---

[153] Saline, *The Emotional Experience of ADHD*.

- **Grab a notebook or use a notes app on your phone.** Make this your "alternative metrics log."
- **Ask yourself one or more of these questions:**
  - How did I honour my needs today?
  - What brought me joy today?
  - Where did I show self-compassion instead of pushing harder?
  - What did I say no to that protected my energy?
  - When did I feel most like myself?
- **Write your answers down—short, honest, and judgment-free.**

Over time, this creates a new feedback loop that celebrates how you live, not just what you check off. It's a small shift, but it changes how you define a "good" day. And that change matters.

DOPAMINE MENU

Overworking is often our default dopamine source. It's intense and rewarding, and it gets stuff done—that is, until it burns us out. The goal here isn't to stop seeking dopamine. It's to find better ways to get it.

Here's how to build your own dopamine menu:

Step 1: Choose your categories.

Use at least three of these:

- Physical movement
- Music or audio
- Sensory comfort (warm drinks, soft textures)
- Creativity
- Connection
- Quick wins (tiny tasks that give you instant satisfaction)
- Novelty or humour
- Rest and reset

Step 2: List three to five items under each.

Keep it realistic. No aspirational stuff here. Choose things you actually enjoy and can access easily. For example:

- **Physical:** Stretch, take a short walk, jump rope.
- **Audio:** Listen to one song at full volume, listen to nature sounds.
- **Quick Wins:** Tidy one drawer, delete ten emails.
- **Connection:** Voice note a friend, hug your dog.

Step 3: Post it somewhere visible.

Stick it on your desk. Add it to your phone notes, or turn it into a shortcut widget.

Step 4: Use it before you crash.

Set a reminder midmorning and midafternoon. Choose one item, and give yourself five minutes to actually enjoy it.

This isn't indulgent. It's neurological maintenance. Your brain needs stimulation, and if you don't give it healthy options, it'll go looking for intensity in all the wrong places.

Research on ADHD self-management and recovery strategies shows that brief, simple activities can help restore energy and reduce burnout.[154] Keeping a short list of easy reset activities is one practical way to apply this evidence.

---

[154] Amanda J. Williamson, J. Jeffrey Gish, and Ute Stephan, "Let's Focus on Solutions to Entrepreneurial Ill-Being! Recovery Interventions to Enhance Entrepreneurial Well-Being" (working paper, Social Science Research Network, May 14, 2021), https://papers.ssrn.com/sol3/papers.cfm?abstract_id=3844146.

HYPERFOCUS BOOKENDING

Hyperfocus can be a superpower until it becomes a trap. When you're in it, time disappears. Hunger, fatigue, and boundaries? Gone. What starts as productivity can quietly slide into burnout.

One of the most effective ways to prevent that crash is using a strategy called *hyperfocus bookending*. It's a simple way to work *with* your brain instead of letting it run the show.

Here's how to do it:

- **Step 1: Set a clear start time.** This signals to your brain that you're entering a focus period. Bonus if you use a small ritual to anchor it, like putting on noise-cancelling headphones or turning off notifications.
- **Step 2: Choose a hard stop time.** Decide in advance when you'll end. Not "when I feel like it" but something specific like "at three" or "after one Pomodoro round."
- **Step 3: Set external cues.** Use a loud timer, calendar alert, or text check-in with an accountability buddy. Pick something strong enough to get your attention even if you're deep in the zone.
- **Step 4: Honour the stop—even if it's mid-flow.** This part is hard. But stepping away helps you build the muscle of cognitive flexibility and protects your energy long term.
- **Step 5: Build in a transition.** Don't just yank yourself out. Give your brain a soft landing. Stretch. Drink water. Step outside. Do something grounding.

This approach is backed by research showing that ADHD brains benefit from external scaffolding to manage time blindness and maintain sustainable focus.[155]

---

[155] Hupfeld et al., "Living 'in the Zone'"; Barkley, *Executive Functions*; Radek Ptacek et al., "Clinical Implications of the Perception of Time in Attention Deficit Hyperactivity Disorder (ADHD): A Review," *Medical Science Monitor* 25 (May 2019): 3918–3924, https://doi.org/10.12659/MSM.914225.

PERMISSION SLIPS FOR REST

For those of us who struggle with rest, reframing it isn't optional; it's survival. Rest is not the opposite of productivity. It's part of it.

One way to internalise that truth is through physical "permission slips" for rest. These are simple cards you can place somewhere visible—on your desk, on your mirror, inside your planner—with affirming statements like:

- "Rest makes me more effective."
- "Downtime is necessary for my brain to function."
- "I'm allowed to pause without earning it."

To turn this into a practise:

1. **Start paying attention:** Notice the moments you feel resistance to rest, whether it's taking a break, ending your workday, or even just doing nothing for a few minutes.
2. **Each time you catch it, write yourself a new permission slip:** Use a note card, sticky note, or index card.
3. **Include a sentence that speaks directly to your inner critic:** Something you need to hear in that moment. Be specific.
4. **Collect notes over a few days:** Keep them somewhere visible, such as a jar, corkboard, or notebook, or even turn it into a small art project or display in your home.
5. **Revisit them often:** These reminders help retrain your nervous system to associate rest with safety, not guilt or shame.

Giving yourself permission to rest isn't lazy; it's an act of resistance against burnout and a step toward working *with* your brain, not against it.[156]

---

[156] Neff, *Self-Compassion*.

REDEFINE SUCCESS

Many ADHD women tie success to output, time worked, or how closely they've followed a neurotypical standard. But those measures often leave us feeling like we're always behind, no matter how much we've actually done.

This exercise is about shifting the definition of success so it reflects your reality, not someone else's rule book.

Start by reading through the examples below and choose one or two that feel most relevant to where you're currently stuck. Then write down your current belief and create your own personal reframe. Keep these reframes somewhere visible or revisit them at the end of the day.

If you're journaling, you can use a reflection prompt like:

- What felt successful today, even if it wouldn't look that way to someone else?
- Where did I honour my capacity?
- What did I do that moved things forward, even a little?

Here are practical ways to start redefining success for yourself:

- **Ditch the all-or-nothing mindset:** Instead of "I didn't complete my to-do list, so I failed today," try "I tackled two important tasks that moved me forward."
- **Prioritise energy management over time management:** Pay attention to your natural energy cycles, and build your day around them. When energy dips, lean on body doubling, timers, or check-ins to stay grounded.
- **Redefine productivity as impact, not hours worked:** Replace "I only worked for three hours today, so I wasn't productive" with "I made real progress in three focused hours."
- **Use strengths-based goal setting:** Instead of rigid goals like "I will work out five days a week," try "I'll experiment with different types of movement and see what feels good."
- **Measure success in small wins:** Don't wait until the project is fin-

ished to feel accomplished. Celebrate brainstorming, outlining, or creating a first draft. Progress counts.
- **Let go of neurotypical timelines:** Change "I should have figured this out by now" to "My path is different, and that's okay."[157]

The more you practise reframing success this way, the more space you create for sustainable motivation. This does not mean you're lowering the bar. Instead, you're building a different one—one you can actually reach.

---

[157] Sedgwick et al., "The Positive Aspects of Attention Deficit Hyperactivity Disorder"; and Mahdi et al., "An International Qualitative Study of Ability and Disability in ADHD Using the WHO-ICF Framework."

Chapter Eight

Emotional Flooding and Anxiety

THE EMAIL DIDN'T SEEM LIKE A BIG DEAL—JUST A ROUTINE QUEStion from her manager about yesterday's presentation: "Could you clarify the numbers on slide fifteen? They don't quite match what we discussed."

No big deal, right?

For Megan, a late-diagnosed ADHD woman, it hit like a freight train. Her stomach dropped. Her heart started hammering. The walls felt like they were closing in. She thought, *Oh jeez, I messed up. The whole thing was wrong. Everyone noticed. They're probably talking about it right now. I'm going to get fired. Lose my house. My kids will have to switch schools.*

One second, she was sipping coffee. The next, her body was in full-blown survival mode.

"My heart was racing, and my brain immediately jumped to, 'I screwed up. I'm getting fired.' I couldn't think straight," Megan told me later. "I spent the next hour rereading my own email over and over, trying to find a mistake I wasn't even sure existed."

If you have ADHD, you probably know exactly what this feels like.

A casual comment from a friend. An unexpected schedule change. A small mistake at work. Something that should be minor, except it doesn't feel minor. It feels like the world is caving in.

For ADHD women, emotional flooding isn't just a rough day. It's an everyday reality. One small trigger, and suddenly your emotions are at full volume, drowning out all logic. Add anxiety, which affects up to 50 percent of adults with ADHD, and the reaction gets even bigger. Once that flood starts, it's almost impossible to stop.[158]

I remember sitting in a meeting when a colleague casually pointed out a mistake in my report. It wasn't a big deal. Easily fixable. But in that moment? Shame hit me like a brick wall. My face burned. My chest tightened. My vision blurred. I could barely hear the conversation over the spiral in my head.

Later, I found myself in the bathroom, fighting back tears yet again, thinking, *Why am I like this? Why can't I just shake it off?*

Understanding emotional flooding and anxiety changed everything for me. It didn't make the feelings go away, but it helped me recognise what was really happening. It's not a personal failing. It's not proof that I'm broken. It's just how my brain is wired. And once I understood that, I could finally start working with it instead of fighting against it.

EMOTIONAL FLOODING

Research shows that people with ADHD struggle with emotional regulation because of differences in the prefrontal cortex, the part of the brain responsible for impulse control, decision-making, and rational thought.[159] When we experience intense emotion, this part of the brain often goes offline. Logic doesn't just take a back seat. It vanishes. We're

---

[158] Shaw et al., "Emotion Dysregulation in Attention Deficit Hyperactivity Disorder"; Ronald C. Kessler et al., "The Prevalence and Correlates of Adult ADHD in the United States: Results from the National Comorbidity Survey Replication," *The American Journal of Psychiatry* 163, no. 4 (2006): 716–23, https://doi.org/10.1176/ajp.2006.163.4.716; and Patricia O. Quinn, "Treating Adolescent Girls and Women with ADHD: Gender-Specific Issues," *Journal of Clinical Psychology* 61, no. 5 (2005): 579–87, https://doi.org/10.1002/jclp.20121.

[159] Barkley, ed., *Attention-Deficit Hyperactivity Disorder*.

launched into fight-or-flight mode before we've even processed what's happening.

This is what emotional flooding feels like. It's that sudden, overwhelming rush of emotion that hits like a tidal wave. You might feel like you can't think straight, you can't breathe, or like you need to react right now. For ADHD women, this often shows up as tearfulness, panic, snapping in anger, or completely shutting down. The common thread is that it feels unmanageable in the moment and deeply confusing or even shameful afterward.

If this sounds familiar from the section on rejection sensitivity, that's because it is. Emotional flooding and RSD often feel the same in the body. Tight chest, flushed face, racing thoughts, and that intense pressure to say something or fix something right away.

But they're not the same.

RSD tends to be about perceived rejection or criticism. Emotional flooding is broader. It can be triggered by conflict, overstimulation, shame, or just being pushed past your limit. Both hijack your nervous system. Both make it hard to think clearly. But the source is different.

One of my clients put it perfectly. "I started noticing the early signs of flooding," she told me. "My chest would tighten. My face would get hot. My thoughts would speed up. And instead of reacting on autopilot, I started giving myself permission to pause."

What makes it worse is that the flooding often comes from things that might seem small to others. A short tone in an email. A suggestion that something be done differently. A glance from someone you care about. These little things can feel like huge emotional threats when your nervous system is already overtaxed.

Many ADHD women don't realise this is what's happening. They think they're "being too sensitive" or "overreacting." In reality, it's a neurobiological response. Your brain is not broken. It's reacting to perceived danger without enough time to process context or intent. And once you understand that, you can start working with it instead of against it.

ADHD AND ANXIETY: THE PERFECT STORM

Sarah had always been a worrier. As a kid, she'd lie awake at night, convinced something terrible was about to happen. As a teenager, she'd rehearse conversations in her head, trying to plan for every possible response. By adulthood, she had backup systems for everything, including multiple alarms, sticky notes everywhere, and endless checklists because forgetting something important felt like a disaster waiting to happen.

For the longest time, she thought this was just how everyone operated. Didn't everyone get a sinking feeling when the phone rang? Didn't everyone's brain replay awkward moments from ten years ago while trying to fall asleep?

It wasn't until she was diagnosed with ADHD in her forties that she finally understood. This wasn't just anxiety. It was the way her ADHD brain had been coping all along.

"I've been anxious my entire life," Sarah told me after her diagnosis at forty-two. "I always thought it was just my personality, that I was a worrier. But now I realise I was anxious because I couldn't trust my own brain. Every day felt like walking through a field of land mines, never knowing when I'd make a mistake or forget something important."

For many of us, ADHD and anxiety are tangled together in ways we don't even recognise at first. Research suggests that up to 50 percent of adults with ADHD also struggle with an anxiety disorder.[160] But for a lot of us, that anxiety isn't a separate condition. It's a response to the unpredictability of living with ADHD.

For Sarah, it wasn't random. It was the constant fear of her brain letting her down. Would she forget an important meeting? Miss a deadline? Lose her keys yet again? Say something awkward without realising it? Every day felt like a mental obstacle course, and her anxiety was her way of trying to stay ahead of the next disaster.

So she developed habits to compensate:

---

[160] Barkley, ed., *Attention-Deficit Hyperactivity Disorder*.

- Checking (and rechecking) everything because she'd made careless mistakes before.
- Over-preparing for meetings because thinking on the spot felt impossible.
- Showing up ridiculously early because she'd lost track of time too many times before.
- Avoiding social situations because she was terrified of saying the wrong thing.
- Apologising constantly even for things that hadn't actually gone wrong.

She wasn't just being "overly cautious" or "too sensitive." These were survival strategies, built over years of struggling with an unpredictable brain. But they came at a cost. Constantly bracing for failure drained her energy, leaving her exhausted.[161]

ADHD itself doesn't cause anxiety, but the daily struggles that come with it do. The unpredictability of executive dysfunction, social challenges, and years of being misunderstood create the perfect storm for chronic worry and overthinking.[162]

Emotional flooding and anxiety often get lumped together, but they're not the same. Anxiety is the chronic mental loop of worry, what-ifs, and worst-case scenarios. Emotional flooding is more like a surge. It's when your nervous system gets overwhelmed all at once, and you can't think clearly because your brain is too busy reacting.

For ADHD women, both show up often, and often *together*. Emotional flooding can trigger anxiety, and anxiety can prime the brain for emotional flooding. The shared link is a dysregulated nervous system.

---

[161] Van Dijk et al., "Do Cognitive Measures of Response Inhibition Differentiate Between Attention Deficit/Hyperactivity Disorder and Borderline Personality Disorder?"

[162] Marija Maric, Anika Bexkens, and Susan M. Bögels, "Is Clinical Anxiety a Risk or a Protective Factor for Executive Functioning in Youth with ADHD? A Meta-Regression Analysis," *Clinical Child and Family Psychology Review* 21, no. 3 (September 2018): 340–353, https://doi.org/10.1007/s10567-018-0255-8;. and Van Dijk et al., "Do Cognitive Measures of Response Inhibition Differentiate Between Attention Deficit/Hyperactivity Disorder and Borderline Personality Disorder?"

When executive function breaks down and internal coping systems are overloaded, we quickly move into panic, shutdown, or both.[163]

That's why they're both in this chapter. They often feed into each other and need similar supports: nervous system regulation, realistic expectations, and compassion-based self-talk instead of shame.

Some thoughts you might recognise if ADHD and anxiety team up in your brain:

- Did I say something weird in that conversation? (RSD-driven anxiety)
- What if I forget to follow up on this? (Executive dysfunction–driven anxiety)
- Why is this so hard for me when everyone else seems fine? (Masking-driven anxiety)

It's a vicious cycle: Anxiety makes ADHD symptoms worse, and ADHD symptoms fuel even more anxiety. When I'm anxious, my executive function tanks. I forget more, focus less, and make more mistakes. And of course, that only makes me more anxious.[164]

When we stop fighting our ADHD and start working with it, we keep the anxiety from feeling so overpowering.

MANAGING EMOTIONAL FLOODING AND ANXIETY

Jana shared that one spring afternoon, she sat in her car in a grocery store parking lot, tears streaming down her face. The trigger: a text from her daughter's teacher about a forgotten permission slip. Not a crisis. Not even a big deal. But her body reacted like the world was crashing down.

---

[163] Barkley, ed., *Attention-Deficit Hyperactivity Disorder*; and N. H. Zainal and M. G. Newman, "Executive Functioning Constructs in Anxiety, Obsessive-Compulsive, Post-Traumatic Stress, and Related Disorders," *Current Psychiatry Reports* 24, no. 12 (December 2022): 871–880, https://doi.org/10.1007/s11920-022-01390-9.

[164] Marija Maric, Anika Bexkens, and Susan M. Bögels, "Is Clinical Anxiety a Risk or a Protective Factor for Executive Functioning in Youth with ADHD? A Meta-Regression Analysis," *Clinical Child and Family Psychology Review* 21, no. 3 (September 2018): 340–353, https://doi.org/10.1007/s10567-018-0255-8.

"As I sat there crying, part of me was watching it happen, almost like an outsider," Jana said. "I remember thinking, *Why am I falling apart over this? This is a five-minute fix, not a disaster.* But that logical voice couldn't break through. It was like my emotions had completely hijacked me."

Later, after working with an ADHD therapist, she finally had a name for what was happening: emotional flooding, when the ADHD brain gets stuck in an intense emotional response and can't regulate it.

"My therapist explained it like this: Most people's brains have a fire alarm system. It goes off when there's a fire, but once the danger is gone, the alarm stops. But with ADHD, the alarm just keeps blaring, even after the problem is over."[165]

That explanation hit home. Jana realised she wasn't choosing to overreact. Her brain was wired to struggle with emotional regulation. Understanding that was one thing, but learning how to manage it really changed the game.

The first thing that made a difference for Jana was naming what was happening. "When I felt that wave of emotion hit, I started saying, out loud if I could, 'This is emotional flooding. This is my ADHD brain. This will pass.' It sounds almost too simple, but it helped. Just acknowledging what was happening created some space between me and the reaction, like my rational brain was stepping in before my emotions could take over completely."

Jana also learned that physical interventions worked better than mental ones when she was overwhelmed.

"Trying to *think* my way out of it never worked. But doing something physical could interrupt the spiral."

She found that cold water was the quickest reset. "When I felt myself spiralling, I would splash cold water on my face, run my wrists under the faucet, or even hold an ice cube. That jolt of cold immediately cut through the emotional intensity and gave me a moment to reorient."

Research shows that the mammalian diving reflex activated when

---

[165] Dodson, "How ADHD Ignites RSD."

cold water touches the face slows the heart rate and engages the parasympathetic nervous system, helping the body shift out of a heightened emotional state.[166] This physiological response can disrupt emotional flooding, giving the brain a chance to reset.

Another game changer: creating space before reacting—*the power of the pause.*

That pause doesn't make the feelings disappear. But it gives us just enough space to stay with ourselves instead of reacting in ways we regret.

"I need a minute" became one of the most useful phrases in Jana's life. "Those four words helped me hold the boundary between my emotions and my actions. They gave me time to process before I said something I'd regret."

Having these tools ready before an emotional flood hits made them easier for her to access in the moment.[167]

THE SCIENCE BEHIND ADHD, EMOTIONAL FLOODING, AND ANXIETY

Learning about the brain science behind anxiety and emotional flooding can be a turning point for many women with ADHD.

That's what happened for Casey. One evening in her ADHD support group, a specialist pulled out a whiteboard and drew a simple diagram of the brain, pointing to two key areas: the prefrontal cortex and the amygdala.

"In ADHD brains," she explained, "the prefrontal cortex, which helps regulate emotions and impulses, doesn't communicate as efficiently with the emotional centres of the brain. When the amygdala, the brain's alarm system, gets triggered, the prefrontal cortex struggles to send the 'all clear' signal. That's why emotions can feel so intense and take longer to settle."

Casey felt something shift.

---

166 W. Michael Panneton, "The Mammalian Diving Response: An Enigmatic Reflex to Preserve Life?," *Physiology* 28, no. 5 (2013): 284–97, https://doi.org/10.1152/physiol.00020.2013.

167 D. Giwerc and B. Luther, "Module A4: Filtering Thoughts and Beliefs," in *Advanced Coach Training Program Resource Guide*, version 5.0 (ADD Coach Academy, 2023), https://addca.com/adhd-coach-training/Module-Details-Advanced/.

So this isn't just me? she thought. *This is actually how my brain works?* Research shows that people with ADHD have higher emotional reactivity due to structural differences in the prefrontal cortex and limbic system, making it harder to regulate emotions once they're triggered.[168]

Later, Casey shared how that knowledge changed everything.

"Finding out that my emotional intensity had a neurological basis was freeing," she said. "For years, I thought I was just immature because I couldn't 'control myself' like other people. Now I understand. My brain isn't broken. It just works differently."

Casey also learned that dopamine, a neurotransmitter already in short supply in ADHD brains, plays a key role in emotional regulation. That explained why emotions often felt extreme. Without enough dopamine, the brain struggles to modulate emotional highs and lows, making small disappointments feel devastating and minor criticisms feel unbearable.[169]

Understanding ADHD's impact on emotions helps break the cycle of shame. When Casey finally saw the pattern, she stopped blaming herself for feeling things so deeply. Instead, she focused on strategies that helped her manage emotional intensity.

Visual modelling, or using simple brain diagrams that explain how ADHD affects emotional regulation, can be an effective tool. For example, a basic diagram of the ADHD brain that shows how the prefrontal cortex and emotional centres interact can help make abstract neuroscience more concrete. Showing how low dopamine affects the brain's ability to regulate big emotions makes it easier to connect the dots between symptoms and brain function. When you can see what's actually happening in your brain, it becomes easier to pause and respond with self-compassion instead of self-criticism.

---

[168] A. M. Soler-Gutiérrez, J. C. Pérez-González, and J. Mayas, "Evidence of Emotion Dysregulation as a Core Symptom of Adult ADHD: A Systematic Review," *PLoS ONE* 18, no. 1 (2023): e0280131, https://doi.org/10.1371/journal.pone.0280131.

[169] Amy F. T. Arnsten and Katya Rubia, "Neurobiological Circuits Regulating Attention, Cognitive Control, Motivation, and Emotion: Disruptions in Neurodevelopmental Psychiatric Disorders," *Journal of the American Academy of Child & Adolescent Psychiatry* 51, no. 4 (2012): 356–67, https://doi.org/10.1016/j.jaac.2012.01.008; Paolo Fusar-Poli et al., "Striatal Dopamine Transporter Alterations in ADHD: Pathophysiology or Adaptation to Psychostimulants? A Meta-Analysis," *American Journal of Psychiatry* 169, no. 3 (March 2012): 264–272, https://doi.org/10.1176/appi.ajp.2011.11060940.

DIFFERENTIATING BETWEEN ADHD OVERWHELM AND ANXIETY DISORDER

"Is this ADHD overwhelm or anxiety?" That question became crucial for me after my diagnosis. The two felt almost identical: racing thoughts, physical tension, total mental paralysis. But learning to tell them apart made all the difference in choosing the right coping strategies.

I remember one afternoon sitting at my desk, staring at a never-ending list of tasks. I needed to get them done. My heart was pounding. My thoughts were scattered. I felt completely stuck. Was this ADHD task paralysis? Or was I having an anxiety attack? The symptoms overlapped so much that in the moment, I had no idea.

Over time, with the help of my ADHD coach (yes, even coaches have coaches), I began noticing subtle differences between the two:

ADHD overwhelm usually hit when I had too many tasks and no clear starting point. The main feeling was mental clutter, a jumble of competing thoughts that made it impossible to decide what to do first. It wasn't about fear; it was about executive dysfunction. *There's too much to do, and I don't know where to start.*

Anxiety was different. Even if I had only one clear task, my brain would spiral into worst-case scenarios. *What if I fail? What if everyone realises I don't know what I'm doing? What if this ruins everything?* My body would respond immediately—tight chest, shallow breathing, racing heart—all before I'd even started.[170]

Recognising this distinction completely changed how I handled these moments.

The overlap between ADHD overwhelm and anxiety can be confusing, but the root causes are different. ADHD overwhelm is often tied to executive dysfunction. It shows up when our brains are overloaded and can't prioritise, initiate, or break down tasks. It's not fear-driven. It's a traffic jam of mental tasks with no green light.

Anxiety, on the other hand, is more future-focused. It's driven by fear and uncertainty. It activates the body's threat response even when there's

---

[170] Young et al., "The Economic Consequences of Attention-Deficit Hyperactivity Disorder in the Scottish Prison System."

no real danger in front of us. While ADHD overwhelm leaves us frozen from mental chaos, anxiety sends us into a spiral of worst-case scenarios.

Telling them apart matters. If I respond to executive dysfunction with anxiety tools like grounding or deep breathing, I still might not get the task done. And if I respond to anxiety with productivity hacks, I just end up pushing through the fear without addressing it. Knowing what I'm actually dealing with lets me choose the right support for my brain in that moment.

Recognising this distinction completely changed how I handled these moments.

CHOOSING THE RIGHT STRATEGY

For ADHD overwhelm, activation strategies worked best, such as breaking things down into tiny steps, body doubling (working alongside someone), or creating artificial urgency to kick-start dopamine production and get moving.[171]

For anxiety, calming techniques were more effective, including deep breathing, grounding exercises, or actively questioning my catastrophic thoughts.[172]

But the hardest moments were when both hit at the same time, which happened *a lot*.

I'd freeze because I had too many tasks and no clear plan (ADHD overwhelm), then immediately start catastrophising about how stuck I felt (anxiety). The worse my anxiety got, the harder it became to think clearly, which made the ADHD overwhelm even worse.

That was the real struggle. Not just ADHD, not just anxiety, but the way they fueled each other. Learning to separate them didn't make them

---

[171] Rua Mae Williams and Chorong Park, "Cyborg Assemblages: How Autistic Adults Construct Sociotechnical Networks to Support Cognitive Function," in *Proceedings of the 2023 CHI Conference on Human Factors in Computing Systems* (New York: ACM, 2023), 1–15, https://doi.org/10.1145/3544548.3581556.

[172] Phoebe Chin et al., "A Systematic Review of Brief Respiratory, Embodiment, Cognitive, and Mindfulness Interventions to Reduce State Anxiety," *Frontiers in Psychology* 15 (2024): 1412928, https://doi.org/10.3389/fpsyg.2024.1412928.

disappear, but it gave me a way out of the spiral before it completely took over.

For many of us with ADHD, it's not one or the other; it's both. Research shows that nearly 50 percent of adults with ADHD also have an anxiety disorder.[173] Our ADHD-related challenges (like missed deadlines, social struggles, or task paralysis) can create anxiety, while anxiety can further fuel our avoidance and overwhelm.

WHEN SMALL THINGS FEEL BIG: DECISION PARALYSIS AND MENTAL CLUTTER

Connie, an artist I spoke with, shared, "Yesterday, I spent three hours researching planners, comparing layouts, reading reviews, and watching YouTube comparisons. By the time I had twenty tabs open, I felt so overwhelmed that I closed my laptop in frustration and bought nothing. I knew I needed a planner, but the pressure of choosing the right one left me completely stuck."

This is decision paralysis. If you have ADHD, you probably know it all too well. It's rarely talked about, but for many of us, especially women, it's a constant struggle. What seems like a simple choice can quickly become an emotional minefield. Too many options, too much information, and a brain that's already busy managing a dozen other things create the perfect storm.

That storm doesn't just slow us down. It can trigger emotional flooding. The pressure to make the "right" choice activates the brain's stress response. Your heart races. Your thoughts speed up. Suddenly you're frozen. Not because you don't care or can't decide but because the decision feels loaded with risk.

Anxiety piles on quickly. It whispers things like, "What if I waste money?" or "What if I pick the wrong one and regret it?" That's how a planner becomes a threat. Not logically but neurologically. The combi-

---

[173] Kessler et al., "The Prevalence and Correlates of Adult ADHD in the United States."

nation of mental clutter, emotional intensity, and fear of failure hijacks the brain's ability to move forward.

And yes, this is procrastination too. It's not a character flaw or laziness. It's a protective response. Our ADHD brains avoid what feels emotionally intense or mentally draining. The longer we avoid it, the more pressure we feel. That pressure increases the emotional charge, which makes it even harder to begin. It's a loop we know too well.

Maya, a mom of two, described a moment that felt painfully familiar. "Sometimes even the smallest decisions feel impossible. One day, I found myself standing in the grocery aisle, staring at all the milk options, completely frozen. Instead of picking one, I just…left the store. It was too overwhelming."

Our brains don't filter information efficiently, so when we're making a decision, we're considering too many factors, overanalyzing potential outcomes, and feeling too many emotions all at the same time.

Even minor choices can send us into a mental gridlock.

Emily, a college student with ADHD, shared how this played out in her academic life. "I procrastinate on registering for courses every semester. I stress about picking the 'perfect' schedule, so I keep putting it off—then suddenly, I'm out of options and stuck with the worst time slots. It's a disaster every single time."

The fear of making the wrong choice keeps us stuck. And ironically, in trying to avoid a bad decision, we often make no decision at all. Which inevitably leads to even more stress later.

Executive dysfunction, a core feature of ADHD, affects the brain's ability to organise thoughts, weigh options, and make decisions. The prefrontal cortex, which handles these functions, doesn't filter information efficiently in our ADHD brains. This leads to difficulty prioritising what matters most.[174]

For many of us, decision paralysis is often compounded by perfectionism and fear of regret. *What if I choose wrong? What if another option*

---

[174] Barkley, ed., *Attention-Deficit Hyperactivity Disorder*.

would have been better? These thoughts can turn even trivial decisions into sources of significant anxiety.

COACHING STRATEGY: THE DECISION-MAKING TOOL KIT

This strategy offers practical approaches for overcoming decision paralysis. Here's what I teach my clients:

- **The Reduce Options Rule:** Immediately eliminate all but two to three choices before beginning detailed comparison. This prevents the overwhelm that comes with too many options.
- **The Two-Column Method:** For medium-sized decisions, create just two columns: "Requirements" and "Nice-to-Haves." Focus only on the requirements first to narrow options quickly.
- **The "Good Enough" Principle:** For low-stakes decisions, identify the first option that meets basic criteria rather than searching for the "perfect" choice. This counters perfectionism that drives paralysis.
- **The Decision Timer:** Set specific time limits based on decision importance: sixty seconds for small decisions, five minutes for medium ones, and scheduled decision sessions for truly important choices.
- **The Decision Delegate:** Identify categories of decisions that can be outsourced to others or to randomisation (like a coin flip) without significant negative consequences.[175]

THE INVISIBLE WALL: ADHD AND TASK INITIATION

Lizzy sat at her desk, staring at an email she needed to send. It wasn't complicated, just a quick follow-up with a client, but her fingers hovered over the keyboard, frozen. Instead of typing, she clicked over to social media, scrolled for a bit, and told herself she'd get back to the email in a few minutes.

---

[175] D. Laureiro-Martínez et al., "The Neuroscientific Foundations of the Exploration–Exploitation Dilemma," *Journal of Neuroscience Psychology and Economics* 3, no. 2 (2010): 95–115, https://psycnet.apa.org/doi/10.1037/a0018495.

Minutes turned into hours, while the weight of the unfinished task loomed over her. It wasn't that she didn't want to send the email. She knew it was important. But actually starting felt impossible, like there was an invisible wall between her and the task.

This wasn't laziness. It was task initiation difficulty, something many of us with ADHD experience daily. Starting a task, especially one that isn't intrinsically interesting or urgent, can feel physically uncomfortable. Sometimes it even feels painful.

For Lizzy, time blindness only made things worse. She knew she had a report due next week, but the deadline felt distant, almost unreal. Every time she thought about working on it, her brain reassured her, *You have time.* Then suddenly, it was the night before the deadline, and panic set in.

The neurological explanation: dopamine.

Dopamine plays a key role in motivation, and as I've mentioned before, our ADHD brains have lower baseline dopamine levels. Without enough dopamine, even simple tasks can feel overwhelming, leading to avoidance and procrastination. Tasks don't feel *important* until urgency kicks in, often at the last possible moment.

The ADHD brain is wired for interest-based performance rather than importance-based performance. This means we struggle to engage with tasks based on their importance alone. Our brains need interest, novelty, urgency, or immediate rewards to generate the dopamine necessary for activation.[176]

But the longer we wait, the heavier it feels. That pressure builds into overwhelm. Our bodies react like we're in danger: heart pounding, brain racing, chest tightening. Emotional flooding kicks in fast, and we go into escape mode. What should be a simple task now registers as a threat.

This is procrastination, but not in the way most people think. It isn't carelessness or lack of motivation. It's a way of coping with discomfort. We avoid the task because starting feels unbearable, even if we care about the outcome. The longer we avoid it, the more anxious we become, and

---

[176] Dodson, "How ADHD Ignites RSD."

by the time we finally get moving, we're already worn down from the stress of holding it off.

For many of us with ADHD, this explains why we can easily spend hours researching a new interest but can't make ourselves start a simple work task. It's why deadlines are often our only reliable motivator. The urgency creates a dopamine rush that temporarily overcomes our executive dysfunction.

Charlotte, a freelance writer in my professional sphere, often found herself unable to begin assignments, even when she was passionate about the topic. She would tell herself she needed the perfect opening sentence, but in reality, she was stuck in a cycle of avoidance. By the time she finally started, she was already exhausted from the stress of delaying it.

CREATING ADHD-FRIENDLY ENVIRONMENTS TO MANAGE OVERWHELM

Jessica had tried everything: bullet journals, colour-coded filing systems, productivity apps that swore they'd "fix" her disorganisation. But no matter what she did, her desk remained a chaotic mess of forgotten bills, half-used notebooks, and an ever-growing pile of *I'll deal with it later* items.

She'd sit down to work, only to get distracted by the clutter around her. Next thing she knew, she'd spent an hour rearranging instead of actually getting anything done. She felt exhausted, but somehow still behind on her real tasks.

Then one day, a friend gave her a simple but life-changing piece of advice: "Stop fighting your brain. Set up a space that actually works for your ADHD."

Instead of forcing herself into systems that never stuck, she started designing her workspace based on what her brain actually needed: visibility, accessibility, and structured flexibility. Her desk stopped being a source of distraction and became a place she could focus. She started paying her bills on time. She finally had the energy for her real work instead of battling clutter all day.

This made something crystal clear: *Most traditional organisation systems actually work against ADHD brain wiring.*

You know that minimalist, out-of-sight organising style that productivity gurus swear by? For ADHD brains, it's a disaster because for us, "out of sight" literally means "out of mind." Even writing this brings up tension as I recall all those unpaid bills from when I was married. Important papers, neatly tucked into folders? Forgotten. Tasks written in a closed planner? Might as well not exist.

ADHD brains struggle with working memory and object permanence, which means if something isn't visually present, it basically ceases to exist. Research confirms that this isn't a lack of effort. It's a neurological reality.[177]

One of the most effective ways to reduce ADHD overwhelm is to design a space that supports how your brain actually works. An environment that helps you remember, stay focused, and feel calm becomes part of your support system. For many of us, that means visible storage, clear organisation, and easy access to what we use most. Instead of relying on working memory (which is often unreliable), we rely on the space itself to hold the cues and reminders we need.

Natalie, an architect with ADHD in a coaching group, reworked her home office based on this principle.

"I swapped closed cabinets for open shelving, used clear containers for supplies, and set up a giant whiteboard for tracking projects," she explained. "For someone else, it might look cluttered. But for me, it was exactly what I needed: an external memory system that actually worked with my brain."

It doesn't have to be Pinterest-perfect. It just has to work.

Beyond organising physical space, many of us need to rethink how our environment affects our focus. ADHD brains are often hypersensitive to sensory input. This means that sounds, lights, textures, smells, and visual clutter are not just background details. They are active signals our brains process all at once, without an effective filter. That constant

---

[177] Barkley, ed., *Attention-Deficit Hyperactivity Disorder.*

influx can quickly lead to overwhelm, especially when we're already trying to focus or make decisions.

For Jessica, total silence actually made it harder to concentrate. Her brain needed a little background noise, something to engage just enough of her attention without becoming a distraction.

Now, she plays instrumental music, rainfall sounds, or the quiet hum of a coffee shop in the background. Just the right amount of stimulation keeps her brain engaged without pulling her off track.

Other women I've worked with wear noise-cancelling headphones, swap harsh lighting for warm lamps or coloured LEDs, or keep a fidget nearby to stay grounded. Some chew gum to keep their nervous system regulated, wear weighted lap pads, or diffuse calming scents like lavender while working.

It's about finding that sensory sweet spot—enough input to stay present but not so much that it tips into overwhelm.

EMBRACING MY EMOTIONAL NATURE

If you had told me five years ago that I'd be sitting here writing about how I've "embraced my emotional intensity," I would have laughed. Or rolled my eyes. Or both. For most of my life, I thought my emotions were the problem. I thought if I could just "get it together" or "stop being so sensitive," I'd finally feel normal. But here's what I've learned: I was never supposed to feel less. I just needed better ways to manage it.

I still remember the first time I used cold water to stop an emotional spiral. I was standing at my bathroom sink, hands shaking, face burning with shame after a tough conversation with a university professor who'd pointed out that I tend to catastrophise situations. I turned on the faucet and splashed cold water on my face, and something shifted. It didn't erase my feelings, but suddenly, I wasn't drowning in them. This was long before I knew I had ADHD, but somehow, intuitively, I already knew how to soothe myself.

That moment was the first time I realised: I'm not powerless over my emotions. I just need different ways to regulate them.

For so long, I tried to follow neurotypical advice that never worked. I told myself to "just let it go" or "calm down," but no amount of willpower ever made that happen. I thought something was wrong with me. But I wasn't broken. I just needed different tools.

And that's what this journey is about.

SELF-COACHING EXERCISES: EMOTIONAL FLOODING AND ANXIETY

NAME IT TO TAME IT

A simple but powerful way to manage emotional flooding is the "Name It to Tame It" approach. When you feel yourself spiralling, say it out loud:

"I'm experiencing emotional flooding right now."

That small act of naming it creates space between you and the emotion, making it easier to step out of the overwhelm. I encourage my clients to practise saying this aloud when they feel emotions taking over.

WORRY DECISION TREE

One way to break the emotional overwhelm cycle is by separating helpful worry from unhelpful worry. I teach my clients to use a Worry Decision Tree to ask:

"Is this something I can control?"

- If yes, we pick one small action step to take right away. That might mean sending a quick email, jotting down a to-do list, setting a calendar reminder, or asking someone a clarifying question.
- If no, practise worry postponement by literally scheduling a fifteen-minute "worry time" later in the day. This turns worrying into an intentional act rather than an unconscious habit of ruminating.

Separating worry helps acknowledge the concern without getting stuck in an endless spiral.[178] It's a small change, but it makes a real difference.

---

[178] Annika Dippel, Jos F. Brosschot, and Bart Verkuil, "Effects of Worry Postponement on Daily Worry: a Meta-Analysis," *International Journal of Cognitive Behavioral Therapy* 17, no. 1 (March 2024): 160–178, https://doi.org/10.1007/s41811-023-00193-x.

EMOTIONAL FIRST AID KIT

One tool many women with ADHD find helpful is an Emotional First Aid Kit, a literal box or a note filled with grounding tools for emotional overwhelm. Here are some of the things you might include:

- Sensory items (a stress ball, scented lotion, a smooth stone)
- Written reminders of grounding techniques
- A list of supportive people to text or call
- Affirmation cards with self-compassionate statements
- A playlist of calming or uplifting music
- Photos or notes that bring a sense of comfort

You can keep your Emotional First Aid Kit in a small box, in your purse, or as a note on your phone. The format doesn't matter. What matters is that it's easy to access when things start to spiral. Choose things that actually work for you. If your overwhelm shows up at work, keep something in your desk. If transitions are where you unravel, have a version you can take with you. The goal isn't to have a perfect kit. It's to avoid scrambling when you're already overloaded.

DIFFERENTIATING QUESTIONNAIRE

I help my clients create a personal Differentiating Questionnaire to determine if they're experiencing primarily ADHD overwhelm or anxiety in the moment. Here are some questions we might include:

- Am I afraid of something specific happening or just feeling generally overwhelmed?
- Is my main feeling fear, or is it confusion/frustration?
- Am I experiencing physical symptoms like a racing heart or shortness of breath?
- Would breaking this task into smaller steps help, or do I need to address my fears first?

The answers can guide us to choose the most effective intervention for our current state.

TASK ACTIVATION TOOL KIT

This tool kit offers ADHD-friendly approaches to overcome procrastination. I use these strategies myself and share them with my clients:

- **The Five-Minute Rule:** Commit to working on a task for just five minutes with permission to stop after that time. This significantly lowers the barrier to starting, and momentum often carries forward once begun.
- **The Body Double Technique:** Work alongside someone else (in person or virtually) to provide accountability and the social dopamine that can jump-start task initiation.
- **The Stimulation Boost:** Pair boring tasks with dopamine-generating activities like listening to upbeat music, using a fidget tool, or working in a novel environment.
- **The Impossible to Tiny Method:** Break down overwhelming tasks into ridiculously small first steps that feel impossible to fail at (e.g., "open the document" rather than "write the report").
- **The Artificial Urgency Approach:** Create self-imposed deadlines with social accountability or meaningful consequences to generate the urgency your ADHD brain responds to.[179]

ENVIRONMENTAL DESIGN ASSESSMENT

This exercise helps create spaces that support your unique neurological needs. Here's what I do with my clients:

- **Visual Accessibility Audit:** Evaluate storage systems with the question

---

[179] Russell A. Barkley, "The Important Role of Executive Functioning and Self-Regulation in ADHD," (2010), https://russellbarkley.org/factsheets/ADHD_EF_and_SR.pdf.

"If I can't see it, will I remember it exists?" Create visual reminders for anything important that must be stored out of sight.
- **Friction Reduction Map:** Identify daily friction points (items frequently needed but not easily accessible) and redesign based on frequency of use rather than traditional categories.
- **Sensory Input Inventory:** Document which environmental factors (sounds, lighting, textures, temperatures) help versus hinder focus, and modify accordingly.
- **Transition Zone Creation:** Designate specific spaces for transitional items (incoming mail, items to be returned, things to remember tomorrow) to prevent "doom piles" without requiring immediate processing.
- **Body-Mind Connection Setup:** Incorporate movement opportunities (standing desk options, fidget tools, designated movement breaks) to support your ADHD brain's need for physical activity to maintain focus.[180]

---

[180] Joshua M. Langberg et al., "Prevalence, Patterns, and Predictors of Sleep Problems and Daytime Sleepiness in Young Adolescents with ADHD," *Journal of Attention Disorders* 24, no. 4 (2020): 509–523, https://doi.org/10.1177/1087054717690810.

Chapter Nine

Mastering Emotional Regulation as an ADHD Woman

I REMEMBER THE EXACT MOMENT I REALISED MY EMOTIONAL REACtions weren't just a personality flaw.

I was sitting across from my therapist, my face hot with tears, trying to explain how *devastated* I felt when a friend cancelled our plans at the last minute. "It feels like I'm drowning," I told her. "Like I can't get enough air because the disappointment is sitting on my chest."

She nodded. And then she said something that had a lasting impact on me.

"Your brain processes emotions differently. It's not your fault."

And just like that, the shame cracked open, just a little. Because for the first time, I started to see the truth. This isn't a matter of *overreacting*. It's neurology.

For years, I thought my emotional reactions were a *personal failure*, that I was "too sensitive," "too reactive," "too much." I blamed myself for not handling things better, for letting small things ruin my day. But

ADHD makes emotional regulation different, compelling us to focus not just on our emotions but on how our brains process those feelings.[181]

In the previous chapter, we looked at how emotional flooding and anxiety show up in our lives. Here, we're going deeper into the science behind those reactions and, more importantly, what actually helps us regulate them.

THE SCIENCE BEHIND OUR EMOTIONAL STORMS

When I first started looking into ADHD research, I assumed my emotional ups and downs were just a side effect, something extra on top of the attention issues. But the deeper I dug, the more I realised that emotional regulation isn't just part of ADHD. It's central to it.

As explained in *Attention-Deficit Hyperactivity Disorder*, edited by Dr. Russell Barkley, and as previously mentioned in this book, ADHD isn't just about paying attention; it's about self-regulation as a whole, including our emotions.[182] Our prefrontal cortex, the part of the brain responsible for putting the brakes on impulsive reactions, functions differently from the neurotypical prefrontal cortex. That's why emotions don't simply come and go for us.

Instead, they hit with full force and don't easily let go. It's also why being told to "just calm down" feels as impossible as being asked to "just grow taller."

One of the most validating things I've ever learned comes from Dr. Russell Barkley's research: Our emotional development can be delayed by a two to three year lag in physical development compared to our actual age.[183] That means if you're thirty-five, your ability to regulate emotions might be more like that of a twenty-four-year-old.

When I first read that, I had to sit with it for a moment. It explained so much.

---

181 Barkley, ed., *Attention-Deficit Hyperactivity Disorder*.

182 Barkley, ed., *Attention-Deficit Hyperactivity Disorder*.

183 Russell A. Barkley, "The Importance of Emotion in ADHD" (presentation, Canadian Attention Deficit Disorders Resource Alliance [CADDAC], 2011), https://adhdtreat.caddra.ca/wp-content/uploads/2025/01/Emotion-in-ADHD_Barkley_CADDAC-2025-treat.pdf.

This delay specifically affects "hot" executive functions, the ones tied to emotional control and motivation, far more than "cool" executive functions like organisation and planning. That's why many of us can handle intellectually complex tasks but still struggle with emotional triggers that seem small from the outside.

For years, I beat myself up for "overreacting," for feeling like my emotions were too big, too overwhelming, too much. I thought I just needed to "grow up" and handle things better. But learning that my brain was still catching up completely changed how I saw myself. This wasn't a character flaw. It was a neurological reality.

Leah, a woman I interviewed, had the same reaction. As soon as she read about this, she messaged me. "I'm literally crying right now. I thought I was just emotionally immature. Knowing there's a neurological reason makes me feel so much less broken."

That's exactly why this information matters. Understanding this developmental gap doesn't mean we give up on emotional growth. It means we stop shaming ourselves for not being "there" yet. It gives us permission to work with our brains rather than constantly feeling like we're failing at emotions we "should" have mastered by now.

When we recognise this difference, we can start building emotional regulation skills at a level that actually aligns with where we are instead of expecting ourselves to have already figured it out.

Few things are more frustrating than being told to "just take a deep breath" or "calm down." If it were that simple, we'd already be zen masters. And let's be real: When in the history of humanity has telling a woman to "just calm down" ever ended well? Exactly. Never.

For people with neurotypical brains, emotional regulation works differently. Their prefrontal cortex, the part of the brain responsible for pausing and assessing a situation before reacting, communicates effectively with the limbic system, which processes emotions. This connection acts as an internal brake,[184] helping them slow down their reaction *before* emotions take over.

---

184 Stephen M. Collins, Michael Surette, and Premysl Bercik, "The Interplay between the Intestinal Microbiota and the Brain," *Nature Reviews Microbiology* 10, no. 11 (November 2012): 735–742, https://doi.org/10.1038/nrmicro2876.

But for us, that connection isn't as strong. By the time someone tells us to "calm down," the emotional train has already left the station. Full speed ahead.

I remember trying to explain this to my partner once. I used a traffic analogy: "Imagine your brain has well-functioning traffic lights that stop emotional traffic when needed. With my brain, the signals are faulty. By the time I realise I should stop, I'm already speeding through the intersection."

That clicked for him. And honestly, it clicked for *me* too.

This is why "just calm down" doesn't work for ADHD brains. Emotional regulation isn't about willpower. It's about how our nervous system processes emotions. Instead of trying to *shut down* our reactions, we need strategies that actively engage and regulate our nervous system in the moment.

It's not about suppressing emotions. It's about learning how to ride the wave without getting pulled under.

ADHD brains have what researchers call a lower emotion stimulation threshold.[185] In simple terms, we feel emotions more intensely and more quickly than neurotypical individuals. It's not a personality flaw. It's a neurobiological difference in how our amygdala (our emotional processing centre) and prefrontal cortex (our regulatory centre) communicate.

Brain imaging studies confirm this. When we're exposed to emotional situations, the regions of the brain responsible for processing emotions light up like a firework show, while the areas meant to regulate those emotions stay relatively quiet.[186]

This lower threshold means that something mildly annoying to someone else, like an offhand comment, an unexpected schedule change, or a frustrating email, can trigger a full emotional storm for us. Not because we're dramatic or overreacting but because our brains process emotional information differently.

---

[185] Barkley, ed., *Attention-Deficit Hyperactivity Disorder*.

[186] Shaw et al., "Emotion Dysregulation in Attention Deficit Hyperactivity Disorder."

My friend Jasmine once described it perfectly. She said, "It's like having your emotional skin rubbed raw. Everything just hurts more when you don't have that protective layer."

And that's exactly it. It's not that we *choose* to feel things so deeply. It's that our brains are wired to experience emotions in high definition.

THE HORMONAL ROLLER COASTER THAT MAKES EVERYTHING HARDER

If just having ADHD wasn't complicated enough, throw in the hormonal fluctuations that come with being a woman. It's like trying to drive a car with unpredictable brakes while someone randomly changes the road conditions.

Our ADHD symptoms don't exist in a vacuum. They interact with our hormones in ways many of us were never told about.

Oestrogen plays a direct role in dopamine production, and since our ADHD brains already struggle with dopamine regulation, natural hormonal fluctuations can significantly impact our focus, mood, and emotional stability.[187]

For many of us, ADHD feels *harder* right before our periods. Research suggests this happens because dropping oestrogen levels weaken our already vulnerable dopamine system.[188] For me, PMS isn't just bloating and chocolate cravings. It's a full-on ADHD storm. My rejection sensitivity skyrockets. My focus tanks. Suddenly, emotional regulation feels like an impossible task.

Pregnancy and postpartum bring their own challenges. Some of us actually feel better during pregnancy (thanks to rising oestrogen levels), while others experience mood swings that make PMS look mild by comparison. Then comes the postpartum crash. When oestrogen plummets

---

[187] Madhoo and Quinn, "A Review of Attention Deficit/Hyperactivity Disorder in Women and Girls."

[188] Ronit Haimov-Kochman and Itai Berger, "Cognitive Functions of Regularly Cycling Women May Differ Throughout the Month, Depending on Sex Hormone Status; a Possible Explanation to Conflicting Results of Studies of ADHD in Females," *Frontiers in Human Neuroscience* 8 (2014): 191, https://doi.org/10.3389/fnhum.2014.00191.

after birth, emotional dysregulation can hit *hard*, but instead of recognising it as ADHD-related, many of us are told it's just "baby blues."[189]

And then there's perimenopause and menopause. The time when many of us finally get diagnosed.

Melissa, who was diagnosed in her forties, described perimenopause as a betrayal.

"I used to be able to manage it, keep my emotions in check. But once I hit my forties, I'd cry in meetings out of nowhere, snap at my kids, and feel like I was losing control of my own brain. That was when I finally got diagnosed."

She's not alone. Many women don't realise they have ADHD until perimenopause, when plummeting oestrogen makes symptoms impossible to ignore or mask.[190] What once felt manageable can suddenly spiral into overwhelm, leaving us wondering why our brains aren't cooperating anymore.

Understanding this connection matters.

It's more than *hormones*. It's how our shifting brain chemistry interacts with ADHD. And when we know what's happening, we can stop blaming ourselves and start finding strategies that actually help.

WHEN PMS BECOMES A MONSTER: PMDD AND ADHD

For some of us, what we're feeling is not just typical PMS. We're experiencing premenstrual dysphoric disorder (PMDD), a severe form of PMS that brings intense mood swings, depression, and anxiety during the luteal phase of our cycle. Research suggests that women with ADHD may be more vulnerable to PMDD because of our heightened sensitivity to hormonal fluctuations.[191]

---

189 Stephen P. Hinshaw et al., "Annual Research Review: Attention-Deficit/Hyperactivity Disorder in Girls and Women: Underrepresentation, Longitudinal Processes, and Key Directions," *Journal of Child Psychology and Psychiatry* 63, no. 4 (April 2022): 484–496, https://doi.org/10.1111/jcpp.13480.

190 Madhoo and Quinn, "A Review of Attention Deficit/Hyperactivity Disorder in Women and Girls."

191 Sari Solden and Michelle Frank, *A Radical Guide for Women with ADHD: Embrace Neurodiversity, Live Boldly, and Break Through Barriers* (New Harbinger Publications, 2019).

Tara spent years feeling like something was *off* but couldn't figure out what. When she finally got diagnosed with both ADHD and PMDD, she said it was like finding the missing pieces of a puzzle. "For two weeks every month, I wasn't just distracted. I was a completely different person. Now I understand why, and I can actually plan for it."

That's the power of knowing what's really going on. It's not just hormones. It's not just ADHD. It's how the two interact. And when we finally have that understanding, we can stop feeling blindsided every month and start working *with* our brains instead of feeling at war with them.

THE MANY FACES OF EMOTIONAL DYSREGULATION

Our emotional regulation challenges come in different forms. Here are some of the most common patterns I've seen in myself and other ADHD women.

THE ZERO-TO-SIXTY EMOTIONAL MELTDOWN

"I didn't mean to raise my voice," Aisha admitted during our chat together. "My partner forgot to text me back, and suddenly I was going off about how no one respects my time. I knew I was overreacting even while it was happening, but I couldn't stop the words from coming out."

Most of us know that feeling all too well. The moment when we recognise we're overreacting, but it's already too late. Our ADHD brains struggle with emotional impulsivity, meaning the gap between *feeling* and *reacting* is practically nonexistent.[192] Without that built-in buffer, small frustrations can trigger full-blown emotional responses before logic even has a chance to catch up.[193]

It's not that we *want* to overreact. It's that our emotions fire at full volume before we have a chance to turn the dial down.

---

[192] Barkley, ed., *Attention-Deficit Hyperactivity Disorder.*

[193] Hallowell and Ratey, *ADHD 2.0.*

THE SHAME SPIRAL: WHEN EMBARRASSMENT WON'T LET GO

Keisha couldn't stop replaying an awkward moment from a work meeting where she *talked too much*. Days later, she still felt physically uncomfortable just thinking about it.

"I keep remembering everyone's faces. Were they annoyed? Bored? I feel like I should quit my job and move to another country."

Most of us have been there, stuck in an emotional flashback, where a past mistake refuses to fade, dragging us into a spiral of shame and self-criticism.[194] While neurotypical people might cringe at an awkward memory and move on, our ADHD brains don't let us off the hook that easily. Instead, we replay the moment in painful, high-definition clarity, analyzing every detail, convinced that everyone else remembers it just as vividly.[195]

It doesn't fade like a normal thought. It's a loop we can't shut off.

SHUTDOWN MODE: WHEN EVERYTHING BECOMES TOO MUCH

Not all emotional dysregulation looks like outbursts or explosive reactions. Sometimes, it's the exact opposite.

"When things get overwhelming," Sonya admitted, "I just...shut down. I stop answering texts. I avoid responsibilities. I can't make decisions. It's like my brain goes offline."

Many of us know this feeling. Instead of reacting outwardly, we freeze, emotionally paralysed by the sheer weight of our feelings. This happens when our emotions become so intense that our only way to cope is to disconnect completely.[196]

From the outside, we might look calm, even indifferent. But inside, we're drowning in emotional overload. Our system hits its limit, and

---

194 Madhoo and Quinn, "A Review of Attention Deficit/Hyperactivity Disorder in Women and Girls."

195 Hallowell and Ratey, *ADHD 2.0*.

196 Stephen V. Faraone et al., "Practitioner Review: Emotional Dysregulation in Attention-Deficit/Hyperactivity Disorder—Implications for Clinical Recognition and Intervention," *Journal of Child Psychology and Psychiatry* 60, no. 2 (February 2019): 133–150, https://doi.org/10.1111/jcpp.12899.

it's like a circuit breaker flips, shutting everything down to protect us from the overwhelm.

This isn't laziness. It's not apathy. It's a neurological response to too much, too fast, all at once.

THE SLEEP–EMOTION CONNECTION NOBODY TALKS ABOUT

"I can always tell when I haven't slept enough," Lisa told me. "Everything makes me cry. A cute dog video? Tears. My partner asking what I want for dinner? Somehow that's overwhelming. A minor work setback? Complete despair."

Most of us know this feeling all too well.

Sleep issues are practically universal for us ADHD women. Whether it's struggling to fall asleep (despite being exhausted), waking up repeatedly throughout the night, or feeling physically glued to the bed in the morning, poor sleep makes everything harder, especially emotional regulation.[197]

When we're running on empty, our brains have even fewer resources to manage emotions. What might have been a mild frustration on a well-rested day can feel like the end of the world after a night of tossing and turning.

It's not that we're overreacting. It's that our exhausted brains can't filter, regulate, or process emotions the way they should.

The problem is the dopamine–sleep paradox. Our ADHD brains crave dopamine, but sleep deprivation actually lowers dopamine production.[198] This sets up a vicious cycle: The more tired we are, the harder it becomes to regulate our emotions, focus, and resist impulsive behaviours.

And here's another issue: We're often the ones keeping ourselves awake. Many of us stay up chasing dopamine, scrolling, reading, or hyperfocusing on work or creative projects because late at night, when distractions are minimal, we finally feel engaged and productive. But that

---

[197] K. B. van der Heijden et al., "Sleep, Chronotype, and Sleep Hygiene in Children with Attention-Deficit/Hyperactivity Disorder, Autism Spectrum Disorder, and Controls," *European Child & Adolescent Psychiatry* 27 (2018): 99–111, https://doi.org/10.1007/s00787-017-1025-8.

[198] Barkley, ed., *Attention-Deficit Hyperactivity Disorder*.

lost sleep only makes our dopamine deficit worse the next day, leading to even more emotional dysregulation, brain fog, and impulsivity.

Leila described it perfectly.

"I can stay up working until two without even noticing the time. But then the next day, I'm emotionally all over the place, snappy, foggy, just struggling. I tried melatonin, but it didn't work until I also changed my nighttime routine to reduce stimulation before bed. Now I know if I want to feel emotionally stable tomorrow, I have to start winding down by ten tonight."

For ADHD brains, sleep isn't just about rest. It's about giving our nervous system the reset it desperately needs.

NUTRITION: THE EMOTIONAL REGULATION HACK WE OFTEN MISS

"I used to think I was just a moody person," Maya admitted. "Then I realised I was having emotional meltdowns every day around three—exactly when my blood sugar would crash after skipping breakfast and having a sugary lunch."

For so many of us, food and mood are directly linked, yet we don't always make the connection right away. When we don't fuel ourselves properly, our emotional regulation takes a hit.

Food isn't just fuel for the body. It's fuel for the brain. And the right nutrition can make a huge difference in how we manage emotions, focus, and energy throughout the day.

BLOOD SUGAR SWINGS AND MOOD CRASHES

Our ADHD brains are highly sensitive to blood sugar fluctuations. Skipping meals or eating too many refined carbs can cause rapid spikes and crashes, leading to irritability, anxiety, and brain fog.[199] Many of us

---

[199] Julia J. Rucklidge and Jeanette M. Johnstone, "The Role of Diet and Nutrient Supplementation in the Treatment of ADHD," *The ADHD Report* 24, no. 8 (2016), https://doi.org/10.1521/adhd.2016.24.8.1.

know the feeling of intense *hanger*—that moment when hunger turns into an emotional meltdown that feels way bigger than the situation calls for.

The connection between blood sugar and ADHD symptoms is particularly strong because glucose is the brain's primary fuel. Stable glucose levels help maintain consistent dopamine production, which is already in short supply for us. When blood sugar crashes, it triggers a stress response and weakens executive function, making emotional regulation even harder.

Maya realised that starting her day with protein instead of skipping breakfast made her afternoon crashes *way* less severe. For me, keeping protein-rich snacks on hand has saved me from many emotional spirals, especially when meetings run long or plans shift unexpectedly.

Yes, eating regularly is important, but the real key is fuelling your ADHD brain the right way.

ADHD-FRIENDLY EMOTIONAL REGULATION TECHNIQUES

I've tried all the classic emotional regulation advice: Take a deep breath. Count to ten. Think positive thoughts. And for years, I wondered why none of it actually worked.

Now I know.

Most emotional regulation strategies were created for a neurotypical brain with a fully functional prefrontal cortex that can naturally "pause and reflect" before reacting. But for us ADHD women, that's exactly where we struggle.[200] Logic doesn't override emotions in real time. By the time someone tells us to "just calm down," the emotional floodgates have already burst wide open.

So instead of fighting our brains, we need strategies that actually work with our nervous system, not against it.

---

[200] Barkley, ed., *Attention-Deficit Hyperactivity Disorder*.

DOPAMINE-BOOSTING BREAKS TO RESET EMOTIONS

Use quick, enjoyable activities (music, movement, sensory stimulation) to reset emotions in real time.

These activities provide a fast dopamine boost, helping our brains shift out of emotional overwhelm and into a more regulated state.[201]

When I feel emotions bubbling up, I take a "dopamine break": two minutes of dancing to an upbeat song, stepping outside for fresh air, or even just playing with my dogs. These quick dopamine hits interrupt the emotional spiral before it takes over.

One woman I spoke to kept a dopamine menu on her phone (a strategy I explained earlier in the book), a list of small, enjoyable activities she can do when emotions threaten to overtake her.

"Sometimes I just need to jump on the spot for thirty seconds or eat something sour to snap out of it," she said.

These quick shifts don't suppress emotions. They help us ride them out without drowning in them.

PLANNED SCRIPTS FOR REJECTION SENSITIVITY MOMENTS

Write out self-validating responses for rejection-sensitive situations to help override negative self-talk.[202]

When rejection hits, our brains go into panic mode. Pre-written responses provide a lifeline when our thoughts turn dark.

When RSD kicks in, it can hijack my brain. I've learned to keep a note in my phone with phrases that talk me down:

- This feeling will pass.
- One person's opinion isn't the truth.
- I am worthy, regardless of others' reactions.
- One moment in time does not define me.

---

[201] Marja-Leena Juntunen and Katja Sutela, "The Effectiveness of Music–Movement Integration for Vulnerable Groups: A Systematic Literature Review," *Frontiers in Psychology* 14 (August 2023): 1127654, https://doi.org/10.3389/fpsyg.2023.1127654.

[202] Hallowell and Ratey, *ADHD 2.0*.

Reading these when RSD hits interrupts the spiral of negative thoughts. It's a small shift, but it stops me from believing every painful thought my brain throws at me.

BODY-BASED REGULATION TECHNIQUES

Use physical strategies to regulate your nervous system when emotions feel overwhelming.

ADHD emotions live in our bodies. Physical movement, deep pressure stimulation (weighted blankets, compression gear), and cold exposure help regulate intense feelings.[203]

I discovered this by accident when I borrowed a friend's weighted blanket during a stressful moment on a holiday visit. The instant calming effect was so profound that I bought my own the next day.

Other strategies that help me include:

- Splashing cold water on my face.
- Wearing compression clothing.
- Doing vigorous exercise to release emotional tension.

Camille kept an "emotional regulation kit" at work: a stress ball, chewing gum, and a small spray bottle of rose water.

"People think I'm just into self-care," she laughed. "Really, I'm trying to stop emotional overwhelm during meetings."

THE POWER OF THE PAUSE: TRANSFORMING REACTIONS INTO RESPONSES

Create a deliberate pause before reacting emotionally.

---

[203] Yang Siyuan et al., "Effects of Physical Exercise on Anxiety Depression and Emotion Regulation in Children with Attention Deficit Hyperactivity Disorder: A Systematic Review and Meta-Analysis," *Frontiers in Pediatrics* 12 (2025), https://doi.org/10.3389/fped.2024.1513727.

Introducing a structured pause gives our prefrontal cortex time to activate, creating space between stimulus and response.[204]

"I used to react immediately to any criticism with defensiveness," Rebecca admitted. "Learning to pause, even for a few seconds, completely changed my relationships."

The pause stops us from reacting on autopilot. Some ways we can practise it include:

- Wearing a specific bracelet to touch when emotions rise.
- Using the 5-5-5 technique (inhale for five, hold for five, exhale for five).
- Repeating back the last thing someone said to naturally slow the conversation.

Research shows that practising the pause strengthens neural pathways over time, improving emotional regulation even when we're not consciously using the technique.[205]

THE SECOND PATH STRATEGY: REDIRECTING THE IMPULSE

Create an alternative behaviour for when you feel an emotional impulse.

ADHD brains resist suppression but respond well to redirection.[206] Instead of trying to fight an emotional reaction, redirect it:

- Instead of sending an emotional email, draft it in a separate document first.
- Instead of lashing out, shift your focus with a dopamine booster (music, movement).

---

204 Adam R. Aron, "The Neural Basis of Inhibition in Cognitive Control," *Neuroscientist* 13, no. 3 (2007): 214–28, https://doi.org/10.1177/1073858407299288.

205 Richard J. Davidson and Sharon Begley, *The Emotional Life of Your Brain* (Avery, 2012).

206 Edmund J. Sonuga-Barke et al., "Do Executive Deficits and Delay Aversion Make Independent Contributions to Preschool Attention-Deficit/Hyperactivity Disorder Symptoms?," *Journal of the American Academy of Child & Adolescent Psychiatry* 42, no. 11 (2003): 1335–42, https://doi.org/10.1097/01.chi.0000087564.34977.21.

- Instead of reacting immediately, commit to a thirty-minute waiting period.

The key isn't fighting the emotional energy. It's channelling it somewhere else.

PATTERN RECOGNITION: TRACKING EMOTIONAL CYCLES

Track emotional highs and lows alongside hormonal cycles.

By predicting tough emotional days, we can proactively manage them.[207] After months of tracking, I noticed clear patterns. My emotional regulation is more challenging about five days before my period starts, and I'm much more resilient during ovulation.

This information isn't just interesting; it's empowering. Now I can:

- Plan important conversations or challenging work for my "emotionally stable" weeks.
- Build in extra support during vulnerable times.
- Give myself permission to *expect* more emotional sensitivity and treat it with care.

"I literally have weeks marked 'hormonal fluctuation, extra self-care needed' in my calendar," shared Dani. "My partner can see my calendar, and he's actually grateful for the heads-up."

PERMISSION TO FEEL: RIDING THE WAVE

Instead of forcing "calm down" strategies that don't work for you, acknowledge your emotions as valid and ride the wave.[208]

Resistance to emotions often intensifies them. Accepting an emotion

---

[207] Haimov-Kochman and Berger, "Cognitive Functions of Regularly Cycling Women May Differ Throughout the Month."

[208] Madhoo and Quinn, "A Review of Attention Deficit/Hyperactivity Disorder in Women and Girls."

as a temporary experience reduces our shame and allows us to process it more naturally.

"I spent years fighting against my emotions," said Rachel. "When I felt hurt or angry, I'd immediately try to talk myself out of it or push it down. That never worked. It just made the feeling more intense and last longer. Now I say to myself, 'This is a big feeling, and that's okay. I can feel this without acting on it. It will pass.' And you know what? It actually does pass faster when I don't fight it."

Instead of battling our emotions, we can learn to move through them with awareness, self-compassion, and patience.

This is how we work with our ADHD brains instead of against them. These strategies aren't about suppressing emotions. They're about building a better relationship with them.

THE "FUTURE ME" TEST: MAKING CONSEQUENCES REAL

Many of us struggle to see future consequences when we're caught up in emotion. In the moment, the only thing that feels real is right now. Future regret, fallout, or alternative choices seem distant and irrelevant.

Rebecca knew this pattern well. She'd send angry emails, make impulsive decisions, or burn bridges in the heat of the moment, only to regret it later. She needed something to bridge the gap between impulse and foresight.

That's when she started using the Future Me test:

- Before making a decision, she writes down how she expects to feel about it in twenty-four hours.
- She keeps a sticky note on her desk that says, "Would future me thank me for this?"
- She records voice notes, talking herself through the decision before acting on it.

Our ADHD brains struggle with mental time travel, meaning future consequences feel vague, abstract, and disconnected from the present.[209] But research shows that externalising future consequences through writing or verbal processing activates the prefrontal cortex, making our decisions more deliberate.[210]

Since our talk, Rebecca has started using this technique before sending emotional texts, and it has saved her from many regrets. Just asking herself, "How will I feel about this tomorrow?" is often enough to disrupt the impulse and bring clarity.

That said, she still occasionally texts me at odd hours with "Talk me down from this ledge. I'm about to text my ex."

And without fail, I reply, "Put the phone down and step away slowly."

Because sometimes accountability saves us before logic kicks in.

REFRAMING OUR EMOTIONAL SENSITIVITY AS A STRENGTH

What if our emotional intensity isn't a flaw but a gift we haven't fully understood?

Cloe, a woman I interviewed, remembered sitting in her therapist's office, exhausted after yet another emotional roller coaster of a week.

"I just wish I didn't feel everything so deeply," she told her therapist. "It's exhausting."

Her therapist studied her for a moment before responding.

"Your emotional sensitivity is also what makes you an incredible friend," she said. "It's why you notice when others are hurting. It's what makes you passionate about your work. It's why your writing connects with people."

Cloe sat there, stunned. She had never thought about it that way before.

For so long, she had seen her emotional intensity as something to fix,

---

209 Kate B. Metcalfe, Corinna D. McFeaters, and Daniel Voyer, "Time-Perception Deficits in Attention-Deficit/Hyperactivity Disorder: A Systematic Review and Meta-Analysis," *Developmental Neuropsychology* 49, no. 1 (2024): 1–24, https://doi.org/10.1080/87565641.2023.2293712.

210 Russell A. Barkley, "The Important Role of Executive Functioning and Self-Regulation in ADHD," fact sheet, accessed October 29, 2025, https://russellbarkley.org/factsheets/ADHD_EF_and_SR.pdf.

as the reason she struggled with overwhelm, rejection, and emotional burnout. But she had never stopped to consider what she would lose if she didn't feel so deeply.

While emotional dysregulation can be challenging, it also comes with strengths that many neurotypicals don't have. ADHD women tend to be deeply empathetic, intuitive, and passionate.

Our ability to feel deeply makes us:

- Powerful advocates who fight for what we believe in.
- Creative thinkers who connect ideas in ways others don't.
- Emotionally connected friends and partners who notice the unspoken and care deeply.[211]

Cloe is still learning to manage the intensity of her emotions, but she's also learning to honour the gifts that come with them.

Maybe we weren't meant to be less emotional. Maybe we were meant to feel deeply so we can bring something unique into the world.

FROM BURDEN TO VALUABLE ASSET

What if instead of fighting against our emotions, we learned to lean into their wisdom?

For me, embracing emotional awareness meant seeing my sensitivity as a form of intuition. I pick up on things others miss: the slight change in someone's tone, unspoken tension in a room, the deeper meaning behind someone's words. This has been an asset in my relationships and my work.

Learning to manage this emotional depth wasn't about feeling less. It was about not getting lost in what I feel.

One strategy I regularly teach my clients and personally rely on is intentionally anchoring myself in my own emotional clarity.

When someone else's emotions start to overwhelm me, I consciously

---

[211] Hallowell and Ratey, *ADHD 2.0*.

remind myself that empathy doesn't mean absorbing their feelings as my own.

This practise allows me to hold space for others without compromising my own emotional balance. It's a powerful method for developing resilience and strong emotional boundaries.

In my opinion, many of us with ADHD have a heightened ability to detect subtle social and environmental cues, which contributes to exceptional empathy, creativity, and intuitive understanding. Brain imaging studies show that ADHD brains often have increased connectivity between emotional processing centres and creative thinking regions.[212]

This might explain why so many of us excel in fields that require emotional intelligence, creative problem-solving, and deep intuitive thinking.

Rather than seeing our emotional intensity as something to fix, we might consider it an inherent cognitive strength that, when properly channelled, allows us to connect deeply, think uniquely, and perceive the world in ways others don't.

BUILDING EMOTIONAL RESILIENCE: PRACTICAL STRATEGIES

Since emotions hit us harder, having self-soothing techniques is essential. I've found that these strategies help me regulate my emotions without suppressing them:

- **Deep pressure stimulation** (weighted blankets, compression clothing) helps calm my nervous system.
- **Sensory grounding techniques** (holding an ice cube or textured object, scented oils) bring me back to the present.
- **Movement-based regulation** (dancing, walking, stretching) helps process emotions physically when my brain feels stuck.

---

[212] Thomas Armstrong, *The Power of Neurodiversity: Unleashing the Advantages of Your Differently Wired Brain* (Da Capo Press, 2010).

Rather than trying to numb out my emotions, I've learned to channel them in ways that work for me.

Our ability to feel deeply isn't a flaw. It's a strength. The key is learning to honour our emotions without being consumed by them.

TAKEAWAY: WORKING WITH OUR ADHD BRAINS, NOT AGAINST THEM

For us, emotional regulation isn't about suppressing feelings. It's about understanding them, honouring them, and building systems that support our emotional resilience.

With the right strategies, our emotional intensity can become one of our greatest strengths.[213]

By making small, ADHD-friendly adjustments, we can create conditions for better emotional balance:

- **Tracking hormonal cycles** so we can anticipate mood shifts and adjust accordingly.
- **Improving sleep hygiene** so we're not running on emotional fumes.
- **Stabilising blood sugar** so we don't mistake physical crashes for emotional ones.

The goal isn't perfection. It's to create sustainable habits that support both our mental and physical well-being.

Zoe, an interviewee, captured this perfectly over coffee one day.

"I used to think my emotions were too much, too big, too intense, too unpredictable," she said. "Now I realise they're exactly the right size for the person I'm meant to be. I just needed the right tools to work with them instead of against them."

And that's the real shift. This isn't about shrinking who we are. It's about supporting ourselves so we can thrive.

---

[213] Dodson, "Emotional Hyperarousal in ADHD."

EMBRACING OUR EMOTIONAL NATURE

After interviewing countless late-diagnosed women and reflecting on my own experiences as both an ADHDer and an ADHD coach, I've realised just how many of us share a similar story: We've spent years battling against our emotions. We've tried to rein them in, quiet them down, and shape them into something society deems acceptable. We carry the memories of shame from being labelled "too sensitive," as though feeling deeply is something to apologise for. We remember vividly the frustration of being blindsided by intense emotions and the exhaustion from constantly masking our true reactions to fit into a world that often feels unequipped for our depth.

For a long time, we believed the solution was to fix this perceived flaw, to control and suppress our emotional intensity. But that approach missed the truth.

What I've discovered, and what I want you to take away, is that our emotional intensity is not a problem to solve; it's an integral part of who we are. When we stop fighting our ADHD brains and start embracing and working with them, everything changes. Our emotional depth reveals itself not as weakness but as an extraordinary strength.

In my coaching practise, I've witnessed women from our community transform their emotional intuition into powerful art that resonates deeply, advocacy efforts that drive meaningful change, and connections built on profound empathy and understanding. I've seen firsthand what happens when we shift from suppressing our emotions to learning how to channel them effectively.

We don't just survive. We thrive. We become unstoppable.

True emotional regulation isn't about feeling less. It's about feeling with intention.

It's about:

- Creating space between feeling and reaction.
- Developing tools that work with our unique brains.
- Recognising that our emotions aren't just vulnerabilities; they hold value.

So tonight, as you sit with your own emotions, I hope you see your sensitivity for what it really is. Not something to manage, apologise for, or shrink down.

But something to honour.

Because the world doesn't need us to feel less.

It needs us to feel fully and to show up exactly as we are.

Yes, our emotions run deep and fast. But they also connect us to ourselves, to others, to the world in ways that enrich our lives immeasurably.

When we embrace all of who we are, including our emotional intensity, we don't just survive as ADHD women. We thrive.

SELF-COACHING STRATEGIES: EMOTIONAL REGULATION

If you struggle to regulate your emotions, it is not because you lack willpower. ADHD affects the systems in the brain responsible for pausing, processing, and recovering from intense emotional states.[214] Self-coaching strategies are not about avoiding emotions. They are about supporting your nervous system in real time so that you can move through those emotions without being hijacked by them.

Here are five evidence-based strategies I teach clients to use when overwhelm hits.

REGULATE THROUGH THE BODY BEFORE TRYING TO PROBLEM-SOLVE

When your nervous system is dysregulated, cognitive strategies like reframing, perspective-taking, or positive self-talk often fail. The brain's prefrontal cortex, which manages logic and impulse control, temporarily goes offline during high-stress emotional states.[215] Physical interventions are often more effective in the moment.

Start with one of the following:

- Splash cold water on your face.
- Hold an ice cube.
- Run your hands under cool water.
- Step outside and feel your feet on solid ground.

This activates the parasympathetic nervous system and calms the fight-or-flight response. The mammalian diving reflex in particular can slow heart rate and improve emotional regulation quickly.[216]

---

[214] Barkley, ed., *Attention-Deficit Hyperactivity Disorder*.

[215] Arnsten, "Stress Signalling Pathways That Impair Prefrontal Cortex Structure and Function."

[216] Panneton, "The Mammalian Diving Response."

EXTERNALISE WHAT IS HAPPENING WITH A LABEL

When emotions surge, try naming what is happening as it happens. This gives the prefrontal cortex something to do and introduces a brief pause between the trigger and your response.

Try saying aloud or writing down: "This is emotional flooding. It is my ADHD brain reacting fast. It will pass."

This technique is based on the Name It to Tame It approach from affect labelling research. Labelling emotional states has been shown to reduce activity in the amygdala and support cognitive regulation.[217]

USE A PREDECIDED DELAY PHRASE

When someone triggers you or you feel emotionally off-centre, default to one short phrase that buys you time. I often coach clients to practise this line: "I need a minute."

You can walk away, pause the conversation, or breathe before reacting. Even a short delay allows the prefrontal cortex to reengage. This is the foundation of impulse regulation and is supported by findings from executive function research.[218]

CREATE A DOPAMINE RESET LIST

Because ADHD brains are under-stimulated during boredom, stress, or emotional overload, adding quick dopamine hits can help shift emotional state. This works especially well when combined with movement or sensory input.

Keep a short list of activities that boost your mood or help you reset:

- Listen to two minutes of upbeat music.
- Play with a pet.

---

[217] Lieberman et al., "Putting Feelings into Words."

[218] Adam R. Aron et al., "Inhibition and the Right Inferior Frontal Cortex," *Trends in Cognitive Sciences* 8, no. 4 (2004): 170–77, https://doi.org/10.1016/j.tics.2004.02.010.

- Squeeze a sensory object.
- Taste something sour.
- Do ten jumping jacks.

These do not fix the situation. They help calm the nervous system so you can engage with the situation more effectively.[219]

TRACK VULNERABLE PATTERNS TO BUILD AWARENESS

Many ADHD women experience emotional dysregulation cyclically or in predictable patterns. Start tracking yours. Are your hardest days tied to hormone shifts, skipped meals, poor sleep, or transitions between activities?

Keeping a brief journal can help identify which patterns are physiological, environmental, or behavioural. For example:

- Mid-cycle rejection sensitivity often correlates with dropping oestrogen and dopamine levels.[220]
- Blood sugar crashes can trigger emotional meltdowns due to reduced dopamine and executive function.[221]
- Poor sleep reduces emotional control and raises emotional reactivity across the board.[222]

The goal is not to eliminate emotion. It is to create more space for intentional responses rather than reactive ones.

---

[219] Robert E. Thayer et al., "Self-Regulation of Mood: Strategies for Changing a Bad Mood, Raising Energy, and Reducing Tension," *Journal of Personality and Social Psychology* 67, no. 5 (1994): 910–25, https://doi.org/10.1037/0022-3514.67.5.910.

[220] Madhoo and Quinn, "A Review of Attention Deficit/Hyperactivity Disorder in Women and Girls."

[221] Qian Zhao et al., "Executive Function and Diabetes: A Clinical Neuropsychology Perspective," *Frontiers in Psychology* 11 (2020): 2112, https://doi.org/10.3389/fpsyg.2020.02112.

[222] Cara A. Palmer et al., "Sleep Loss and Emotion: A Systematic Review and Meta-Analysis of over Fifty Years of Experimental Research," *Psychological Bulletin* 150, no. 4 (2024): 440–63, https://doi.org/10.1037/bul0000410.

Chapter Ten

Owning Your ADHD and Letting Go of Comparison

I SEE IT IN MY COACHING SESSIONS EVERY DAY—THAT MOMENT when an ADHD woman realises she's been measuring herself with the wrong ruler her entire life. We've all felt that gnawing sense of inadequacy when comparing ourselves to neurotypical peers.

It happens in meetings when everyone else seems effortlessly organised while our brains feel like browsers with forty-seven tabs open. It happens at home when our friend's kitchen is spotless but our sink is overflowing with dishes. It happens on social media platforms like Fakebook. Oops, I mean Facebook. We see perfectly curated morning routines while we are still searching for our keys again. We'll dig more into social media shortly.

At first, we use comparison as a motivation tool. We think, *If I just try harder, I can be like them.* But over time, the constant self-criticism chips away at our confidence, leaving us exhausted and defeated.

The reality: Holding ourselves to neurotypical standards is like judging a fish by its ability to climb a tree. It is not just unfair. It is impossible. Poor fishy. I see you.

Many of my clients describe feeling "behind" in life, as though they missed an invisible memo on how to be an adult. We watch neurotypical peers effortlessly excelling in careers, managing their homes, and balancing social lives, and wonder, *Why is it so much harder for us?*

This struggle is compounded by a lifetime of masking, hiding our ADHD traits to fit in. Like many of you, I've spent years forcing myself into rigid structures not designed for my brain, which inevitably led to burnout.

The issue isn't that we're not trying hard enough. It's that neurotypical strategies simply don't work for how our brains operate.

Research shows that women with ADHD are more likely to struggle with self-esteem due to a lifetime of perceived failures.[223] Because ADHD symptoms in women are often dismissed as "flakiness" or "laziness," many of us develop deep-seated shame around our differences. The more we compare ourselves to neurotypicals, the more these internalised beliefs take root.

THE "TOGETHER" MOM VERSUS THE ADHD MOM

Isabelle, one of the women I interviewed and a mother of two, messaged me distraught one day. "I feel like the worst mom at school," she confessed.

She described watching other moms arrive on time, with their kids neatly dressed and lunches packed with homemade sandwiches and perfectly cut fruit. Meanwhile, she rushed in five minutes late, her daughter's hair hastily tied in a messy ponytail and a lunch packed with whatever snacks she could find that morning.

"This morning, I overheard another mom talking about how she preps a week's worth of meals on Sundays," Isabelle told me, her voice breaking. "I felt this immediate wave of shame wash over me. Why can't I do that? Why does meal prep feel impossible?"

---

223 Madhoo and Quinn, "A Review of Attention Deficit/Hyperactivity Disorder in Women and Girls."

Determined to prove herself, Isabelle spent the next weekend forcing herself to do the same. She made lists, bought groceries, and tried to follow through. By Sunday evening, her kitchen was a disaster, and she was mentally drained. She called me again. By Wednesday, she had abandoned the meal plan entirely, overwhelmed by the rigidity of it.

It wasn't that she was lazy or incapable. It was that the neurotypical model of meal prep wasn't designed for her ADHD brain. The executive function demands—planning, sequencing, remembering steps—were too high.

Our ADHD brains struggle with prospective memory, the ability to remember to do things in the future.[224] Neurotypicals can set a plan and execute it without much resistance. Our brains, however, often need more immediate motivation and flexibility. That's why rigid systems can quickly fall apart for us. It's not a character flaw. It's neurobiology.

Well-meaning advice from neurotypicals often sounds like:

"Just make a list and follow it."

"Use a planner."

"Set reminders on your phone."

"You just need more discipline."

By now I bet you can see the problem here. ADHD isn't a discipline issue. It's a difference in executive function. Our brains struggle with task initiation, time management, and working memory not because we lack willpower but because of neurological wiring.

Studies show that ADHD brains have lower dopamine levels, making routine tasks feel physically painful to start.[225] In my own life, I've found that "just do it" advice doesn't work because it ignores the fundamental way our ADHD brains process motivation.

We need interest, novelty, challenge, or urgency, not just a list.

In our coaching group last year, Jenna shared her struggle as a project manager. She constantly compared herself to her coworker, Emma, who seemed effortlessly organised. Emma had colour-coded spreadsheets,

---

224 Barkley, ed., *Attention-Deficit Hyperactivity Disorder.*

225 Volkow et al., "Evaluating Dopamine Reward Pathway in ADHD."

never missed deadlines, and kept a pristine email inbox. Meanwhile, Jenna had thousands of unread emails, relied on last-minute bursts of energy, and constantly felt like she was playing catch-up.

"I'm determined to be more like Emma," Jenna told the group. She bought a planner and tried to use time-blocking. It worked for about a week before she started avoiding her planner entirely. "The structure felt suffocating," she admitted. "Instead of feeling accomplished, I felt like a failure."

Through our work together, Jenna learned that her ADHD brain needed dopamine-driven productivity strategies.

She discovered that she thrived on timers, accountability partners, and breaking tasks into micro steps. Comparing herself to Emma had only led to self-criticism, when in reality she needed different tools to succeed.

Our ADHD brains often need external structure but on our own terms. Traditional organisation systems rely on internal motivation, which our brains struggle with.[226] That's why self-imposed deadlines often fail, while externally imposed ones work. It's also why body doubling (working alongside someone else) and novelty-based approaches are more effective for us. When I realised this myself, I stopped fighting my brain and started working with it.

THE SCIENCE BEHIND ADHD AND COMPARISON

Neuroscience explains why our ADHD brains struggle with comparison. The default mode network (DMN), the part of the brain responsible for self-referential thinking, tends to be hyperactive in ADHD individuals.[227] This leads to excessive rumination and self-criticism, making comparison an automatic habit rather than a conscious choice.

---

[226] Thomas E. Brown, "ADD/ADHD and Impaired Executive Function in Clinical Practice," *Current Attention Disorders Reports* 1 (March 2009): 37–41, https://doi.org/10.1007/s12618-009-0006-3.

[227] F. Xavier Castellanos et al., "Cingulate-Precuneus Interactions: A New Locus of Dysfunction in Adult Attention-Deficit/Hyperactivity Disorder," *Biological Psychiatry* 63, no. 3 (2008): 332–37, https://pubmed.ncbi.nlm.nih.gov/17888409/.

Additionally, our ADHD brains have an impaired ability to regulate dopamine, which impacts reward processing.[228] When we see a neurotypical person succeeding, our brains may register it as a threat rather than an inspiration, reinforcing feelings of inadequacy.

Instead of measuring ourselves against neurotypical success, I encourage my clients (and myself) to try shifting the focus:

- **Recognise Your Unique Strengths:** Our ADHD brains are creative and intuitive and thrive in high-energy environments. We may struggle with spreadsheets, but our ability to think outside the box is invaluable.
- **Reframe "Failure" as Experimentation:** Neurotypical people may thrive on rigid routines, but our ADHD brains often need flexibility. If one system doesn't work, that doesn't mean we failed. It means we need a different approach.
- **Measure Progress, Not Perfection:** Instead of comparing ourselves to others, we can compare ourselves to yesterday's version of ourselves. Did we complete one more task? Find a small win? That's real progress.
- **Lean into ADHD-Friendly Strategies:** Research shows that ADHD motivation is interest-based rather than purely driven by external rewards.[229] Building on this, practical coaching strategies like body doubling, gamification, and accountability partners help translate that motivation framework into daily life, offering alternatives to neurotypical productivity models.[230]

Imagine what would happen if we stopped measuring ourselves against neurotypical people. What if instead of striving for a rigid, linear

---

[228] Volkow et al., "Evaluating Dopamine Reward Pathway in ADHD."

[229] Caryn L. Carlson and Leanne Tamm, "'Responsiveness of Children with Attention Deficit-Hyperactivity Disorder to Reward and Response Cost: Differential Impact on Performance and Motivation," *Journal of Consulting and Clinical Psychology* 68, no. 1 (2000): 73–83, https://doi.org/10.1037/0022-006X.68.1.73.

[230] Kaia Newman et al., "'Get Me In The Groove': A Mixed Methods Study on Supporting ADHD Professional Programmers," in *Proceedings of the 2025 IEEE/ACM 47th International Conference on Software Engineering* (Pittsburgh, PA: IEEE/ACM, 2025).

path, we embraced a path that works for us? Success for an ADHD woman doesn't mean forcing herself into neurotypical expectations.

It means building a life that supports her brain.

Our journey may look different, but that doesn't mean it's less valuable. What if our winding, unpredictable path isn't a flaw but a feature? What if the way we think, feel, and operate isn't broken but brilliant? How's that for a delicious little "what if"?

Next time you catch yourself comparing, ask, *Would I expect a sunflower to grow like a pine tree?*

Then give yourself permission to bloom exactly as you are.

RECOGNISING HIDDEN ADHD STRENGTHS

ADHD often comes with challenges that are impossible to ignore—disorganisation, forgetfulness, emotional intensity—but what about the strengths? We are often so focused on what we struggle with that we fail to recognise the unique abilities we bring to the table.

These strengths might not fit the traditional mould of success, but they are powerful, valuable, and, in many cases, extraordinary.

CREATIVITY: THE BRAIN THAT THINKS IN COLOUR

Our minds refuse to stay inside the lines. We think in big, bold, unexpected ways, connecting ideas that others would never see. Research shows that individuals with ADHD score higher in divergent thinking—a measure of creativity that involves generating multiple solutions to a problem.[231] This means that our brains don't just think outside the box; we reinvent the box entirely.

Example: One of the women I spoke to, Mia, always struggled with structured work environments but thrived when she became a freelance designer. She found that her ADHD-driven ability to make unexpected

---

[231] Holly A. White and Priti Shah, "Uninhibited Imaginations: Creativity in Adults with Attention-Deficit/Hyperactivity Disorder," *Personality and Individual Differences* 40, no. 6 (2006): 1121–31, https://doi.org/10.1016/j.paid.2005.11.007.

creative connections allowed her to develop unique branding ideas that her clients loved. Once she stopped trying to fit into traditional work models, she flourished.

Reframe: Embrace the Chaos. Research shows that adults with ADHD often use a divergent, less structured creative style, which can support innovation.[232] In practise, one way I apply this is by encouraging brainstorming sessions where every idea—no matter how scattered—is captured first and organised later. Personally, I've found this kind of process has led to some of my most innovative coaching techniques.[233]

HYPERFOCUS: THE DEEP WORK ADVANTAGE

Hyperfocus is the ability to deeply immerse ourselves in an activity and is one of ADHD's most misunderstood gifts. When something captures our interest, we can lose ourselves in it for hours, achieving levels of productivity and insight that others struggle to reach. Studies suggest that hyperfocus occurs when the ADHD brain locks onto an engaging task, releasing dopamine that sustains intense concentration.[234]

Example: Natalie, a software engineer, struggled with deadlines until she realised that hyperfocus was her secret weapon. She started structuring her workday around bursts of deep focus, eliminating distractions and diving into coding marathons that allowed her to accomplish in a few hours what used to take her days.

Reframe: Focus Sprints. Schedule your most important work during the times when you naturally hyperfocus. Use noise-cancelling headphones, and set up "focus sprints." Structure your day around your energy rather than the clock. I've learned to write my books and course

---

[232] Holly A. White and Priti Shah, "Creative Style and Achievement in Adults with Attention-Deficit/Hyperactivity Disorder," *Personality and Individual Differences* 50, no. 5 (2011): 673–77, https://doi.org/10.1016/j.paid.2010.12.015.

[233] Shankar Sankaran and Saul Brown, "Coaching Collaborative Creativity and Innovation: An Action-Based Method for Sustainable Innovation, Learning and Development in Business Organizations," in *Action Research for Sustainable Development in a Turbulent World*, ed. Ortrun Zuber-Skerritt (Bingley, UK: Emerald Group Publishing Limited, 2012), 127–52, https://doi.org/10.1108/978-1-78052-823-4.

[234] Hupfeld et al., "Living 'in the Zone.'"

content during my peak hyperfocus hours (usually first thing in the morning) rather than forcing myself to work during traditional hours.[235]

RESILIENCE: THE STRENGTH OF GETTING BACK UP

Many of us have spent our entire lives facing obstacles such as missed deadlines, forgotten appointments, social misunderstandings. But instead of giving up, we push forward. ADHD builds resilience because navigating a world designed for neurotypical brains requires constant adaptation and perseverance.[236]

Example: After being told for years that she was "too scattered" to run a business, my client Ava launched her own online shop. She faced setbacks, missed emails, and inventory mishaps, but her ability to bounce back kept her moving forward. Now, she credits her ADHD-fuelled determination for her success.

Reframe: Resilience Journal. When facing setbacks, remind yourself of all the times you've overcome challenges. Keep a resilience journal, where you record obstacles you faced and how you handled them. I review my own journal whenever I feel discouraged, and it reminds me that I've faced ADHD challenges before and come out stronger.[237]

INTUITION: THE ABILITY TO READ BETWEEN THE LINES

We often have heightened emotional sensitivity, which can translate into deep intuition. We pick up on micro expressions, shifts in tone, and unspoken emotions, making us excellent at reading people. Research suggests that ADHD brains may process emotions more intensely due to differences in dopamine regulation.[238]

---

235 Hupfeld et al., "Living 'in the Zone.'"

236 Barkley, ed., *Attention-Deficit Hyperactivity Disorder.*

237 Shona L. Falon et al., "A Clustered-Randomized Controlled Trial of a Self-Reflection Resilience-Strengthening Intervention and Novel Mediators," *Journal of Occupational Health Psychology* 26, no. 1 (2021): 1–19, https://doi.org/10.1037/ocp0000268.

238 Dodson, "How ADHD Ignites RSD."

Example: Camille always sensed when her friends were struggling, even before they said anything. This skill made her an incredible therapist, where her ability to tune into others' emotions helped her build deep, meaningful connections.

Reframe: Trust Your Gut. If you're in a situation where something feels off, don't dismiss it as overthinking. Your ADHD brain is wired to notice patterns that others miss. I've learned to trust my intuition when working with clients, often picking up on unspoken struggles that they haven't articulated yet.

ADAPTABILITY: THE MASTER OF PIVOTING

Life rarely goes as planned, and we with ADHD are particularly skilled at thinking on our feet. Because we are used to handling forgotten tasks, last-minute changes, and shifting priorities, we develop a high tolerance for unpredictability.[239]

Example: When her carefully planned wedding day was thrown into chaos by bad weather, Lauren didn't panic. She problem-solved on the spot, turning a potential disaster into a cozy, intimate indoor celebration. Her ability to adapt made the day even more special.

Reframe: The Power of Unpredictability. Instead of seeing unpredictability as a problem, view it as an opportunity to be resourceful. Keep backup plans, but also trust that your ability to adjust in the moment is one of your greatest strengths. I've found that my own adaptability has allowed me to navigate career changes, relationship challenges, and business pivots that would have overwhelmed me if I'd expected perfect execution.[240]

---

239 Brown, "ADD/ADHD and Impaired Executive Function in Clinical Practice."

240 Carl Folke et al., "Resilience Thinking: Integrating Resilience, Adaptability and Transformability," *Ecology and Society* 15, no. 4 (2010): article 20, https://doi.org/10.5751/ES-03610-150420.

PATTERN RECOGNITION: THE BRAIN THAT SEES WHAT OTHERS MISS

Our brains are often exceptional at spotting connections and trends that others overlook. Whether it's recognising emerging business opportunities, understanding how different concepts intersect, or noticing shifts in social dynamics, our minds excel at finding patterns.[241]

Example: Olivia, a financial analyst, struggled with standard accounting tasks but had an uncanny ability to predict market trends. She leveraged this strength to move into investment analysis, where her pattern recognition skills gave her an edge over her peers.

Reframe: Connect the Dots. Keep a journal of insights that come to you unexpectedly, whether it's a business idea, a social dynamic, or a creative breakthrough. Your ability to connect the dots is invaluable. I keep a voice memo app handy for those moments when my ADHD brain spots a pattern or connection that I might otherwise forget.[242]

HOW TO REWRITE YOUR PERSONAL SUCCESS METRICS TO ALIGN WITH ADHD

For many of us with ADHD, our success has long been measured against neurotypical standards: consistency, organisation, and the ability to methodically work toward long-term goals. We were praised when we followed routines, met deadlines, and stayed on top of responsibilities without needing external accountability.

But for our ADHD brains that thrive on novelty, urgency, and passion, these definitions of success can feel like an impossible standard.

From an early age, we internalised the idea that our worth was tied to productivity. The straight A student who pulled all-nighters. The

---

[241] Bruce E. Wexler and Ryan Kish, "Using Micro-Cognition Biomarkers of Neurosystem Dysfunction to Redefine ADHD Subtypes: A Scalable Digital Path to Diagnosis Based on Brain Function," *Psychiatry Research* 326 (August 2023): article 115348, https://doi.org/10.1016/j.psychres.2023.115348.

[242] Anvita Bhardwaj and Hailey Ziegelhofer, "Alternative Therapies for Mood Enhancement: Is Laughter Truly the Best Medicine?," *Undergraduate Journal of Psychology at Berkeley* 62 (2015): 62, https://www.researchgate.net/publication/292137100_Alternative_Therapies_for_Mood_Enhancement_Is_Laughter_Truly_the_Best_Medicine.

entrepreneur who burned out trying to keep up with neurotypical peers. The mother who felt like a failure for struggling to keep the house in order. These stories are common among us ADHD women. We try to measure up, only to find ourselves overwhelmed, exhausted, and convinced that we're failing.

But what if the problem isn't us? What if the issue is the definition of success we've been given?

Rather than forcing ourselves into a neurotypical mould, we need to redefine success in a way that actually works for our brains. That means shifting away from rigid, linear expectations and toward an approach that values flexibility, creativity, and progress over perfection.

Let's look at some common ADHD struggles and how we can reframe our success metrics.

REFRAMING PRODUCTIVITY: SUCCESS IS IMPACT, NOT HOURS WORKED

Old Metric: "I must be productive every day to be successful."

ADHD Reframe: "My success is measured by the impact of my work, not how many hours I clock."

People with ADHD often have "burst productivity," where we hyperfocus and accomplish an immense amount in a short period, only to crash later. Instead of measuring success by a traditional nine-to-five workday, we can acknowledge that our energy fluctuates and plan around our strengths.

Research by Dr. William Dodson explains that our ADHD brains operate on an interest-based nervous system, meaning we thrive when tasks are engaging or urgent.[243] I've noticed that I can write ten thousand words in one sitting when inspired but struggle to write one hundred words when forcing myself on a schedule. By embracing this, we can create systems that lean into our strengths rather than fighting them.

---

243 William Dodson, "How ADHD Shapes Your Perceptions, Emotions & Motivation," webinar, ADDitude Magazine, June 6, 2022, https://www.additudemag.com/webinar/adhd-symptoms-emotions-motivation/.

REFRAMING CONSISTENCY: SUCCESS IS ADAPTABILITY, NOT RIGID ROUTINE

Old Metric: "If I can't stick to a routine, I'm failing."

ADHD Reframe: "Flexibility is a strength. My success comes from adapting, not forcing structure that doesn't work for me."

ADHD brains resist monotony. Instead of beating ourselves up for failing at strict schedules, we can build dynamic routines that allow variety. For example, instead of "I will work out every morning at six," we might set a goal like "I will move my body in a way that feels good three times a week." We'll dig more into this later.

Studies show that ADHD brains struggle with habit formation due to lower dopamine levels in the prefrontal cortex.[244] This means traditional habit-building techniques may not work for us. Instead, using novelty (changing up workouts), external accountability (workout buddies), and immediate rewards (a fun playlist) can make routines more sustainable. I've applied this in my own life by creating a "fitness menu" rather than a rigid workout schedule.

REFRAMING FOCUS: SUCCESS IS PROGRESS, NOT PERFECTION

Old Metric: "If I don't finish everything I start, I've failed."

ADHD Reframe: "Every step forward counts. Completion isn't the only marker of success."

Many of us struggle with task initiation and completion. We may start projects with enthusiasm, only to abandon them when boredom sets in. Instead of viewing this as failure, we can recognise that not all tasks need to be finished. Sometimes, starting something is valuable in itself.

Executive function challenges impact our ability to prioritise and complete tasks. Instead of fighting this, we can create strategies like "body doubling" (working alongside someone), using timers, or breaking tasks into smaller chunks. I've found that pairing tasks with something

---

[244] Barkley, ed., *Attention-Deficit Hyperactivity Disorder*.

rewarding, like listening to my favourite podcast while cleaning, makes initiation and follow-through much easier.[245]

REFRAMING TIME MANAGEMENT: SUCCESS IS AWARENESS, NOT PERFECT PUNCTUALITY

Old Metric: "I'm always late, so I'm unreliable."

ADHD Reframe: "Time blindness is real, but I can set myself up for success with tools and strategies."

ADHD time blindness makes it difficult to estimate how long tasks will take or to recognise the passage of time. Instead of labelling ourselves as unreliable, we can acknowledge this as an ADHD trait and use tools to support ourselves, like visual timers, alarms, or planned "transition time" between activities.

Time perception differences in ADHD are linked to deficits in the brain's dopaminergic system.[246] Recognising that time management is a skill, not a moral failing, allows us to seek out strategies that work for us. I've started setting all my appointments fifteen minutes earlier in my calendar than they actually are, which has dramatically reduced my lateness.

BREAKING FREE FROM ALL-OR-NOTHING THINKING

A major ADHD trap is all-or-nothing thinking. Our brains default to absolutes:

- I always mess things up.
- I'm never going to catch up.
- I'll never be successful.

These blanket statements feel real in the moment but aren't objec-

---

[245] Barkley, *Executive Functions*; and Brown, *A New Understanding of ADHD in Children and Adults*.

[246] Brown, "ADD/ADHD and Impaired Executive Function in Clinical Practice."

tively true. This is where a key reframe comes in: "Big T" Truths versus "little t" truths.

In coaching, I use this concept to challenge limiting beliefs. Some things are Big T Truths. They are indisputable, like the law of gravity. Other things are little t truths. They feel true but are actually perceptions, not facts.

For example, "I am always late." Is that a Big T Truth? Have you never once arrived on time? Or does it just feel true because ADHD makes time management harder? When we pause to examine these kinds of automatic thoughts, we can start to break the mental loops that reinforce shame and comparison.

This concept is especially helpful for ADHD women because we're more vulnerable to black-and-white thinking. If something doesn't feel 100 percent successful, we often label it as a failure. That leaves us constantly falling short in our own minds, especially when we compare ourselves to others who seem more consistent or capable. Little t truths often grow out of those comparisons. We assume other people are handling things better, and we start to believe something is wrong with us.

By challenging little t truths, we can replace those distorted beliefs with more accurate and self-compassionate ones. Instead of "I never finish anything," we might say, "I struggle with follow-through sometimes, but I've also finished plenty of things that matter." To support that new thought, I ask clients to track real examples. Even small completions count. This kind of evidence helps retrain the brain and gives us something solid to come back to when self-doubt creeps in.

MANTRAS AND MINDSET SHIFTS

Earlier in this book, I shared two mantras I live by, though it took me time to fully embrace them. I've also added a third bonus mantra that I'm still working on. Changing the way we talk to ourselves is one of the most powerful tools we have. Here are three mantras I regularly teach in my coaching practise:

What you think of me is none of my business. We often compare ourselves to neurotypical expectations, but their metrics don't apply to us.

Progress over perfection. Small, imperfect steps forward are better than being paralysed by an impossible standard.

And the bonus mantra:

Comparison is the thief of joy. The only person you need to measure yourself against is the you from yesterday.

I've found that mantras work better for ADHD brains when paired with visual reminders. I have these phrases as lock screens, sticky notes, and desktop wallpapers. Multiple modalities help reinforce the mindset shifts when our attention wanders.

BREAKING FREE FROM SOCIAL MEDIA COMPARISON AND ADHD GUILT SPIRALS

We've all been there: mindlessly scrolling through social media, seeing images of spotless homes, perfectly curated family moments, and hyper-productive entrepreneurs. A simple glance at someone else's "highlight reel" can trigger an instant wave of comparison and shame. For our ADHD brains, this spiral hits even harder.

ADHD women are especially vulnerable to comparison traps. Research shows that social media delivers fast dopamine hits but is also linked to addictive use and lower self-esteem.[247] For ADHD brains, this cycle reinforces feelings of inadequacy, especially when we see others effortlessly managing life while we struggle with basic routines.[248]

And then comes the guilt cycle:

1. We compare ourselves to others and feel inadequate.
2. That feeling of failure leads to overwhelm and avoidance.
3. Avoidance leads to procrastination.
4. We feel guilty for not "doing better" and start the cycle all over again.

---

[247] Ofir Turel and Antoine Bechara, "Social Networking Site Use While Driving: ADHD and the Mediating Roles of Stress, Self-Esteem and Craving," *Frontiers in Psychology* 7 (2016): article 455, https://doi.org/10.3389/fpsyg.2016.00455.

[248] Julie Hall, "The Role of Social Media on Attention Deficit/Hyperactivity Disorder, Self-Esteem Imposter Phenomenon, and Identity Distress" (master's thesis, University of Central Florida, 2025), https://stars.library.ucf.edu/etd2024/1214.

Social media turns into a self-inflicted emotional roller coaster where our self-worth becomes tied to unrealistic, curated online personas.

Here are real examples of how social media fuels ADHD guilt spirals.

Aimee, a late-diagnosed mom I spoke to, felt like a failure every time she saw perfectly put-together moms on Instagram. She struggled with executive dysfunction and emotional dysregulation, making household management feel impossible. The guilt from comparing herself to neurotypical moms left her feeling inadequate.

During our call, I asked her to look closely at one mom influencer she followed. "Notice how she never shows the mess, the tantrums, the forgotten permission slips," I pointed out. Aimee realised she was comparing her unfiltered reality to someone else's carefully crafted image.

Melanie, an entrepreneur, followed high-achieving business influencers who seemed effortlessly organised. She hyperfocused on their success, then spiralled into shame when she forgot to respond to emails or missed deadlines. The comparison made her doubt her ability to run a business.

We worked together to identify her unique business strengths: creativity, passion, and ability to connect deeply with clients. These qualities were invisible on social media but invaluable in real life.

Madison, a high achiever, was always praised for being put together. But she confessed during our Zoom call that she arrived an hour early to work just to compensate for her chronic forgetfulness. Watching productivity gurus on social media made her feel like she was barely keeping up, even though others admired her organisation.

For ADHD brains, this comparison cycle is more than just insecurity. It's tied to real neurobiological challenges. The research shows why it happens:

- **Dopamine Dysregulation and Social Media Addiction:** Our ADHD brains have lower baseline dopamine levels, making us more likely to seek external validation.[249] Social media provides an easy dopamine hit, but it also reinforces our insecurities.

---

249 Volkow et al., "Evaluating Dopamine Reward Pathway in ADHD."

- **Rejection Sensitivity Dysphoria (RSD):** ADHD individuals experience perceived rejection and criticism more intensely than neurotypicals.[250] Seeing "better" versions of people online can feel like personal proof that we are failing.
- **The Not Enough Narrative:** ADHD women struggle with internalised self-doubt and perfectionism.[251] The curated nature of social media only amplifies these feelings.

I've noticed that RSD affects how my clients engage with social media in unique ways. Many report becoming fixated on a single negative comment while ignoring dozens of positive ones. I encourage them to practise "social media distancing" by physically putting down their phones and walking away when they notice comparison thoughts arising.

I've also found that many of my clients use social media as a form of "productive procrastination." We convince ourselves we're gathering information or inspiration, but we're actually triggering comparison and avoidance. Setting app timers and creating intentional social media breaks can help interrupt this cycle before it spirals.

Understanding that this is not a personal failing but a neurological reality is the first step toward breaking free from this toxic cycle.

BREAKING THE SOCIAL MEDIA CYCLE

How do we stop this destructive cycle? We can't eliminate social media, but we can change how we interact with it.

Reframe Comparison

Instead of seeing social media as proof that others are "doing life better," remind yourself this is a highlight reel, not reality. No one posts their meltdowns, their executive dysfunction, or their struggles with guilt.

---

250 Shaw et al., "Emotion Dysregulation in Attention Deficit Hyperactivity Disorder."

251 Madhoo and Quinn, "A Review of Attention Deficit/Hyperactivity Disorder in Women and Girls."

In my coaching sessions, I often ask clients to imagine what the "behind the scenes" of a perfect post might look like. That immaculate workspace probably has a pile of clutter just outside the camera frame. That mom who seems to have it all together might have cried in her car this morning.

Curate Your Feed Intentionally

If certain accounts make you feel like you're failing, mute or unfollow them. Instead, follow ADHD-friendly accounts that celebrate neurodivergence and self-acceptance.

I did a complete social media audit last year and was shocked to realise how many accounts I followed regularly triggered my feelings of inadequacy. Replacing them with ADHD-affirming content transformed my online experience.

Engage with Purpose

Before opening an app, ask yourself, *Why am I here?* If the answer is boredom or self-soothing, consider a different dopamine-friendly activity like listening to music, doodling, or moving your body.

I've started keeping a list of "dopamine alternatives" on my phone so when I catch myself reaching for social media out of habit, I have quick alternatives that don't lead down the comparison rabbit hole.

Self-Compassion over Perfection

Instead of feeling guilty for not keeping up, remind yourself that your brain is wired differently. ADHD-friendly strategies work with our neurodivergence, not in spite of it.

I've found that creating a "comparison interrupter" helps many of my clients. When they notice comparison thoughts, they have a prepared statement to repeat: "This is my ADHD brain seeking dopamine through comparison. I can redirect this energy." Having this specific language ready short-circuits the shame spiral before it gains momentum.[252]

SHIFTING THE NARRATIVE

ADHD brains don't thrive under impossible standards. We thrive under acceptance and alignment with our strengths.

Instead of measuring success by neurotypical standards, ask yourself:

- What small wins did I achieve today?
- How can I define productivity in a way that works for my ADHD brain?
- Am I using social media for connection, or am I using it to shame myself?

Social media doesn't reflect real life, and we ADHD women are not behind; we are simply wired differently. The more we embrace our differences, the more we free ourselves from the weight of comparison and guilt.

In my own journey, I've learned that my worth isn't measured by how neurotypical I appear online. It's measured by how authentically I live in a way that honours my ADHD brain.

And that's something no Instagram filter can capture.

---

[252] Nora D. Volkow et al., "Evaluating Dopamine Reward Pathway in ADHD: Clinical Implications," *JAMA* 302, no. 10 (2009): 1084–91, https://doi.org/10.1001/jama.2009.1308.

SELF-COACHING EXERCISES: LETTING GO OF COMPARISON

Comparison can pull you away from your own progress and make your wins feel invisible. When you measure yourself against others, you risk ignoring the ways your ADHD brain helps you succeed. This exercise is about shifting that focus back to your unique strengths and redefining success in ways that feel meaningful for you.

REFRAMING OUR ADHD STRENGTHS

If you've spent years focusing on your struggles, it can be hard to shift your mindset to see your strengths. Here are three ways to start:

- **Flip the Narrative:** Instead of saying, "I get distracted easily," say, "I notice things that others miss." Instead of "I can't sit still," say, "I have a high energy level that keeps me engaged."
- **Ask Others:** Sometimes we don't see our own strengths. Ask close friends or colleagues what they think you excel at. You might be surprised.
- **Keep a Wins List:** Every day, write down one way your ADHD brain helped you. Whether it was solving a problem quickly, making someone laugh, or thinking of a creative idea, celebrate it.

What hidden strength will you start embracing today?

MEASURING SUCCESS ON YOUR TERMS

Rather than aiming for unrealistic ideals, create personal success metrics that align with our ADHD strengths. Here are a few examples of ADHD-friendly ways to define success:

- **Engagement over Endurance:** Success is feeling excited about what I'm doing, even if I don't work on it every day.
- **Progress over Perfection:** Success is moving forward, even if the steps are small.

- **Flexibility over Rigidity:** Success is adjusting when needed rather than forcing an unworkable system.
- **Energy Management over Time Management:** Success is knowing when to push forward and when to rest.
- **Authenticity over Compliance:** Success is creating a life that works for my brain, not one that just "looks good" to others.

Chapter Eleven

Create a Thriving Life That Works for You

CHAPTER TEN FOCUSED ON SHIFTING MINDSETS, ESPECIALLY around productivity and comparison, so you can see your ADHD strengths and redefine success on your terms. This chapter is about taking that insight and turning it into action. We'll focus on concrete, ADHD-specific strategies that replace traditional productivity advice with systems designed for your brain.

We'll talk about what makes follow-through hard, why motivation comes in waves, and how perfectionism and shame often hijack our systems before they have a chance to work. You will learn how to build a structure that fits the way your brain works, not one that constantly makes you feel like you are behind.

The focus isn't on output. It's on finding peace in your process.

Earlier, I mentioned how a few years ago I hired a business coach because I was desperate for help with structure and accountability.

Every week, he would assign tasks, and every single week I'd promise myself: *This time will be different. This time I'll actually get the homework done ahead of schedule.* Yet without fail, an hour before our call, I'd be in a cold sweat, frantically trying to finish assignments I'd had the entire week to complete.

What made it worse was that I genuinely cared about my goals. I wanted to succeed. So why couldn't I just do the work? Was I really that lazy? That undisciplined? Those questions haunted me for years.

It wasn't until I understood my ADHD brain that I realised what was happening. Traditional goal frameworks simply aren't built for how our minds operate.

In this chapter, we will look at why traditional goal frameworks often fail ADHD brains and explore alternatives that work with our wiring instead of against it. You will learn how to adapt goals so they feel doable, how to harness interest-based motivation, how to design flexible systems that support follow-through, and how to communicate your needs so you can maintain progress. We will also cover practical tools like the HARD goals approach, dopamine-friendly planning, and accountability strategies that make success more sustainable.

SMART GOALS ARE NOT SO SMART FOR ADHD

Most advice on goal setting revolves around SMART goals: specific, measurable, achievable, relevant, and time-bound. This makes perfect sense on paper. Structure, clear milestones, and accountability should theoretically make goals easier to accomplish.[253]

But for those of us with ADHD, SMART goals often leave us feeling worse than when we started. My own experience with this was painful and confusing before my diagnosis.

We need urgency, novelty, and flexibility, elements that SMART goals rarely accommodate. When I talk with ADHD coaching clients now, almost all of them describe some version of this same experience: feeling stuck despite caring deeply, procrastinating until panic sets in, and abandoning projects after hitting the first obstacle.

---

[253] George T. Doran, "There's a S.M.A.R.T. Way to Write Management's Goals and Objectives," *Management Review* 70, no. 11 (1981): 35–36, https://www.scirp.org/reference/ReferencesPapers?ReferenceID=1459599.

Our brains are wired differently, not deficiently. When we struggle with traditional goal-setting methods, it's not because we're failing but because the methods weren't designed with our neurology in mind.[254] After talking with hundreds of women with ADHD and diving into the research, I've seen several factors that make traditional goal setting particularly challenging for us:

- **Rigidity and Overwhelm:** SMART goals feel like putting on a straitjacket when our brains crave movement and adaptation. "Body doubling" introduces the flexibility we need to actually complete tasks.[255]
- **Executive Dysfunction:** Barkley's work shows that ADHD fundamentally impacts planning, organisation, and task completion.[256] It isn't a matter of preference. Our brains actively fight against structure.
- **Time Blindness:** My clients often say time feels entirely different to them. As Brown describes it, we experience time in a nonlinear way, making those "time-bound" deadlines almost meaningless until they're dangerously close.[257]
- **Dopamine Dependency:** Our brains are wired to respond more strongly to immediate rewards than distant ones. Studies show that delaying rewards diminishes dopamine responses and increases sensitivity to the costs of waiting, making long-term goals harder to sustain.[258]
- **Perfectionism and Rejection Sensitivity:** Many of us have been

---

[254] Katya Rubia, "Cognitive Neuroscience of Attention Deficit Hyperactivity Disorder (ADHD) and Its Clinical Translation," *Frontiers in Human Neuroscience* 12 (2018), https://doi.org/10.3389/fnhum.2018.00100.

[255] Tessa Eagle et al., "Proposing Body Doubling as a Continuum of Space/Time and Mutuality: An Investigation with Neurodivergent Participants," *Assets* (October 2023): 1–4, https://doi.org/10.1145/3597638.3614486.

[256] Russell A. Barkley, "The Important Role of Executive Functioning and Self-Regulation in ADHD," fact sheet, accessed October 21, 2025, https://russellbarkley.org/factsheets/ADHD_EF_and_SR.pdf.

[257] Brown, *Smart but Stuck*.

[258] Alexander Soutschek and Philippe N. Tobler, "A Process Model Account of the Role of Dopamine in Intertemporal Choice," *Neuroscience* (March 8, 2023), https://doi.org/10.7554/eLife.83734; Shunsuke Kobayashi and Wolfram Schultz, "Influence of Reward Delays on Responses of Dopamine Neurons," *The Journal of Neuroscience* 28, no. 31 (2008): 7837–46, https://doi.org/10.1523/JNEUROSCI.1600-08.2008; and Zilong Gao et al., "The Neural Basis of Delayed Gratification," *Science Advances* 7, no. 49 (2021), https://doi.org/10.1126/sciadv.abg6611.

criercised so often that we develop an intense fear of failure. One setback can trigger complete abandonment of a goal.[259]
- **Lack of Flexibility:** Lucina Uddin notes that people with ADHD often thrive with adaptable structures.[260] When a system doesn't bend, we break away from it entirely.

THE ADHD-FRIENDLY ALTERNATIVE: HARD GOALS

After years of bending myself to follow rules that weren't built for me, I've found that a completely different approach works better.

Rather than SMART goals, I recommend what I call HARD goals to my ADHD clients:

- **Heartfelt:** The goal must connect emotionally and personally. I had a client who struggled with exercise until she realised she genuinely loved dance. Once her fitness goals involved dance classes instead of dreaded gym sessions, everything changed.
- **Animated:** It should feel alive and engaging. Static goals on paper rarely motivate us. Goals that evolve, surprise us, or involve other people tend to maintain our interest.
- **Realistic:** The goal needs to account for ADHD challenges. A client once told me, "I finally realised setting a goal to meditate for thirty minutes daily when I can barely sit still for five was setting myself up to fail."
- **Doable:** Steps should be smaller than you think necessary, with room to adjust when hyperfocus or distraction inevitably occurs.[261]

For example, using a SMART goal, you might say, "I will go to the gym three times a week for forty-five minutes."

---

259 Philip Asherson et al., "Under Diagnosis of Adult ADHD: Cultural Influences and Societal Burden," supplement, *Journal of Attention Disorders* 16, no. 5 (2012): 20S–38S, https://doi.org/10.1177/1087054711435360.

260 Lucina Q. Uddin, "Cognitive and Behavioural Flexibility: Neural Mechanisms and Clinical Considerations," *Nature Reviews Neuroscience* 22, no. 3 (2021): 167–79, https://doi.org/10.1038/s41583-021-00428-w.

261 Rubia, "Cognitive Neuroscience of Attention Deficit Hyperactivity Disorder (ADHD) and Its Clinical Translation."

A HARD goal for the same purpose might look like this: "I will move my body in ways that feel good three times a week, whether that's dancing while cooking dinner, taking a walk with my favourite podcast, or joining a class that looks fun. I'll track which activities give me the biggest mood boost."

The second approach still encourages consistent movement but acknowledges the reality of ADHD motivation. It builds in flexibility, follows interest, and incorporates self-compassion, all crucial elements for our neurotype.

MAKING ADHD GOALS WORK

Through both research and personal experience (including many spectacular failures), I've found these strategies make the biggest difference:

- **Connect to What Actually Matters to You:** I spent years setting goals I thought I "should" have rather than ones I genuinely cared about. When I finally aligned my goals with my passions, everything shifted. For example, I struggled to establish a reading habit until I gave myself permission to read graphic novels and sci-fi instead of the business books I thought I "should" be reading.
- **Make Steps Comically Small:** I cannot emphasise this enough. The steps that seem reasonable to neurotypical brains are often overwhelming for us. One of my clients was paralysed by a messy house until we broke down "clean the kitchen" to "put away three items." Just three. That tiny win created momentum.
- **Find Your People:** External accountability changes everything for ADHD brains. I have an accountability partner, and we meet biweekly. Since starting this routine, my productivity has quadrupled. Something about knowing someone else is working alongside me bypasses my executive function struggles in a way nothing else can.
- **Build Flexible Systems:** Hard deadlines often trigger either avoidance or last-minute panic. Instead, I've started setting "commitment windows," like "I'll work on this project for three twenty-five-minute

sessions this week and see where I get." The flexibility reduces the threat response that rigid schedules trigger.
- **Celebrate Literally Everything:** Our ADHD brains need more frequent dopamine hits. I keep dark chocolate at my desk as a tiny reward for completing difficult tasks. A client of mine has a "victory dance" she does after sending emails she's been avoiding. These small celebrations build momentum.

HOW TO LEVERAGE INTEREST-BASED MOTIVATION INSTEAD OF FORCING PRODUCTIVITY

Have you ever sat down to work on an important deadline, everything organised and ready to go, only to find yourself staring blankly at the screen or finding literally anything else to do? Meanwhile, that same week, you probably spent hours absorbed in a new hobby—maybe exploring gardening tips for beginners, planning your dream kitchen remodel, or perfecting gluten-free baking recipes—without even noticing how quickly the hours flew by?

This inconsistency used to make me hate myself. Why couldn't I just focus on what mattered? The question tormented me until I understood that ADHD motivation isn't broken. It's just fundamentally different.

If you've ever had someone tell you to "just try harder" or "just focus," you know how useless that advice is. For our ADHD brains, motivation isn't about willpower. It's about dopamine.

People without ADHD can generally summon steady motivation through routine and external rewards. Their brains respond predictably to importance.

Ours don't.

Instead, our motivation is wildly inconsistent, either fully activated or completely absent. This isn't a character flaw; it's neurobiology.

The science behind this is fascinating. Research shows our ADHD brains have lower baseline dopamine levels and different dopamine processing.[262]

---

[262] Volkow et al., "Evaluating Dopamine Reward Pathway in ADHD."

This makes mundane tasks feel physically painful to start, while high-interest activities feel effortless. As Dr. William Dodson explained, ADHD motivation is driven by interest, challenge, novelty, or urgency—not importance. This explains why we might procrastinate on a career-changing opportunity while spending hours organising our spice rack when the mood strikes.

I've spent the last two years collecting stories from women with ADHD, and they're remarkably consistent:

Jess, a marketing executive, told me, "Last month I deep cleaned my entire apartment in one night because a friend mentioned they *might* stop by. But the report that could determine my promotion? I've been staring at it for weeks, unable to start despite knowing how important it is."

Joanne shared, "I can create an entire curriculum over a weekend when I'm excited about a topic. But grading papers? I'll literally do the dishes to avoid it—and I *hate* doing dishes."

Nicole confessed, "My brain simply doesn't register boring tasks. They're like invisible items on my to-do list, no matter how many reminders I set."

I've experienced this countless times. The tasks I procrastinate doing aren't necessarily difficult or time-consuming—they're just not intrinsically interesting to my brain. Understanding this was the first step toward building systems that actually work.

REFRAMING PRODUCTIVITY FOR OUR ADHD BRAINS

After years of trying to force my ADHD brain into productivity methods that just didn't fit, I finally had an aha moment: What if I started working *with* my brain, instead of constantly fighting against it?

I stopped thinking of productivity as pushing myself to do things I dreaded and started creating environments and routines my brain naturally wanted to engage with. Here are some key mindset shifts that made a huge difference:

- **From Discipline to Curiosity:** Instead of beating myself up whenever

I procrastinated, I got curious. I'd ask myself, "What could I tweak to make this task feel easier or more interesting to my brain right now?"

- **From Rigid Schedules to Flexible Structures:** I finally let go of the myth that I should be productive at the same pace all day long. Instead, I embraced my natural rhythm—intense bursts of focus followed by intentional breaks. This flexibility allowed me to recharge instead of burning out.
- **From Self-Criticism to Self-Accommodation:** Rather than labelling myself as lazy or unmotivated, I started experimenting with my environment and routines. I gently asked myself, "Under what conditions do I genuinely feel motivated to start this task?" and then I created those conditions whenever possible.

Remember, motivation with ADHD isn't about forcing yourself. It's about crafting a supportive environment where your unique brain can thrive.

THE POWER OF SELF-ACCOMMODATION: DESIGNING LIFE AROUND YOUR ADHD NEEDS

One of the most damaging myths we internalise is that accommodating our ADHD needs means "giving up" or "making excuses." Nothing could be further from the truth.

Self-accommodation is an act of self-respect and wisdom. It's saying, "I understand how my brain works, and I'm going to create conditions where I can thrive instead of constantly fighting against my neurology."

You might have heard the word "accommodation" in a school or workplace context—things like extra time on tests or using noise-cancelling headphones. This is the same idea, but you're applying it to your life. Think of it less as special treatment and more as creating a life that matches how your brain works rather than trying to bend to systems that don't fit.

When I stopped forcing myself to use written to-do lists (which I inevitably lost or ignored) and switched to visual reminders and phone alerts, my productivity improved dramatically. I wasn't lowering my standards. I was finally using tools that actually worked for my brain.

A powerful reframe that helped me: Instead of thinking, "I need to get better at following schedules," I started asking, "How can I create a workflow that actually supports how my brain naturally operates?"

Self-accommodation isn't lowering standards. It's creating a more appropriate measuring stick. When we design our lives around our neurological wiring instead of against it, we can often exceed expectations rather than constantly falling short of inappropriate ones.

The practical benefits of self-accommodation are clear: increased productivity, reduced stress, and more consistent results. But the emotional impact can be even more profound.

When we stop fighting our brains and start supporting them, shame begins to dissolve. We realise that we're not broken. We're just different.

And different doesn't mean deficient.

I remember the first time I used noise-cancelling headphones in a coffee shop instead of forcing myself to "just focus" amid the distractions. Not only did I get more done, but I also felt a profound sense of self-acceptance. I was finally treating myself with the same kindness I would show anyone else with different needs.

Through years of working with adults with ADHD and experimenting myself, I've found the following strategies consistently helpful.

DITCH THE PLANNER; BUILD A DOPAMINE-FUELLED WORKFLOW

I've watched countless clients abandon planner after planner, each time feeling like a personal failure. The truth is, many traditional planning systems just don't work for our visual, nonlinear ADHD brains.

Instead, try these:

- **Create Visual Workflows:** Use whiteboards or sticky notes that you can actually see (out of sight truly means out of mind for us).

- **Use Apps Like Todoist or Google Keep:** These apps send reminders and don't require you to remember to check them.
- **Build "If-Then" Triggers:** "If I finish responding to these emails, then I get to spend ten minutes on Instagram."

One client transformed her productivity by creating a "done list" instead of a to-do list. Seeing everything she'd accomplished each day, rather than focusing on what she hadn't done, changed her entire relationship with productivity.

TIME BLINDNESS HACKS: MAKING TIME "VISIBLE"

Time blindness—the inability to sense the passage of time—is one of the most debilitating aspects of ADHD. I can't tell you how many times I've looked up from an interesting task to realise three hours had passed when it felt like twenty minutes.

Strategies that help:

- **Use Visual Timers:** Timer apps show time disappearing in a colourful display.
- **Rely on External Transition Cues:** "When this playlist ends, it's time to start getting ready to leave."
- **Build in Buffer Time:** I always add 50 percent more time than I think I'll need for tasks.

A client who constantly ran late for meetings started setting two alarms—one labelled "start wrapping up" and another called "leave now." This simple accommodation transformed her punctuality without requiring her to magically develop a better time sense.

INTEREST-BASED MOTIVATION: LEVERAGING DOPAMINE

Instead of fighting against our dopamine-driven brains, we can work with them:

- **Pair Boring Tasks with Engaging Inputs:** For example, listen to an audiobook while doing dishes.
- **Gamify Mundane Responsibilities:** Apps like Habitica turn chores into role-playing games.
- **Use Body Doubling:** Help solo tasks feel social and accountable.

One surprising strategy that's worked for me: creating artificial challenges. When filing tax paperwork felt impossible, I challenged myself to get everything sorted in fifteen-minute "sprints" with short breaks. The time constraint turned an overwhelming task into a manageable game.

ENERGY-DRIVEN SCHEDULING: WORKING WITH YOUR ADHD RHYTHMS

The nine-to-five workday rarely aligns with ADHD energy patterns. I've found it far more effective to track when I naturally have the most focus and creativity and then schedule demanding tasks during those windows.

This might mean:

- Doing creative work late at night if that's when your brain comes alive.
- Planning for "low executive function" periods with tasks that require less decision-making.
- Embracing hyperfocus when it arrives, even if it means temporarily rearranging your schedule.

I have a client who realised she has about ninety minutes of clear-headed focus in the morning, followed by a significant slump until late afternoon, when her energy returns. Instead of fighting this pattern, she now schedules her most demanding work during those peak times and uses the slump periods for meetings or simpler tasks.

OUTSOURCE, AUTOMATE, AND ELIMINATE

One of the most powerful forms of self-accommodation is recognising that we don't have to do everything ourselves. If certain tasks consistently drain your energy or trigger overwhelm, consider:

- **Outsourcing:** Meal kit services, virtual assistants, housekeeping help.
- **Automating:** Bill payments, subscription deliveries for essentials.
- **Eliminating:** Ruthlessly questioning which tasks are actually necessary.

One woman I spoke with had struggled for years with grocery shopping until she finally gave herself permission to use a delivery service. The mental energy she saved turned out to be far more valuable than the delivery fee.

Imagine what your life would look like if you stopped forcing yourself into systems that were never designed for your brain. If you stopped attempting to function like everyone else and instead created structures that honoured your unique neurology.

You don't have to follow a morning routine to be successful. You don't have to use a planner if it doesn't work for you.

You don't have to fit into neurotypical boxes to thrive. In fact, it's those very boxes that can feel suffocating.

The real power of self-accommodation isn't just increased productivity. It's the freedom that comes from aligning your life with who you actually are rather than who you think you "should" be.

I now regularly remind myself it's time to stop fighting and start intentionally designing a life that genuinely works for me, and I hope these pages have inspired you to do the same.

In that permission, true success begins.

HOW TO COMMUNICATE YOUR NEEDS TO FAMILY, FRIENDS, AND COLLEAGUES

Sheryl, a woman I met through my interviews, described struggling through an uncomfortable conversation with her partner about missed deadlines and forgotten promises. His frustration was visible as he said, "But this was important. Why couldn't you just remember?" She felt that familiar knot in her stomach: a mixture of shame, defensiveness, and the frustration of not knowing how to explain her brain without sounding like she was making excuses.

If you've lived with ADHD, you've likely experienced similar moments—trying to explain why you were late again, why a "simple" task remained undone, or why you needed accommodations that others didn't seem to require.

These conversations are particularly difficult because:

- We often lack the language to describe our internal experiences.
- We carry the weight of past misunderstandings and criticism.
- We fear being perceived as making excuses or avoiding responsibility.
- We've internalised shame about our differences.

My own journey with these conversations has been messy and imperfect. I've had tearful breakdowns trying to explain why I missed important deadlines despite genuinely caring. I've struggled to request accommodations at work without feeling unprofessional, and I've even lost friendships because I couldn't clearly communicate why certain environments were overwhelming for me.

Research explains why these conversations can be so challenging. ADHD affects multiple aspects of communication, including working memory (making it hard to remember our points), emotional regulation (making feedback feel threatening), and impulsivity (leading to defensive responses).[263] This creates a perfect storm when we're trying to advocate for ourselves, especially when we're already feeling vulnerable.

---

[263] Barkley, ed., *Attention-Deficit Hyperactivity Disorder*.

Understanding the neurological basis for our communication challenges can help us be more patient with ourselves and develop better strategies. Those of us with ADHD often struggle with:

- **Word Retrieval Issues:** ADHD affects our ability to quickly access the right words, especially under pressure.[264] This is why writing out key points before important conversations can be helpful.
- **Emotional Dysregulation:** We may react more strongly to perceived criticism, making it harder to stay calm during difficult conversations.[265]
- **Working Memory Limitations:** We might forget important points mid-conversation or struggle to follow long explanations.[266]
- **Nonlinear Communication Style:** Many of us communicate in a "bottom-up" way (sharing details before the main point), which can confuse linear thinkers.[267]

Understanding these challenges helps explain why conversations about our needs can feel so difficult—and why preparation and patience with ourselves are essential.

UNDERSTANDING WHAT WE NEED BEFORE WE COMMUNICATE

Before we can effectively communicate our needs to others, we first have to identify them ourselves—something many of us struggle with after years of masking and accommodation.

I've found it helpful to start with these questions:

- When do I feel most overwhelmed or frustrated in my daily life?

---

[264] Dodson, "How ADHD Ignites RSD."

[265] Barkley, ed., *Attention-Deficit Hyperactivity Disorder*.

[266] Brown, *Smart but Stuck*.

[267] Dodson, "How ADHD Ignites RSD."

- What environments or expectations consistently trigger my ADHD symptoms?
- What small changes would make the biggest difference in my functioning?

For example, I realised that open-office environments destroy my productivity because of my auditory sensitivity and distractibility. This wasn't about preference. It was about creating conditions where I could actually perform at my best.

Many of my clients discover their needs through "contrast experiences"—moments when things suddenly work better. One woman noticed she could focus beautifully during power outages when all electronic distractions were eliminated. This insight helped her create a low-stimulation work environment that dramatically improved her productivity.

If you struggle to identify your needs, try to notice when you feel resentful or overwhelmed. These emotions often point to boundaries that need to be established or needs that aren't being met.

COMMUNICATING WITH FAMILY AND FRIENDS: SETTING EXPECTATIONS WITH COMPASSION

Family dynamics can be particularly challenging to navigate because they're loaded with history and expectations. The key is to approach these conversations with both self-advocacy and empathy for the other person's experience.

Some approaches that have worked for me and my clients include:

- "I know it's frustrating when I forget things we've discussed. My brain genuinely processes verbal information differently. Would you be willing to text me important dates or decisions? I'm much more likely to remember things I can see."
- "When we have back-to-back social plans, I get overwhelmed and can't be present with you. It's not that I don't enjoy our time together.

My brain just needs recovery periods. Could we build in some downtime between activities?"
- "I'm working on being more punctual, but time perception is genuinely difficult for me. If something has a strict start time, could you give me a fifteen-minute warning text? That external cue really helps me transition."

With romantic partners, clear communication about ADHD's impact on your relationship is crucial. My relationship transformed when I stopped saying, "You're being too demanding!" and started saying, "I feel overwhelmed when I have multiple requests at once because my working memory can only hold so much. Can we create a shared system for household responsibilities?"

For parents with ADHD, modelling healthy self-advocacy shows children that it's okay to ask for what they need. Phrases like "Mommy's brain needs a quiet moment before I can help with homework" demonstrate both boundary setting and self-care.

COMMUNICATING IN THE WORKPLACE: SELF-ADVOCACY WITHOUT SHAME

The workplace can feel particularly intimidating because of power dynamics and concerns about professional perception. However, clear communication about your working style can actually enhance your value rather than diminish it.

Some strategies for workplace communication:

- **Know Your Rights:** ADHD is recognised under disability protections in many countries, including the United States (ADA), Canada (Canadian Human Rights Act), the UK (Equality Act), and Australia (Disability Discrimination Act). This means you *may* be legally entitled to reasonable accommodations.
- **Frame Accommodations as Performance Enhancers:** Instead of saying, "I have trouble staying organised," try "I've found I deliver

my best work when using visual project management tools. Could we implement Trello for our team projects?"
- **Focus on Outcomes, Not Methods:** "I'd like to discuss some adjustments that would help me maximise my productivity" is more effective than "I can't work the way everyone else does."

A client who struggled with interruptions and task switching gave a brief presentation to her team about "deep work" principles and proposed designated no-interruption periods each day. This benefited everyone while accommodating her ADHD needs without specifically labelling them as such.

Another approach is highlighting the strengths that come with your ADHD while acknowledging areas where you need support: "My creative problem-solving is strongest when I have clear deadlines and written instructions. This helps me channel my thinking in the most productive direction."

HANDLING PUSHBACK: WHAT TO DO WHEN PEOPLE DON'T UNDERSTAND

Despite your best efforts, some people will respond with skepticism, dismissal, or outright rejection of your needs. This can be painful, but having strategies ready can help:

- **Stay Calm and Factual:** "ADHD is a neurodevelopmental condition that affects executive function. The accommodations I'm asking for help me work with my brain instead of against it."
- **Connect to Shared Goals:** "I'm bringing this up because I want our relationship/team to thrive, and these adjustments will help me contribute at my best."
- **Set Boundaries When Necessary:** "I understand you may not fully understand my experience, but these accommodations are important for my well-being."
- **Know When to Seek Additional Support:** If workplace accommo-

dations are refused, consider consulting with HR or an employment advocate who understands disability rights.

After a manager repeatedly dismissed her needs, a client of mine documented her accommodation requests and the business cases for them and then scheduled a meeting with both her manager and HR. Having a third party present changed the dynamic and resulted in approved accommodations.

At its core, advocating for our ADHD needs is an act of self-respect. It says, "I understand my needs, and I deserve relationships and environments that support me."

This journey isn't always easy. I still sometimes stumble when explaining my needs, particularly to people who are skeptical about ADHD. But each conversation gets a little easier, and the freedom that comes from creating an ADHD-friendly life is worth the temporary discomfort.

The right people, those who truly care about your well-being, will want to understand and support you. And those who don't? That's valuable information about who deserves your energy and time.

BUILDING A DOPAMINE MENU: A PERSONALISED TOOL KIT FOR SUSTAINABLE MOTIVATION

We've all been there—staring at an important task, knowing it needs to get done, yet feeling completely unable to start. The harder we try to force ourselves to begin, the more our brains resist. Meanwhile, the guilt and anxiety build, creating a paralysis that can last hours, days, or even weeks.

I experienced this recently with tax preparation. Despite knowing the deadline, despite setting aside time, despite understanding the consequences of delay, I simply couldn't get my brain to engage. Yet that same week, I spontaneously reorganised my entire digital photo collection spanning fifteen years, a massive project I hadn't planned or even considered important.

This inconsistency isn't laziness or lack of discipline. It's the result of how our ADHD brains process dopamine, the neurotransmitter responsible for motivation, focus, and reward.

Research shows that people with ADHD have differences in dopamine production, reception, and processing.[268] These differences make it physically harder for us to engage with tasks that don't provide immediate stimulation or reward, regardless of how important they might be.

Think about it this way: A neurotypical person might be able to motivate themselves by thinking about the outcome ("I'll feel relieved when this is done" or "This will help my career"). But for many of us with ADHD, future rewards simply don't activate our motivation centres strongly enough to overcome the initial resistance.

THE POWER OF A DOPAMINE MENU

A dopamine menu is a personalised collection of strategies designed to make tasks more engaging by introducing elements that naturally stimulate our ADHD brains. It's like having a tool kit of motivational strategies tailored specifically to how our unique brains work.

I created my first dopamine menu after a particularly frustrating period of work avoidance. Instead of continuing to berate myself for procrastination, I started documenting what conditions actually helped me focus. I noticed patterns: certain types of music, specific environments, time pressures, and social accountability all seemed to help me bypass my executive function challenges.

By deliberately incorporating these elements, I found I could work on almost anything—not through force of will but by creating conditions that made my brain naturally engage.

Here are the core components I recommend including in an ADHD dopamine menu.

---

[268] Volkow et al., "Evaluating Dopamine Reward Pathway in ADHD."

Body Doubling

Working alongside another person (in person or virtually) creates just enough social accountability to get started and stay focused. Research supports this strategy for ADHD brains.[269]

I discovered the power of body doubling accidentally while working at a coffee shop near a friend. We weren't collaborating, just sitting together working on our own projects, but my productivity tripled compared to working alone. Now I use virtual body doubling through services like Focusmate when I need to tackle difficult tasks.

Gamification

Adding elements of play, competition, or reward to boring tasks can trigger dopamine release.[270]

A client of mine transformed her bill-paying routine by creating a "money game" where she timed herself and tried to beat her previous record. What was once a dreaded monthly task became a challenge she actually looks forward to.

Movement-Based Focus

Physical activity increases dopamine and can enhance cognitive function.[271]

I have a desk treadmill in my office to keep myself moving throughout the day. A coaching client discovered she can process complex information better while walking, so she now takes "thinking walks"

---

[269] Tessa Eagle et al., "'It Was Something I Naturally Found Worked and Heard About Later': An Investigation of Body Doubling with Neurodivergent Participants," *ACM Transactions on Accessible Computing* 17, no. 3 (2024): 1–30, https://doi.org/10.1145/3689648.

[270] Edward L. Deci and Richard M. Ryan, "The 'What' and 'Why' of Goal Pursuits: Human Needs and the Self-Determination of Behavior," *Psychological Inquiry* 11, no. 4 (2000): 227–68, https://doi.org/10.1207/S15327965PLI1104_01.

[271] John J. Ratey, *Spark: The Revolutionary New Science of Exercise and the Brain* (Little, Brown, 2008).

when planning projects. Another uses a standing desk with a balance board to incorporate subtle movement throughout her workday.

Sound Stimulation

The right audio environment can provide just enough stimulation to keep our ADHD brains engaged without overwhelming them.[272]

My audio needs vary by task. For writing, I need instrumental music with no lyrics (lyrics compete with my verbal thinking). For data entry or other monotonous tasks, podcasts keep my brain stimulated enough to stay with the boring work. One of my clients works best with specific white noise frequencies that mask distracting sounds.

Sensory Rewards

Pleasant sensory experiences can boost dopamine and make work environments more engaging.[273]

I keep a collection of fidget tools on my desk and treat myself to scented candles during difficult tasks. One of my clients created a "comfort corner" in her home office with a soft blanket, her favourite tea, and a small fountain—sensory elements that make work time more appealing. These aren't distractions; they're bridges that help our sensory-seeking brains stay engaged.

Novelty and Variety

Changing elements of our environment can refresh attention and stimulate dopamine.[274]

When I notice my focus fading, sometimes simply moving to a dif-

---

[272] Howard Abikoff et al., "The Effects of Auditory Stimulation on the Arithmetic Performance of Children with ADHD and Nondisabled Children," *Journal of Learning Disabilities* 29, no. 3 (1996): 238–46, https://doi.org/10.1177/002221949602900302.

[273] Kooij, *Adult ADHD: Diagnostic Assessment and Treatment*.

[274] Brown, *Outside the Box*.

ferent location can reset my brain. I've written parts of this book at my desk, on my back porch, in coffee shops, and even sitting on the floor of my bedroom. A graphic designer I interviewed keeps three different workspaces in her home and rotates between them throughout the day. Another client uses different coloured notebooks for different projects to create visual novelty.

Urgency Hacks

Creating artificial constraints can trigger the brain's natural response to deadlines and time pressure.[275]

After years of being able to work only when deadlines loomed, I've learned to create helpful urgency without the stress of actual last-minute panic. I use the Pomodoro technique (twenty-five-minute focused work periods) to create manageable sprints. I'll commit to sending a draft to a colleague by noon, creating accountability and a real deadline. A client who struggled with morning routines created an "appointment" with a friend for a daily check-in call, instantly making her mornings more structured.

Emotional Connection

Linking tasks to personal values and emotional meaning can activate motivation.[276]

When I'm struggling to start a task, sometimes I'll take a moment to reconnect with why it matters beyond the immediate outcome. Writing this book became easier when I kept a folder of messages from people who said my previous work had helped them. A teacher I worked with keeps a journal of meaningful student interactions to review when paperwork feels overwhelming. Connecting tasks to our deeper values

---

[275] Barkley, ed., *Attention-Deficit Hyperactivity Disorder*.

[276] Hallowell and Ratey, *ADHD 2.0*.

doesn't always create instant motivation, but it can provide the initial push to get started.

Your dopamine menu isn't just a productivity hack. It's a form of self-compassion! Instead of forcing your brain to function in ways it simply doesn't, you're creating conditions where it can naturally thrive.

I've seen countless clients transform their relationship with work by embracing these strategies. A writer who couldn't finish her novel created a body doubling schedule with another author and completed her manuscript in three months. A graduate student who was falling behind in his program discovered that recording himself explaining concepts (instead of writing traditional notes) worked with his verbal processing style, turning his academic career around.

The question isn't "How can I force myself to be productive?" but rather "How can I create conditions where my brain naturally engages with what matters?" What will you add to your dopamine menu today?

THE IMPORTANCE OF COMMUNITY AND SUPPORT SYSTEMS FOR LONG-TERM SUCCESS

I'll never forget sitting in a circle of adults at my first ADHD support group, tears streaming down my face as others described experiences that mirrored my own. For decades, I'd believed I was uniquely flawed, uniquely disorganised, uniquely unreliable, uniquely unable to do what seemed effortless for others.

In that moment, I wasn't just hearing my story reflected back to me. I was experiencing the profound relief of understanding I wasn't alone.

Many of us with ADHD have spent years in isolation, believing our struggles were character flaws rather than symptoms of a neurological difference. We've internalised messages from teachers who called us lazy, partners who labelled us careless, and family members who dismissed our difficulties as excuses. Over time, these experiences have taught us to hide our struggles and attempt to manage them alone, often with devastating effects on our self-worth.

The truth is, ADHD was never meant to be a solo journey. Our brains are literally wired for connection, and community support isn't just helpful but essential for long-term success.

When we connect with others who share our neurotype, something transformative happens. The shame that's been our constant companion begins to dissolve. We recognise our struggles as shared experiences rather than personal failures.

And perhaps most importantly, we gain access to strategies and insights from others who truly understand.

I watched this transformation happen with Johannah, a forty-three-year-old executive who received her ADHD diagnosis after her daughter was evaluated. Before finding community, she described feeling like "the world's worst imposter." She was successful on paper but constantly struggling with invisible challenges.

"I thought I was just chronically underperforming," she told me. "I had no idea other people's brains worked differently. I just assumed everyone else was better at hiding their chaos."

After joining an online community for professional women with ADHD, Johannah found not just emotional support but practical strategies from others who'd navigated similar challenges. She discovered she wasn't alone in struggling with certain aspects of her high-powered career, nor was she alone in developing creative work-arounds.

"These women get it in a way no one else has," she explained. "They don't judge when I talk about setting five alarms to make a meeting or needing to create elaborate systems to remember basic tasks. They offer solutions that actually work for brains like ours."

My own experience was similar. Finding my ADHD community felt like finally coming home to myself. These people didn't raise an eyebrow when I jumped topics mid-conversation or showed up with mismatched socks. More importantly, they offered understanding without judgment when I talked about the darker aspects of ADHD: the rejection sensitivity, the chronic self-doubt, the exhaustion of constant masking.

Finding community doesn't just provide emotional support. It literally rewires our understanding of ourselves. When we see others thriving with ADHD, we begin to believe it's possible for us too.

WHY COMMUNITY MATTERS

The research on this is captivating. Studies show that social connection plays a vital role in both mental health and executive function, areas in which many of us with ADHD struggle.

Peer connection is helpful for many adults with ADHD: Recent qualitative work reports that people deliberately seek peer spaces to improve coping and social connection, and the wider mental health literature links peer support with gains in self-esteem and empowerment.[277]

Barkley's 2015 research suggests that social support can serve as an "external executive function system," helping us maintain motivation and follow through on intentions when our internal systems falter.[278] This explains why many of us find it easier to complete tasks with an accountability partner or in group settings.

Here's why community becomes such a powerful force for ADHD management:

- **External Motivation:** When our internal motivation fails (as it often does with ADHD), external accountability from understanding peers can bridge the gap. Unlike accountability from people who don't understand ADHD, community accountability comes without judgment or shame.
- **Dopamine Boost:** Social connection naturally increases dopamine levels—exactly what our ADHD brains need for focus and motivation. This is why working alongside others (even virtually) can make difficult tasks more accessible.
- **Shared Strategies:** Learning from others who think like us provides solutions we might never discover through conventional advice.

---

277 Callie M. Ginapp et al., "The Experiences of Adults with ADHD in Interpersonal Relationships and Online Communities: A Qualitative Study," *SSM Qualitative Research in Health* 3 (June 2023): 100223, https://doi.org/10.1016/j.ssmqr.2023.100223; and Julie Repper and Tim Carter, "A Review of the Literature on Peer Support in Mental Health Services," *Journal of Mental Health* 20, no. 4 (2011): https://doi.org/10.3109/09638237.2011.583947.

278 Russell A. Barkley, "Behavioral Inhibition, Sustained Attention, and Executive Functions: Constructing a Unifying Theory of ADHD," *Psychological Bulletin* 121, no. 1 (1997): 65–94, https://doi.org/10.1037/0033-2909.121.1.65.

Our community becomes a living laboratory of ADHD-friendly approaches.
- **Emotional Safety:** In a world that often pathologises our differences, ADHD communities provide rare spaces where we can be fully ourselves. This emotional safety reduces the cognitive load of constant masking, freeing up mental resources for growth.

I've seen these benefits firsthand in the ADHD coaching groups I facilitate. Members often arrive feeling broken and leave understanding they're part of a heart-centred community with unique strengths and challenges. The transformation isn't just emotional. It's reflected in tangible improvements in functioning and quality of life.

FINDING ADHD-FRIENDLY COMMUNITIES

Building a support system might feel overwhelming, especially if past social experiences have been difficult (as they often are for those of us with rejection sensitivity and social challenges). The good news is that there are more ADHD-specific communities available than ever before.

Here are some places to start.

Online ADHD Communities

Facebook groups, Reddit forums (r/ADHD and r/ADHDwomen are particularly active), and Discord servers provide accessible entry points. The How to ADHD community founded by Jessica McCabe offers particularly compassionate support. In Canada, the Centre for ADHD Awareness (CADDAC) provides resources and community connections specifically relevant to the Canadian context.

I found my first ADHD communities on LinkedIn and Facebook after my diagnosis, and they became a lifeline during those early days of processing what ADHD meant for me. Being able to ask questions at two in the morning when my mind wouldn't quiet was invaluable.

ADHD Coaching and Support Groups

Many ADHD coaches (including those who are members of the International Coaching Federation) offer group programs that combine professional guidance with peer support. The combination can be particularly powerful for developing practical skills alongside emotional resilience.

A client who struggled with one-on-one coaching found a group program that finally clicked for her. "Seeing others work through similar challenges made the strategies feel more relevant," she explained. "And there's something about collective problem-solving that generates more creative solutions."

Meetups and Local ADHD Groups

Before the pandemic, in-person meetups were common in major cities. While many have shifted online, these gatherings are beginning to return in modified forms. Local ADHD organisations often host events or can connect you with regional resources.

Body Doubling and Accountability Partnerships

Services like Focusmate facilitate virtual coworking sessions designed specifically for people who benefit from working alongside others. ADHD-specific Discord servers often include channels for body doubling and accountability check-ins.

I have clients who use Focusmate and credit it with helping them complete projects that would have otherwise languished. The simple act of saying out loud what you're about to work on and knowing someone else can see you doing it helps bypass many of the executive function challenges that typically get in the way.

Therapeutic Support Networks

Group therapy specifically for ADHD can provide structured support with professional guidance. Many therapists now offer virtual groups, making this option more accessible across geographic areas.

OVERCOMING BARRIERS TO SEEKING SUPPORT

Despite the clear benefits, many of us hesitate to reach out for support. Common barriers include:

- **Fear of Rejection:** After years of social difficulties, many of us develop protective isolation. We avoid potential connection to prevent potential hurt.
- **Shame:** Believing our struggles are character flaws rather than neurological differences can make us afraid to be vulnerable with others.
- **Imposter Syndrome:** Especially for those diagnosed as adults, there can be a sense of not being "ADHD enough" to claim space in the community.
- **Practical Challenges:** Executive function difficulties can make finding and consistently participating in communities difficult.

If these barriers resonate, consider starting with smaller steps:

- Join online communities as an observer first, absorbing support without feeling pressure to contribute.
- Reach out to just one person who seems to understand ADHD, and start a conversation.
- Try time-limited commitments (like a single workshop or event) before ongoing groups.
- Remember that seeking support is a strength, not a weakness.

I struggled with imposter syndrome after my late diagnosis, feeling like I hadn't "earned" my place in ADHD spaces. What helped was realising that the very doubts I experienced were common among late-diagnosed women, another way my experience confirmed rather than contradicted my diagnosis.

Success with ADHD isn't about "fixing" ourselves to fit into neurotypical expectations. It's about creating lives that work with our unique brain wiring rather than against it. And that journey becomes significantly easier when we travel it together.

The isolation many of us have experienced isn't inevitable. It's the result of navigating a world that wasn't designed for minds like ours. By finding our communities, we create spaces where our differences are understood, our strengths are celebrated, and our challenges are met with compassion rather than criticism.

As one member of my support group beautifully expressed, "Finding my ADHD community didn't just help me manage my symptoms better. It helped me finally like who I am."

SELF-COACHING EXERCISES: THRIVING WITH ADHD

In these exercises you'll explore practical ways to build sustainable motivation, advocate for yourself, and create a dopamine menu tailored to your brain. Think of this section as your tool kit for putting ideas into practise and making them part of daily life. You don't need to get it perfect. What matters is finding what clicks for you.

SUSTAINABLE MOTIVATION

The next time you're struggling with motivation or with completing a task, try out these approaches that have worked for many of my clients:

- **Make It a Game:** Turn mundane tasks into fun challenges using timers, points, or rewards. Right now, I earn "tokens" for completing tedious tasks, and then I trade these in for guilt-free fun activities. Sure, it might sound silly, but trust me, adding that bit of novelty and challenge can really help your dopamine-hungry brain get going.
- **Work Alongside Others:** Body doubling is genuinely game changing. Having another person, even virtually, working alongside you can create just enough social accountability to spark your productivity. Personally, I love using Focusmate; it's amazing how much more I accomplish when someone else is quietly working beside me.
- **Sandwich Boring Tasks Between Interesting Ones:** Pair boring tasks with something enjoyable, like listening to a captivating podcast while doing household chores. The dopamine hit from the podcast makes the chore far more manageable. This "interest sandwich" turns low-dopamine tasks into something surprisingly doable.
- **Prime Your Brain with Dopamine First:** Kick-starting tasks with something enjoyable, whether that's listening to your favourite song, taking a quick walk, or enjoying a little chocolate, helps give your brain the dopamine boost needed to ease into less-appealing tasks.
- **Create a Task Menu Instead of a Rigid List:** For days when your brain refuses to tackle your main project, keep a list of alternative productive tasks handy. This strategy respects your need for variety,

allowing you to pivot without guilt while still getting meaningful things done.
- **Build in External Accountability:** If left completely to myself, I might never complete difficult tasks. However, simply texting a friend "I'm working on this report for the next half hour" instantly boosts my likelihood of following through. The gentle pressure of social accountability creates just enough urgency to propel action.

SELF-ADVOCACY

Use the following questions to help yourself create a plan for self-advocacy:

- Where in my life am I struggling to communicate my needs?
- What's one small step I could take this week to advocate for myself?
- How can I reframe self-advocacy as a strength rather than a burden?

YOUR PERSONAL DOPAMINE MENU

Your own dopamine menu will be unique to your brain, interests, and challenges. Here's how to create one that works for you.

1. Identify Your Natural Dopamine Triggers

Pay attention to when you effortlessly engage with tasks. What conditions are present? Are you working alongside others? Is there music playing? Is there a sense of urgency or novelty? These patterns provide valuable clues about what activates your motivation.

For example, I noticed that I easily hyperfocus when:

- I'm slightly under time pressure (but not panicked).
- I have background noise (but not conversation).
- The task involves creativity or problem-solving.
- I've recently physically moved.
- I've explained the task to someone else.

2. Experiment with Different Strategies

Try various approaches to see what works best for specific types of tasks. You might find that body doubling helps with administrative work, while music enhances creative tasks.

Keep track of what you try and how it affects your focus and productivity. I literally kept a journal of focus experiments for a month, noting what conditions helped with different types of work. The patterns that emerged were fascinating and sometimes surprising.

3. Make It Accessible

Create a physical or digital list of your most effective strategies, organised by the type of task or the specific motivation challenge. When you feel stuck, you can consult your menu instead of falling into shame or procrastination.

I keep my dopamine menu as a colourful mind map on my wall where I can easily see it. A client created hers as a deck of strategy cards she can shuffle through when feeling stuck. The format doesn't matter as long as you'll actually use it when motivation lags.

4. Adjust Based on Context

Our needs change based on the environment, our energy levels, and the nature of the task. What works perfectly one day might not work the next. Having multiple strategies allows for flexibility when circumstances change.

I've found that my morning brain needs different motivation strategies than my afternoon brain. I've also noticed seasonal shifts—what helps me focus in winter differs from what works in summer. Embracing this variability rather than fighting it has made maintaining motivation much easier.

Chapter Twelve

The ADHD Awakening: We Are More Than Enough

YOU'VE ALREADY DONE THE HARD PART. YOU'VE MADE IT THROUGH the stories, the science, the unpacking. You've started to see your life through a different lens. Not a broken lens, just a clearer one.

This chapter isn't where your ADHD story begins. It's where everything starts to come together because by now, you're not just reading. You're recognising yourself.

You're remembering the moments that never made sense. You're connecting the dots. You're starting to see that this thing you've been battling your whole life has a name. And it was never laziness or failure or not trying hard enough.

What comes next isn't about fixing yourself. It's about finally meeting yourself.

By now, you do not just know what I am talking about. You have most likely felt it in your own story.

I remember Rachel sitting across from me at a café in Kelowna last winter, stirring her tea obsessively while she told me, "I would make these elaborate planning systems—colour-coded, the works—and then abandon the bloody things within days." She looked up with tired eyes. "Every single time, I'd beat myself up. Why can't I just follow through like a normal adult?"

Or Melissa, who crushed it at her tech job but felt like she was drowning at home. "I could hyperfocus at work for eight hours straight, but at home? Couldn't even remember to put the wet laundry in the dryer. For three days! I was absolutely convinced I was failing as a mom and partner." Been there, done that, bought the T-shirt (and forgot to wash it).

These stories might feel like the old movie *Groundhog Day*, but the truth is that our similarities are far greater than our differences. This book is a collection of validation and shared lived experiences as late-diagnosed ADHD women.

For loads of us, diagnosis day isn't some tragedy. It's this massive, cosmic relief. "You mean there's an actual *reason* I've been struggling? I'm not just fundamentally lazy or broken or unmotivated?" This realisation kicks off our journey from all that shame to something approaching self-acceptance. It's a wonky path, for sure, but at least we're on it together, holding each other up when one of us stumbles.

And stumble we do!

The path from shame to self-acceptance is anything but a straight line. Some days I wake up feeling like I've got this ADHD thing sorted, and by lunchtime I'm back to calling myself an idiot for forgetting an important call. But acceptance isn't about never having bad days. It's about meeting those days with a bit of understanding instead of the usual self-flagellation.

Acceptance also isn't the same as accommodation. Self-accommodation is about working with your brain. It's the systems, supports, and strategies that help you function day to day. Self-acceptance goes deeper. It's about how you see yourself when the systems fall apart. It's the voice you use when things go sideways. It's the difference between saying, "I need a different way to do this," and "I'm broken because I can't do it the way others do." This chapter is about that deeper shift. Not just managing ADHD but living with it without shame.

In the pages ahead, we will explore how self-acceptance can transform both how you feel about yourself and how your brain functions day to day. You will learn why this shift matters neurologically, how to navigate the grief and relief that often follow a late diagnosis, and how to move from shame toward pride in your ADHD identity. We will look at ways to reframe old stories, recognise and use your strengths, and practise habits that make acceptance a lived experience rather than an abstract idea.

Thriving might look like progress. Acceptance is what holds you steady when you feel like you're sliding backward.

When we feel that shame spiral starting (and oh boy, do I know that feeling), we can try to pause, take a deep breath, and remind ourselves our brains work differently, not deficiently.

Barkley's 2015 research shows that those of us diagnosed as adults go through this "retroactive sense-making" thing—suddenly understanding years of struggles through a completely new lens.[279] It can bring up grief for all the opportunities we missed, but also a profound relief and budding self-compassion. We might find ourselves revisiting memories: the half-finished crafts gathering dust in the spare room, the impulsive decisions (like that midnight turquoise ukulele purchase I *clearly* thought would launch my indie folk career...until it retired in the corner of my closet after a single rendition of *Ode to Joy*), the emotional outbursts that still make us cringe, but this time, with *understanding* instead of the usual shame hangover.

For so many of us, shame runs deep as a frozen Canadian lake in February. We've internalised all these messages that say we're not trying hard enough, we're just making excuses, we simply need more bloody discipline. But as we've been unpacking throughout this book, ADHD isn't a character flaw. It's a neurological difference in how our brains handle attention, motivation, and time.

---

[279] Margaret Weiss, Lily Trokenberg Hechtman, and Gabrielle Weiss, *ADHD in Adulthood: A Guide to Current Theory, Diagnosis, and Treatment* (New York: Taylor & Francis, 2001).

Self-acceptance starts when we truly, actually get that our difficulties aren't moral failings but neurological realities.

When we finally wrap our heads around this truth, we can stop fighting ourselves and start supporting ourselves instead.

The journey to self-acceptance often includes these milestones:

- **Acknowledgment:** We recognise ADHD's impact on our lives without minimising or exaggerating it. We say to ourselves, "Yeah, this is real, and it affects me significantly."
- **Education:** We understand the neurological basis of our experiences. We learn that our struggles with focus, organisation, and emotional regulation have biological roots.
- **Compassion:** We extend the same kindness to ourselves that we'd offer to a friend. We speak to ourselves with gentleness: "This is hard. We're doing our best with what we've got."
- **Community:** We find others who share our experiences and validate our struggles. We discover we aren't alone, and our weirdness isn't actually that weird.
- **Advocacy:** We learn to speak up for our needs without shame or apology. We say, "This is what I need to succeed," without feeling we need to justify our neurology.

Each of these steps pushes us further from shame and closer to self-acceptance.

This journey isn't just psychological. It's neurological too.

Chronic shame activates our threat response, keeping the prefrontal cortex offline—which, as mentioned earlier, is already a challenge for ADHD brains. Self-acceptance, on the other hand, activates neural pathways associated with safety, allowing our executive functions to work more effectively. When we practise self-acceptance, we're not just being kind to ourselves. We're creating the optimal neurological conditions for our brains to do their thing.

I'll never forget Lisa, a forty-two-year-old teacher I met online who was diagnosed at thirty-eight. She described her transition from shame to self-acceptance while nervously picking at her cuticles. "I spent most of my life thinking I was just crap at being an adult. Now I understand that my brain works differently, and that's not a *moral failing*. I don't need to hide my struggles anymore. I can acknowledge them and find solutions that actually work for me." When Lisa shared this with our group, everyone collectively exhaled—like they could finally breathe after holding their breath for decades.

This shift from seeing ourselves as broken to understanding ourselves as being wired differently marks the essential first step toward thriving with ADHD. The goal isn't excuses. It's approaching our challenges with clarity and compassion.

When we chuck off the weight of shame, we free up enormous mental and emotional resources that can be redirected toward growth, creativity, and authenticity.

ADHD ISN'T JUST A STRUGGLE BUT ALSO A STRENGTH

As we've seen for way too long, the narrative around ADHD has focused exclusively on what's wrong with us. We're constantly hearing about what we can't do, what we struggle with, what makes us different in challenging ways. But this one-sided story misses the full picture of what it means to have an ADHD brain.

Yeah, we struggle with certain aspects of daily life—no argument there!

But our unique neurological wiring also gives us remarkable strengths that neurotypical folks often don't possess to the same degree. When we embrace our whole selves, both our challenges and our gifts, we discover that ADHD isn't just something to manage; it's something that makes us uniquely valuable.

Research on positive psychology and neuroscience has begun to identify distinct cognitive advantages associated with ADHD.[280] These include:

---

[280] Hallowell and Ratey, *ADHD 2.0*.

- **Divergent Thinking:** We have the ability to generate multiple ideas and see connections others miss. While others focus on finding the "right" answer, our minds naturally explore dozens of possibilities (sometimes simultaneously and chaotically, but still!).
- **Hyperfocus:** We have the capacity to become fully immersed in tasks that capture our interest. When engaged, we can achieve a state of flow that produces exceptional results and insights. I once wrote for thirteen hours straight and forgot to eat. Not healthy, but definitely productive!
- **Cognitive Flexibility:** We have a skill for shifting perspectives and adapting to new information. We naturally think outside conventional boundaries, mainly because we can't see the boundaries in the first place.
- **Resilience:** Our experience navigating challenges has often built remarkable resilience. We've developed grit through necessity. After you've forgotten your keys 147 times, you develop some creative problem-solving skills!
- **Creativity:** Our nonlinear thinking often leads to innovative solutions and approaches. We make connections others might never consider because our minds dance across topics that seem unrelated to everyone else.
- **Empathy:** Our heightened emotional sensitivity can make us deeply attuned to others' feelings. We notice emotional nuances that others might miss or dismiss.
- **Energy:** Our dynamism and enthusiasm can inspire and motivate those around us. Our passion is contagious when we're engaged in something we actually care about.

We've seen these strengths in action throughout history. Lots of innovators, artists, entrepreneurs, and change-makers showed classic ADHD traits. Their divergent thinking helped solve complex problems when boring linear approaches failed. Their hyperfocus allowed them to delve deep into subjects of passion. Their cognitive flexibility helped them adapt when everything went pear-shaped.

I remember talking with Emma, an engineer whose ADHD manifests as both a challenge and an asset. "In meetings, I'll notice connections between seemingly unrelated projects that no one else picks up on. My mind makes these leaps that honestly freak people out sometimes." She laughed, tugging at her unruly curls. "Yeah, I struggle with deadlines and paperwork, and my inbox is a horror show, but my creative thinking has earned me recognition. I'm learning to value this aspect of my ADHD instead of just focusing on what's hard." When Emma shared this insight at our workshop, I swear I could physically see her confidence growing and her shoulders relaxing as she stopped apologising for her brain.

Take Catherine, an ER nurse whose ADHD helps her thrive in emergencies. "I might forget to complete routine paperwork—my supervisor has to chase me down every bloody time—but in a crisis? Everything sharpens. I can track multiple patients, make quick decisions, and stay calm when everything's gone to hell. That's my ADHD superpower." As she told me this over burnt hospital coffee at three in the morning, her eyes lit up with that recognition of how valuable her supposedly "disordered" brain could be in the right context.

As we think about our own lives, we might ask when our ADHD traits have actually helped us.

Perhaps our creativity has led to artistic expression or unusual solutions to problems. Maybe our energy has lifted others during tough times. Or our empathy has created deeper connections with people who need understanding.

This isn't about denying the challenges. It's about embracing the full picture of who we are. Both sides of the coin matter.

The same neurological differences that create our challenges also create our strengths. Our heightened response to novelty that makes routine tasks difficult also fuels our creativity. Our sensitivity that can overwhelm us also makes us deeply empathetic. Our energy that can seem "too much" for some people also drives our passion and enthusiasm. We aren't dealing with separate traits but with different expressions of the same neurological differences.

Dr. Edward Hallowell, a psychiatrist with ADHD who has dedicated his career to understanding the condition, describes ADHD as having "a Ferrari engine with bicycle brakes." The power and potential are extraordinary. We just need to learn how to harness and direct that energy effectively. We don't need a different engine; we need better brakes and a road that suits our vehicle. (And maybe a good mechanic who understands Ferraris!)

In research conducted with adults with successfully managed ADHD, Dr. Hallowell found that those who thrived didn't eliminate their ADHD traits; they channelled them. They found environments, careers, and relationships that valued their strengths while accommodating their challenges. They built systems that supported their executive function weaknesses while maximising their creative, energetic strengths.

By recognising and leveraging our ADHD strengths, we begin to see our neurodivergence not as a deficit to overcome but as a different way of experiencing and interacting with the world. One with both challenges and remarkable gifts.

We stop trying to be neurotypical (which I think we can all agree is exhausting) and start embracing our neurodivergent potential.

Working with our brains means designing our environments, tasks, and relationships around what actually helps us thrive. It means solving for our specific needs rather than trying to conform to standards that weren't created with ADHD brains in mind. It's a radical act of self-advocacy and self-respect.

Jamie, a business consultant with ADHD, shared how this shift transformed her work when we spoke over coffee (her third double espresso of the morning): "I used to try to work like my colleagues, sitting at a desk for eight hours straight, methodically going through tasks. I'd inevitably fail and feel terrible about myself. Now I break my day into twenty-five-minute focused sprints with short breaks for movement. I use noise-cancelling headphones and work standing up when I need to. My productivity has doubled, and my stress has halved." When Jamie demonstrated her new work setup during our coaching session, fiddling with her standing desk while talking a mile a minute, I could see the relief on her face. Finally, a system built for her brain, not someone else's expectation of how work "should" look.

Similarly, Diane, a mom of three, redesigned her home life. "I realised I was spending more energy fighting my ADHD than working with it. Now I have baskets in every room so items can be quickly collected and returned to their proper places later. I set timers for household tasks so I don't get lost in hyperfocus. I meal plan using a rotating schedule of simple recipes instead of trying to reinvent dinner every night." She laughed. "Life isn't perfect—you should see the state of my junk drawer—but it's so much better since I stopped trying to be neurotypical." As Diane walked me through her home, pointing out these solutions with pride while simultaneously fishing a toy dinosaur out of the toilet, I could feel how these small adaptations had restored her sense of capability.

Dr. William Dodson's concept of the "interest-based nervous system" helps explain why this approach works, as we worked through earlier in this book. Our ADHD brains are primarily motivated by interest, challenge, novelty, and urgency, not by importance.[281] When we design our lives around these motivators rather than fighting against them, we unlock our potential. We stop trying to force motivation and start creating conditions where motivation naturally emerges.

As Dr. Russell Barkley notes in his research, ADHD is not a disorder of knowing what to do. It's a disorder of doing what you know.[282] By creating systems that bridge the gap between knowing and doing, systems aligned with our neurological needs, we can achieve results that previously seemed impossible. We don't need more information or more willpower; we need better bridges.

---

281 Dodson, "How ADHD Ignites RSD."

282 Russell A. Barkley, "Attention-Deficit/Hyperactivity Disorder, Self-Regulation, and Time: Toward a More Comprehensive Theory," *Journal of Developmental & Behavioral Pediatrics* 18, no. 4 (1997): 271–79.

THE IMPORTANCE OF SELF-COMPASSION AND CELEBRATING SMALL WINS

If one message emerges consistently in conversations with thriving ADHD women, it's to be gentle with yourself. The harshness with which many of us judge our every mistake, setback, and struggle doesn't make us more productive or successful. It just adds suffering to an already challenging experience.

Our inner critic doesn't motivate us; it paralyses us.

"I spent thirty years beating myself up for every mistake," said Naomi, a professor diagnosed with ADHD at forty-five. "It didn't make me better at anything. It just made me absolutely miserable. Learning to treat myself with kindness has been the greatest gift of my diagnosis journey." As she shared this with me over a coffee meeting (spilling half of it on her papers in a perfectly ADHD moment), I watched years of tension melt from her face, replaced by a gentle acceptance I hope to see in every woman I work with.

Self-compassion isn't self-indulgence or laziness or letting ourselves off the hook. Research by Dr. Kristin Neff has shown that self-compassion actually enhances motivation, emotional resilience, and overall well-being.[283] For those of us with ADHD, cultivating self-compassion isn't just nice; it's necessary. It creates the emotional safety our brains need to function optimally.

Self-compassion has three components that are particularly relevant for our ADHD brains:

- **Mindfulness:** Acknowledging our struggles without exaggerating or minimising them. We see our challenges clearly without being overwhelmed by them. "Yes, I forgot that appointment. It happened."
- **Common Humanity:** Recognising that we're not alone in our challenges—millions of others with ADHD face similar experiences. We understand that our difficulties aren't personal failures but shared experiences. We belong to a circle of people with similar brains.

---

283 Neff, *Self-Compassion*.

- **Self-Kindness:** Treating ourselves with the same warmth and understanding we would offer a good friend. We speak to ourselves with gentleness rather than criticism. "I know this is hard for you. What do you need right now?"

Practising self-compassion might look like:

- Acknowledging when executive function challenges are making a task difficult without judging ourselves for it. "This is hard for my brain, and that's okay. It doesn't mean I'm lazy or stupid."
- Recognising that forgetting appointments doesn't make us bad people. It's a common ADHD experience related to time blindness. "My time perception works differently. This doesn't reflect my character or how much I care."
- Speaking to ourselves with kindness after a setback. "This is hard, but I'm doing my best with the brain I have. How can I support myself right now?" We become our own allies rather than our own worst critics.

Self-compassion becomes especially crucial when we consider the emotional impact of ADHD. Many of us experience rejection sensitivity dysphoria (RSD). This sensitivity, combined with years of negative feedback about our ADHD symptoms, creates a perfect storm of self-criticism. We need to actively counter this pattern with deliberate self-compassion.

I'll never forget when Alicia, a marketing executive with ADHD, described how self-compassion transformed her relationship with mistakes. "I used to spiral into shame over every error. Even a typo in an email could ruin my entire day. I'd obsess about it, convince myself I was going to get fired, the whole nine yards." She rolled her eyes at her former self. "Now I acknowledge the mistake, fix it if possible, and remind myself that I'm human. It's not that I care less about quality. I'm just not destroying myself over imperfection anymore." The day Alicia shared this breakthrough with our group, the collective sigh of relief was almost audible as women realised they, too, could put down the back-breaking burden of perfectionism.

Alongside self-compassion, celebrating small wins becomes a powerful practise for our ADHD brains. Our dopamine-driven reward systems often make it hard to acknowledge progress unless it's dramatic or complete. We finish a project and immediately move on to the next one without pausing to recognise our accomplishment. (Sound familiar? I'm already thinking about my next project as I finish writing this book.) But intentionally celebrating small wins like completing a difficult email, remembering an appointment, or breaking a procrastination cycle builds confidence and momentum. Each celebration releases dopamine, reinforcing the neural pathways that make progress possible. It goes beyond emotional satisfaction; it's neurologically strategic.

Try these ADHD-friendly ways to celebrate small wins:

- **Keep a done list instead of just a to-do list:** Record everything you accomplish each day, no matter how small. I have a bright yellow notebook just for this.
- **Create a visual representation of progress:** Use stars on a chart, marbles in a jar, ridiculous stickers—whatever works. Make your progress tangible and noticeable.
- **Take a moment to literally say "I did it!" out loud:** Use your voice to acknowledge your achievement. (I sometimes do a little dance too. The cats judge me for it.)
- **Text a supportive friend to share your accomplishment:** Make celebration social, which amplifies its impact.
- **Take a short break to do something enjoyable as a reward:** Give yourself permission to experience pleasure after effort. Two chapters written? That's a chocolate break!

Our ADHD brains are often wired to focus on what's going wrong rather than what's going right. This negativity bias combined with rejection sensitivity dysphoria can make it hard to recognise our own progress. Intentionally celebrating small wins rewires this tendency over time.

Think of it as training your attention to notice success with the same intensity it naturally notices failure.

STEP INTO YOUR POWER AND LIVE AUTHENTICALLY

Throughout this book, we've explored strategies for managing ADHD challenges, leveraging ADHD strengths, and creating lives that work with, rather than against, our unique neurology. Now it's time to bring it all together with a final invitation: to step into your power and live authentically.

Living authentically with ADHD means embracing who we are, both our challenges and our gifts. It means releasing the exhausting mask of neurotypicality that many of us have worn for years. (Mine was getting pretty sweaty and uncomfortable anyway!) It means designing lives that honour our needs while nurturing our potential. It means saying, "This is who I am, and I'm not apologising for it anymore."

Stepping into our power might feel scary at first. Many of us have spent decades trying to hide our ADHD traits, afraid that if people saw the real us, with our time blindness, our emotional intensity, our nonlinear thinking, they would reject us. But authenticity actually draws the right people closer while creating a healthy distance from those who don't respect our neurological differences. When we show up as our full selves, we give others permission to do the same.

Here are some ways to step into your ADHD power:

- **Advocate for accommodations at work or school:** Say, "This is what I need to succeed," with confidence and without shame or apology.
- **Create systems that support your unique brain:** Design your life around your actual needs, instead of forcing yourself into one-size-fits-all approaches and idealised standards.
- **Set boundaries around your energy, attention, and time:** Protect your resources instead of depleting them.
- **Find people who appreciate your ADHD traits rather than trying to change them:** Seek connections that energise rather than deplete you.

- **Pursue paths that align with your passions and strengths:** Rather than forcing yourself into a conventional but ill-fitting role, build your life around what works for you.
- **Speak your truth about your experiences:** Share authentically, without minimising or exaggerating, and create space for others to do the same.
- **Help others understand and accept neurodiversity in all its forms:** Become an advocate not just for yourself but for all differently wired individuals.

We see this transformation in women like Sophia, who left a structured corporate job that constantly triggered her ADHD challenges to start a creative business that leverages her strengths. "For years, I shaped myself to meet others' expectations. Now I've shaped my world to meet mine. My creativity, my ability to connect diverse ideas, and my enthusiasm are all the things that made me 'too much' in my old job but are assets in my business."

When Sophia invited me to her new workspace—a chaotic but clearly functional jumble of projects, inspiration boards, and multiple seating options—I could feel how every element was designed to work with her brain, not against it. The joy in her eyes spoke volumes about the power of authenticity.

We also see it in women like Theresa, who stopped hiding her ADHD at work and instead advocated for accommodations. "I was spending so much energy masking my struggles. When I finally disclosed my ADHD and requested simple accommodations such as written instructions, permission to use noise-cancelling headphones, and flexibility to stand during meetings, my performance improved dramatically. Being authentic freed up the mental resources I needed to excel." That changed everything. Watching Theresa's confidence grow as she embraced her needs was one of the most rewarding moments in my work with ADHD women.

Living authentically doesn't mean never struggling; it means acknowledging the struggle without being defined by it. It means recognising that our worth isn't determined by our productivity, our organisation, or our ability to meet neurotypical expectations. We are inherently valuable exactly as we are—messy calendars, forgotten appointments, and all.

Authenticity isn't just psychologically healthy. It's neurologically efficient. Masking ADHD traits consumes enormous cognitive resources, leaving less mental energy for what truly matters.[284] When we live authentically, we free up those resources for growth, connection, and purpose. We spend less energy hiding and more energy contributing our unique gifts to the world.[285]

Stepping into our power also means becoming advocates, not just for ourselves but for all neurodivergent individuals. As we embrace our authentic selves, we create space for others to do the same. We contribute to a world that recognises neurological diversity as a natural and valuable variation in human cognition.

This ripple effect can be profound. When we stop apologising for our ADHD and instead demonstrate how our unique cognitive style contributes to innovation, creativity, and progress, we change the narrative around neurodiversity. We show that difference isn't deficit. It's diversity.

The path to authentic living isn't always smooth. We'll face misunderstanding, skepticism, and resistance. But with each step toward authenticity, our confidence grows. We discover that the acceptance we truly need, acceptance of ourselves, has been within our reach all along.

WE ARE MORE THAN ENOUGH

As we close this journey together, I want to leave you with this truth: We are more than enough. Not despite our ADHD but because of it. Our worth isn't measured by completed to-do lists, punctuality, or uninterrupted focus. Our worth is intrinsic, unchangeable, and complete.

The path forward isn't about becoming someone different. It's about

---

[284] Jacob T. Fisher et al., "Cognitive and Perceptual Load Have Opposing Effects on Brain Network Efficiency and Behavioral Variability in ADHD," *Network Neuroscience* 7, no. 4 (2023): 1483–96, https://doi.org/10.1162/netn_a_00336.

[285] Fisher et al., "Cognitive and Perceptual Load."

becoming more fully ourselves. It's about embracing our neurodivergent brains with all their challenges and gifts. It's about designing lives that work for us, not against us.

Remember:

- Your sensitivity is also your empathy.
- Your distractibility is also your awareness.
- Your impulsivity is also your spontaneity.
- Your intensity is also your passion.
- Your restlessness is also your energy.
- Your nonconformity is also your innovation.

These aren't contradictions. They're two sides of the same neurological coin. By accepting both sides, we step into the fullness of who we are and what we can contribute to the world.

Throughout my work with ADHD women—in support groups and one-on-one coaching—I've witnessed remarkable transformations.

Women who once defined themselves by their struggles now lead with their strengths.

Women who spent decades hiding their ADHD now advocate openly for neurodiversity.

Women who believed they were fundamentally flawed now recognise their inherent value and unique contributions.

These transformations weren't about becoming "more normal" or "less ADHD." They were about becoming more authentically themselves, about aligning their external lives with their internal wiring. About creating environments where their challenges were accommodated and their strengths were celebrated.

The world needs our unique perspectives, our creative solutions, our passionate energy, and our authentic selves. Let's not dim our lights to fit into spaces that weren't designed for us. Instead, let's shine brightly and create new spaces where all kinds of minds can thrive.

To every woman with ADHD reading these words, I extend my deepest gratitude. It has been an absolute honour to share this journey with you, to witness your struggles, your triumphs, your resilience, and your growth. You are not broken or deficient; you are beautifully, brilliantly neurodivergent.

Your challenges are real, but they don't define you.

Your strengths are powerful, and they deserve to be celebrated.

As you close this book and continue your journey, carry this truth with you: You have always been enough. Now it's time to live like you believe it.

Acknowledgments

A HEARTFELT THANK-YOU TO ALL THE ADHD WOMEN EVERYWHERE who are discovering that we're not broken, just misunderstood. Thank you for your courage in seeking answers, for your vulnerability in sharing your experiences, and for your persistence in creating lives that honour your authentic selves.

Your journey has not been easy. Many of you spent years, even decades, without answers, blaming yourselves for challenges that were never your fault. You've navigated criticism, disbelief, and dismissal. You've pushed through fog and overwhelm to advocate for yourselves in systems that weren't designed with your needs in mind.

And still, you persist. You adapt. You innovate. You connect. You create solutions not just for yourselves but for others travelling similar paths.

It's been an absolute honour to share this journey with you, to reflect on the power of embracing your neurodivergent mind. The resilience, creativity, compassion, and determination shown by women like you is nothing short of inspiring. Your stories remind us all of what's possible when we stop masking and start thriving.

Together, we're changing the narrative around ADHD, moving

from a deficit-focused model to one that recognises both challenges and strengths. We're creating spaces where neurodiversity is understood not as a disorder to be fixed but as a natural variation in human cognition to be supported and celebrated.

I cherish the ADHD awakening that has unfolded uniquely for each of us.

Thank you for your willingness to be seen, to share your stories, and to build community. The world is better because you're in it, exactly as you are, with all your beautiful ADHD complexity.

www.ingramcontent.com/pod-product-compliance
Lightning Source LLC
Chambersburg PA
CBHW030513080526
44586CB00011B/180